THE COMPLETE BOOK OF INDIAN COOKING

Premila Lal

ACKNOWLEDGEMENTS

I wish to thank all my readers for their great enthusiasm and encouragement in inspiring me to write this book. The editors of *Femina* and *Eve's Weekly* for allowing me to republish some of the recipes in my column; the late Frene Talyerkhan for the birth of Premila Lal; Home Vakeel for helpful suggestions; my secretary Lena Dias for her willing support with the manuscript; my brother Sukhi for bearing with me while I experimented in his kitchen in London; my mother who taught me to cook; and last, though not least, my husband and three sons for their rowdy but indulgent criticism of the numerous experiments in our kitchen.

THE COMPLETE BOOK OF INDIAN COOKING

Premila Lal

Drawings by
Mario Miranda

Edited by
Christine Smeeth

foulsham

LONDON • NEW YORK • TORONTO • SYDNEY

foulsham

Bennetts Close, Cippenham, Berkshire, SL1 5AP

ISBN 0-572-02264-6

Copyright © 1994 and 1996 W. Foulsham & Co. Ltd

All rights reserved

Printed in Great Britain by
St Edmundsbury Press Ltd.,
Bury St Edmunds, Suffolk.

Contents

Introduction

One of the wonders of Indian cuisine is that every meal is a feast in itself. There is no end, it would seem, to the variety of the dishes served at each meal, not to mention the exotic pickles, chutneys, salads and fried crispies which are a must at every Indian table. Perhaps this is because India is a country of fasts and festivals. For each day of religious fasting there must be at least two days of feasting. So it comes as no surprise that sitting down to an ordinary Indian dinner is a delightful and appetizing ceremony.

It is almost impossible to keep track of the innumerable recipes that are used exclusively for particular ceremonies and festivals. There are dishes that are prepared only for marriages or birth festivities, for naming ceremonies or seasonal and religious festivals. There are also special dishes served only for death and post-mourning ceremonies. Then there are other dishes which are eaten before or after fast days.

A traditional dinner in India is served on a thali, a large round silver or brass salver (today stainless steel thalis have become very popular), on which are placed a set of small individual katoris (serving bowls). There may be as few as three or as many as eight katoris, depending on the variety of the dishes cooked for the meal. All the dishes are served together. In some parts of India, the meal begins with a sweet dish. Again, in most of India, rice is served first and is followed by chappatis or other varieties of Indian bread. However, there are places where chappatis are served at the beginning of the meal and are followed by rice.

Then there is the gracious, traditional custom of serving pan, (a combination of chopped betel nut and spices wrapped up in green betel leaf), after each meal. It is believed that pan acts as a digestive, much like the after dinner brandy or mints served in the West. The hookah, a smoking device invented and perfected by the Muslims, is an after-dinner luxury in many Indian homes. Many a nabob of the East India Company used to enjoy his hookah each evening after dinner.

I have introduced each chapter with some information about a particular Indian holiday or festival. I have done this because I feel that to appreciate the art of Indian cooking truly and to eat it in the spirit with which food is prepared in India, one must have some feeling for the people and their customs. In India, as in most Eastern countries, food and festivity are almost synonymous.

PREMILA LAL

GLOSSARIES

Utensils

Ingredients

Measurements

Methods

This book has not been planned for the inexperienced cook but an effort has nevertheless been made to make the recipes as easy to follow as possible. As an additional guide, the basic recipes for rice and dhal on which this book's more elaborate recipes are built, are given in 'Glossary 4 - Methods'. In the same place, slightly more esoteric procedures are explained, like making coconut milk (which is NOT coconut water), tamarind water, and chhana. The adventurous cook who will try anything once has been afforded all the help she may need. But remember - the art of cooking, like the art of loving, can be perfected only after a lot of practice and a lot of heartache.

1: *Utensils*

Dekchi: Indian word for a saucepan. Usually a saucepan without a handle, but any saucepan may be substituted.

Grinding stone: Rectangular shaped piece of stone, approximately 61 x 30 cm/2ft x 1ft on which spices are ground with a stone pestle or rolling-pin.

Idli steamer: Large steaming pot with inside racks on which to place the katoris when steaming.

Katori (or idli katori): Small serving bowls.

Kerai: A shallow, round-bottomed saucepan made of iron and used for deep-frying. Any deep-frying pan may be substituted.

Sevanazhi: Device for making vermicelli, same as for spaghetti, macaroni, etc. Use a forcing-bag if not available.

Sigri: Small charcoal stove, on the same principle as a charcoal barbecue.

Tandoor: A mud or clay country oven, built in the shape of a barrel. Tandoori cooking is done out of doors and a charcoal barbecue is the best substitute.

Tava: Flattish iron plate with a slightly rounded bottom, used for breads such as chappatis. A heavy iron frying-pan or the plate of an electric stove may be substituted.

Thali: A round silver or stainless steel salver, usually 4.0 cms/11/2 inches deep, that is used as a serving plate or tray. Any baking tray or flat salver may be substituted.

2: Ingredients

Aniseed (sonf) - small oval seeds, light brown in colour, with a licorice taste. Used to flavour food, tea and sweetmeats; also used medically for digestive complaints. It is always served after a meal, either in the form of roasted seeds or wrapped in a betel leaf (pan).

Asafoetida (hing) - resinous gum with strong smell of garlic, used in cookery and in medicine. Also used in preparing pickles.

Bay leaf (tejpatta) - an aromatic dried leaf, used to flavour curries and rice - also known as curry leaf.

Besan - flour made from gram dhal.

Betel leaf (pan) - a leaf served and chewed as a digestive. The nut of the plant 'areca nut' is also chewed, either in pieces or finely chopped and wrapped in the leaf.

Bitter-gourd (karela) - one of the many Indian vegetables belonging to the gourd family. Somewhat bitter in taste, it is supposedly a blood purifier.

Black cardamom (bara elaichi) - large black-skinned variety of cardamom with a very strong flavour; used in meat dishes and pulaos.

Capsicum (Simla mirch) - globe-shaped capsule with seeds - also known as sweet pepper. It has a mild chilli flavour and is cooked as a vegetable.

Cardamom (elaichi) - spice from seed-capsules of an Indian plant. Used in sweets and some foods, it has a cool eucalyptus-scented flavour.

Chana dhal - a variety of pulses or dhal known as gram or chick peas. Used in the preparation of sweetmeats and other dishes.

Charoli or Chironji - small, round, lightly-flavoured nuts used to garnish sweetmeats. Can be substituted with melon seeds.

Chhana - a soft cheese obtained by adding lime juice to warm milk and straining through muslin (See Glossary 4.)

Chilli (mirch) - a hot fiercely-flavoured pepper which turns bright red when ripe. Chilli powder is made from dried red chillies. Green (fresh) chillies are frequently used.

Cinnamon (dalchini) - thin stick of bark from a tree native to

Malabar and certain parts of Sri - Lanka and India. It is used for either foods and beverages.

Cloves (lavang) - this nail-shaped spice is the dried bud of an evergreen plant grown in the tropics. It is used whole or powdered for flavouring preserves and meat dishes.

Coconut (nariel) - ripe, brown, hard-shelled seed of the palm tree. It has a white edible lining inside, enclosing water. (For 'coconut milk' see Glossary 4.)

Coriander (dhania) - an oval aromatic seed used for flavouring dhals and meat and vegetable dishes. It is used whole or crushed. The leaves of the plant are used for garnishing. It can be grown anywhere, even in a flower-pot, and will sprout within a few days. Parsley can be substituted for coriander.

Curd (dahi) - an important ingredient in meat dishes, for which Western commercial yoghurt may be substituted. It is also eaten plain or garnished with chopped vegetables or fruit.

Curry leaf - see 'Bay leaf'.

Dhal - pulses or lentils - a staple diet of the country, especially among the lower classes. It is rich in protein. A large variety of dhals are grown. The better known, such as moong, maanh or urad, chana, toovar and masoor are available at all Indian grocery stores.

Dill (sui bhaji) - this plant originated in Europe. It is cooked as a spinach or used for flavouring preserves and rice.

Drumstick (seeng) - a long, hard bean that grows on a tree. It is cooked, cut into equal pieces and tied with string into bunches. The marrow has a very delicate flavour. If not available, celery may be substituted.

Fenugreek (methi) - small rectangular seeds used for flavouring vegetables and pickles.

Garam masala - A mixture of powdered peppercorns, cloves, cinnamon and cardamom. Used to flavour meats and vegetables.

Garlic (lausen) - a bulb made up of sections called cloves. This pungent herb is used to make the basic masala of most curries.

Ghee - clarified butter. A widely-used cooking medium. The term ghee is also applied to hydrogenated oil, usually groundnut oil. Any cooking medium available may be substituted.

Ginger (adrak) - a tangy-flavoured root, essential in blending the basic masala for curry. Fresh ginger or dried powdered ginger is used in cooking.

Jackfruit (kathahal) - the raw fruit is cooked as a vegetable. It is similar to bread-fruit but a little coarser.

Jaggary (gur) - unrefined brown sugar.

Khoya - fresh milk boiled until all the liquid has evaporated and a solid mass remains. Also known as mava.

Lentils - Applied to all varieties of dhals or pulses.

Mace (javitri) - the outer skin of the nutmeg, used for flavouring pulsus and curries.

Mango (aam) - a fleshy fruit, yellowish-red in colour. Raw mango is used in chutneys, pickles and for flavouring dishes.

Mango powder (amchoor) - raw mango slices dried in the sun and then ground to a powder. Used to flavour dhals and other dishes.

Masala - the paste, made from ground spices, that is the base of a curry.

Mustard seed (rai) - pungent, round black seed used to flavour vegetables and other dishes. The leaf of the plant, sarson, is cooked like spinach.

Nutmeg (jaiphal) - a hard, dried seed with a pleasing fragrance. Used in powdered form for flavouring.

Oil - different kinds of cooking oils are used in Indian cooking: sweet oil or til oil, i.e., sesame oil, coconut oil and, ocasionally, mustard oil.

Parvel - an Indian vegetable, looking like a gherkin.

Peppercorn (kali mirch) - round, black hot-flavoured seeds, used in most dishes.

Pistachio (pista) - nuts with a greenish edible kernel, used to garnish sweet dishes.

Pomegranate seed (anardhana) - dried seeds of the pomegranate fruit. Used for flavouring dhals and breads.

Poppy seed (khus khus) - small tasty seeds from the poppy. Used to make masalas and sweetmeats and to sprinkle on breads.

Saffron (kesar) - orange-coloured stigma of the crocus. Used to add colour and flavour to rice and meat dishes and also as a medicine.

Sesame seed (til) -tiny white seeds that add a milk, nutty flavour to foods.

Silver paper (varak) - this is prepared by beating pure silver to a very fine edible paper leaf. It is used a lot in India and the Middle East to decorate sweets and rice dishes.

Tamarind (imli) - the pods of a tropical tree. The pulp has a piquant sourish taste and is used for flavouring dhal and masalas.

Turmeric (haldi) - a root plant of the ginger family. It is dried and ground to a powder that is a brilliant yellow in colour. Used to blend and to colour food. When available, the fresh root is preferable to the powder.

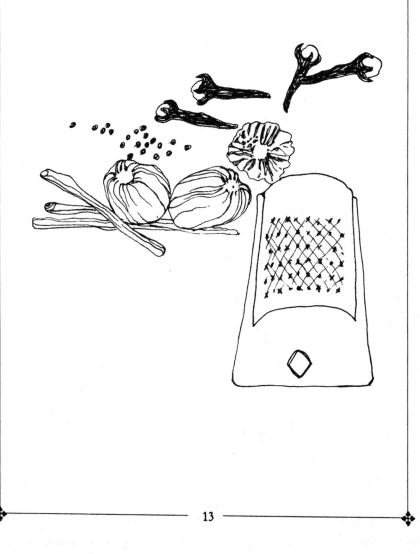

3: Measurements

The amounts specified in these recipes are for the palate of the average 'hot-food eater'. The quantity of chillies, peppery spices and salt can, of course, be varied according to taste. It is similarly hard to lay down how many each recipe will serve, since it depends entirely on how many other dishes you are providing. If however, only one dish is being served, then a pound of meat or fish for two people is a generous estimate.

For housewives who have a distinct preference for weighing as opposed to measuring, or vice versa, the following equivalents may be useful.

1 cup holds   300 ml/½ pint water
              225 g/8 oz sugar
              150 g/5 oz flour

1 tablespoon contains 25 g/1 oz ghee
                        25 g/1 oz sugar

The amounts specified in this book are based on these equivalents.Where cinnamon sticks are specified, unless otherwise stated, a 5 cms/2 - inch stick is intended. (stick of 10 - 15 cms/4 - 6 inches = approximately 5 ml/1 teaspoon powdered cinnamon).

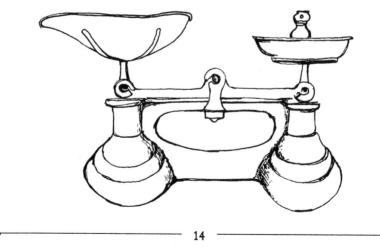

4: Methods

PLAIN RICE

350 g/12 oz rice
1.2 ltrs/2 pints water

1 - 2 tablespoons ghee or butter
¼ teaspoon salt

■ Wash the rice twice. Leave to soak for 5 minutes and drain. Warm the ghee in a saucepan, add the rice and fry, stirring frequently, for 5 minutes. Add the water and salt, stir and cook until ¾ of the water has evaporated. Transfer to an ovenproof dish and place in a moderate oven on a low heat (160°C/325°F/ Gas mark 3) and cook until the water has evaporated and the rice is tender. (The length of time will vary with different types of rice.)

PLAIN DHAL

225 g/8 oz dhal
600 ml/1 pint water
1 onion

1½ tablespoons ghee
¼ teaspoon salt

■ Wash the dhal in water. Drain and add 600 ml/1 pint of fresh water. Add salt and cook until it reaches boiling-point. Boil for 15 minutes, lower heat and simmer for ¾ - 1 hour. Slice the onion and fry in the ghee. Add to the dhal, stir and serve.

CHHANA

Makes 1.7 ltrs/3 pints

1.2 ltrs/2 pints milk   *600 ml/1 pint sour whey*

■ Heat the milk, stirring continuously to prevent the cream forming on the top. Remove from the heat when it boils and gradually stir in the sour whey. Stir until the milk curdles remove from the heat and allow to stand for 20 minutes. Strain through a muslin cloth and squeeze out all the liquid. The cream cheese formed is then called chhana.

COCONUT MILK

Makes 600 ml/1 pint

■ Add 2 cups hot water to 2 cups grated coconut. Leave to cool, squeeze out the milk - this is the thicker milk. Add 1 more cup hot water to the squeezed coconut, cool and squeeze out the thinner milk. When fresh coconut is not available, add 2 cups hot milk to vacuum-packed flaked preserved coconut and squeeze out juice as above.

SAFFRON WATER

■ Soak a pinch of saffron in a tablespoon hot water. When cool, use the coloured water.

TAMARIND WATER

Makes 150 ml/¼ pint

■ For a ball of tamarind 2.5 cms/1 inch in diameter, soak tamarind in 150 ml/ ¼ pint hot water. When cool, strain out the juice and pulp. Substitute lime juice if tamarind is not available.

PICKLES AND CHUTNEYS

PICKLES AND CHUTNEYS

The summer in India is quite unbearable, but it has a saving grace - the mango season. Everyone looks forward to the yearly mango crop, and housewives get busy blending the myriad spices needed for a whole year's supply of mango pickles, as well as pickles and preserves made from other fruit and vegetables. The women are far happier to stay indoors and avoid the heat and they are certainly all too usefully occupied, for pickles and chutneys are an essential feature of the Indian menu.

The exotic mango is no longer as mysterious and unobtainable as it used to be, but the fresh fruit is a bad traveller and various ways of preserving the fruit have been discovered. The mango is unrivalled in smell, colour and taste; the gourmets of the great Emperor Aknbar's court, placed it above muskmelons and grapes. Unfortunately, the mango season is very short and with the first showers of the monsoon, any fruit still on the tree spoils. It is almost impossible to decide between the mango and the monsoon, but after a hot and sultry summer, when all the pickles have been made and stored for the year, the monsoon is most welcome.

In Rajasthan, a special festival is held to celebrate the first monsoon rains. Peasants from the villages bring their families to the cities to take part in the Teej Mela. The gaily coloured turbans of the men and the spectacular costumes of the women symbolise their joy, for rain means food and work on desert land which has for months been barren.

The Teej Mela, or the 'festival of Devi', is essentially a woman's festival. It is also celebrated to strengthen the relationship between the mother and her daughter-in-law (saas bahu). The spirit of the Devi (the wife of Lord Shiva) is worshipped for two days in the home and then sent away with all the love and blessings which are bestowed on a daughter before she leaves for the home of her husband and mother-in-law. The highlight of the day is an elaborate procession of decoratively painted elephants, camels and horses. The colourful people of Rajasthan throng to join the procession which they believe is followed by the spirit of the goddess. This is a day of love, gratitude and worship.

MANGO CHUTNEY

Makes 2.2 kg/5 lb

1 kg/2 lb green mangoes
450 g/1 lb redcurrants
225 g/8 oz fresh ginger
1.8 kg/4 lb sugar

150 ml/ ¼ pint vinegar
3 tablespoons chilli powder
1 tablespoon salt

■ Peel and slice the mangoes. Peel the ginger. Grind half the amount of currants and ginger together. Slice the remaining ginger finely. Put all the ingredients except the mangoes in a saucepan and stirring, cook for 15 minutes. Add the mangoes and simmer until the mixture has a jam-like consistency and the mangoes are tender. Cool and bottle in air-tight jars. The chutney may be eaten immediately.

RIPE MANGO RAITHA

Makes 900 g/2 lb

3 ripe mangoes
600 ml/1 pint curd or
yoghurt
¼ coconut

½ teaspoon mustard seeds
4 green chillies
½ tablespoon ghee
Salt and sugar to taste

■ Peel and chop the mangoes into small cubes. Beat curd to a creamy consistency, add salt and sugar. Grind the coconut and chillies to a paste and add to the beaten curd. Add the mango cubes and mix.
■ Heat ghee in a saucepan and fry the mustard seeds until they splutter. Stir in the chopped onion and fry until light brown in colour. Add the curd-and-mango mixture and remove from the heat. Serve as a side dish with boiled rice or rice pulao.

SWEET MANGO CHUTNEY

Makes 2.7 kg/6 lb

1.5 kg/3 lb green mangoes	*1 tablespoon chilli powder*
1.5 kg/3 lb sugar	*450 g/1 lb plums*
10 cms/4 inch piece ginger	*450 ml/ ³/₄ pint vinegar*
2 pods garlic	*Salt to taste*

■ Peel the mangoes and dice. Sprinkle with salt and keep aside for an hour. Grind the garlic, ginger and chillies with 150 ml/ ¼ pint vinegar to make a smooth paste.

■ Put mangoes and sugar in a saucepan and boil together until the mango is tender and the mixture forms a thick jam. Add the paste and stir gently. Pour in the peeled and chopped plums and cook stirring for 8 minutes. Blend in the vinegar and salt and simmer for 15 minutes. Cool, and bottle in air-tight jars.

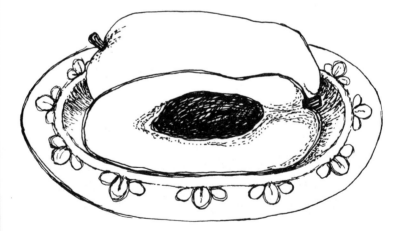

MIXED VEGETABLE PICKLE

Makes 4.4 kg/ 10 lb

1.8 kg/4 lb turnips
1 kg/2 lb cauliflower
1 kg/2 lb young carrots
450 g/1 lb shelled peas
4 pods garlic
100 g/4 oz green ginger
100 g/4 oz onions
2 tablespoons chilli powder

1 tablespoon garam masala
1 tablespoon ground mustard
*   seeds*
1 teaspoon turmeric powder
Salt to taste
600 ml/1 pint mustard oil
450 ml/ ¾ pint vinegar
1 kg/2 lb jaggery

■ Slice turnips into 0.5 cms/¼ inch discs. Quarter carrots lengthways and cut the cauliflower into 5.0 cms/2 inch pieces. Boil 600 ml/1 pint water in a large saucepan, add all the vegetables and cook for 5 minutes to soften. Drain off the water and spread the vegetables on a clean towel to dry. Wipe off any excess water.

■ Grind the garlic, ginger and onions together to a paste. Heat the oil and fry the paste, add remaining spices and salt and fry until the oil floats to the top. Cool and add vegetables. Stir thoroughly. Put in a large jar and keep in a warm place or in the sun if possible for 2-3 days until the vegetables turn a little sour. Shake the bottle well every day.

■ Heat the vinegar with jaggery and boil. Cool and add to the vegetables. Place jar in a warm place for a further 2 days until well-blended and tender. Preserve in air-tight jars.

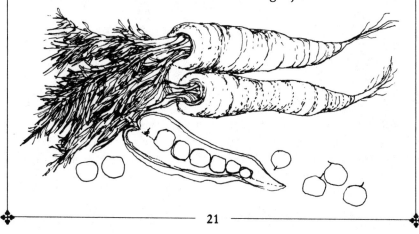

GREEN CHILLI PICKLE

Makes 900 g/2 lb

450 g/1 lb green chillies	2 tablespoons powdered red
100 g/4 oz tamarind	chillies
150 ml/¼ pint gingelly oil	2 tablespoons coriander
2 tablespoons mustard seeds	leaves
4 tablespoons black gram	¼ teaspoon turmeric powder
dhal	100 g/4 oz jaggery
	2 teaspoons salt

■ Cut a hole in the chillies, taking care not to split them. Soak the tamarind in 600 ml/1 pint of water for 30 minutes, and strain the juice.

■ Heat the oil and fry mustard seeds, black gram and coriander leaves. Add green chillies and fry until the chillies are dry. Add tamarind, turmeric, chilli powder, salt and jaggery. Simmer, stirring constantly until the liquid evaporates. Cool and preserve in air-tight jars.

COCONUT CHUTNEY

Makes 450 g/1 lb

½ coconut	1 teaspoon oil
25 g/1 oz gram dhal	½ teaspoon mustard seeds
Pinch of asafoetida	½ teaspoon urad dhal
6 green chillies	1 sprig curry leaves
½ pint curd or yoghurt	Salt to taste

■ Grind the grated coconut, chillies, gram dhal, asafoetida and salt to a smooth paste. Blend this with the curd and keep in a bowl. Heat the oil and fry mustard and urad dhal until it crackles. Add the curry leaves. Pour the oil over the ground chutney and mix. Serve with idlies.

TOMATO CHUTNEY

Makes 900 g/2 lb

1 kg/2 lb large tomatoes	*1½ teaspoons salt*
2 teaspoons raisins	*150 ml/¼ pint vinegar*
175 g/6 oz sugar	*1 teaspoon red chilli powder*
8 cardamoms	*2 bay leaves*

CHOP FINELY:

6 cloves	*1 clove garlic*
2.5 cms/1 inch piece ginger	*25 g/1 oz onion*

■ Use firm ripe tomatoes. Drop in boiling water, cover and allow to stand for 2 minutes. Drain and peel while still warm and chop finely. Combine chopped garlic, ginger and onion and cook, stirring well, until tender. Add the vinegar, sugar, raisins, ground cardamoms, salt, chilli powder and bay leaves. Continue stirring until the chutney thickens. Remove from the heat and cool. Remove the bay leaves before bottling and store in a cool, dry place.

GINGER CHUTNEY

Makes 900 g/2 lb

225 g/8 oz jaggery	*350 g/12 oz raisins*
900 ml/1 ½ pints vinegar	*100 g/4 oz dry red chillies*
4 - 10 cms/4 inch pieces	*1 teaspoon fenugreek*
ginger	*2 tablespoons salt*
3 cloves garlic	

■ Boil the jaggery in 600 ml/1 pint vinegar to make a syrup. Roast and powder the chillies and fenugreek. Pound together in a large mortar the ginger, garlic, stoned raisins, chillies and fenugreek. Mix together the syrup, remaining vinegar, pounded spices and salt. Put into a large earthenware jar and store in a dry place for a fortnight. After that time the chutney will be ready for use.

GARLIC PICKLE

Makes 2.2 kg/5 lb

3 pods garlic
2 dozen lemons
100 g/4 oz dry red chillies

2 teaspoons fenugreek
300 ml/½ pint gingelly oil
2 tablespoons salt

■ Peel garlic, wash and dry well with a towel. Squeeze the juice of the lemons and put in a 1.2 ltrs/2 pint-size jar. Add salt and garlic cloves, shake well and keep aside for 4 days. Meanwhile, prepare the remaining ingredients. Heat 2 tablespoons oil and fry the chillies. Remove from the oil and powder finely. Fry the fenugreek and grind to a powder. On the fourth day add the chilli powder, fenugreek and remaining oil to the garlic. Shake the bottle well and seal. The garlic pickle will be ready for use after 4 days.

LEMON-DATE CHUTNEY

Makes 2.7 kg/6 lb

24 large lemons
100 g/4 oz salt
350 g/12 oz dates
675 g/1 ½ lb jaggery

12 cloves garlic
1 tablespoon cummin seeds
600 ml/1 pint vinegar

■ Wash and wipe the lemons and quarter them. Sprinkle with salt and put the pieces in a large pickling jar. Cover tightly and keep aside for 3 days. On the fourth day, spread the pieces on a large flat tray and dry them in a warm place or in the sun for 5 days. Put the lemon pieces through a mincing machine and mince well. Stone dates and mince the flesh. Grind together the cummin, garlic and jaggery.
■ Put the chutney in a large earthenware vessel, mix in the vinegar, minced lemon and dates to form a thick syrup with a consistency like custard. Use more or less vinegar, as necessary. Pour into air-tight pickle jars and store for 2 weeks before use.

BRINJAL PICKLE

Makes 1.8 kg/4 lb

1.5 kg/3 lb small brinjals (aubergines)	25 g/1 oz dry red chillies
1.75 ltrs/3 pints vinegar	40 g/1 ½ oz green ginger
300 ml/½ pint gingelly oil	12 cloves garlic
1 teaspoon fenugreek	1 tablespoon turmeric powder
1 teaspoon cummin seeds	2 sprigs curry leaves
1 teaspoon mustard seeds	8 green chillies
	Salt and sugar to taste

■ Remove stems and quarter the brinjals. Grind with 150 ml/ ½ pint vinegar, red chillies, turmeric, half the ginger and garlic. Finely slice the remaining garlic and ginger. Heat the oil in a large saucepan, add curry leaves, fenugreek, cummin and mustard seeds, sliced garlic and ginger and fry until brown.
■ Blend in the ground paste and fry until the mixture is dry. Add brinjals, green chillies and mix together. Pour over enough vinegar to cover the vegetables. Add sugar and salt and simmer until the brinjals are tender and the oil floats to the top. Cool and bottle in an air-tight jar.

CAPSICUM COCONUT FRY

Makes 225 g/8 oz

4 capsicums (sweet peppers)	1 tablespoon vinegar
½ coconut	1 teaspoon sugar
2 dry red chillies	1 sprig curry leaves
1 teaspoon mustard seeds	2 tablespoons oil
Pinch of fenugreek	Salt

■ Slice capsicums into strips. Grate the coconut and grind the mustard and fenugreek. Heat the oil in a saucepan and fry curry leaves, ground spices and coconut until brown. Add salt, sugar, capsicums and vinegar and simmer on a low heat until the capsicums are tender. Refrigerate and serve as a fresh pickle.

BRINJAL KASAUNDI

Makes 900 g/2 lb

675 g/1½ lb round brinjals
 (aubergines)
2 tablespoons mustard seeds
1 teaspoon turmeric powder

2 tablespoons salt or to taste
150 ml/¼ pint vinegar
100 g/4 oz jaggery (crushed
 and soaked in vinegar)

GRIND TO A FINE PASTE
WITH A SPRINKLING OF VINEGAR:

10 cloves garlic
5.0 cms/2 inch piece of ginger

10 - 15 dry red chillies

POUND WELL:

7 cardamoms
8 peppercorns
5 cloves

1.4 cms/½ inch piece of
 cinnamon

■ Wash and dry the brinjals and cut into rings 1.4 cms/½ inch thick. Heat the oil and fry ground garlic-ginger-red chilli paste and turmeric powder. Add brinjal rings and cook until soft. Add the jaggery-vinegar solution and finely-ground mustard seeds. Stir and cool. Store in a jar.

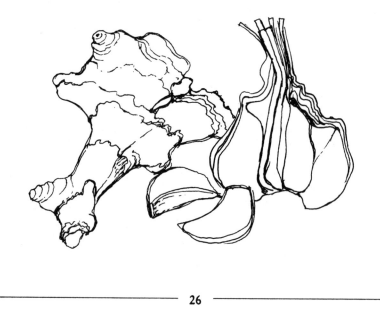

CURD CHUTNEY

Makes 450 ml/¾ pint

450 ml/¾ pint curd
2 level dessertspoons roasted,
   dried, ground green peas
½ teaspoon salt
4 cloves garlic
½ teaspoon cummin seeds

1 small bunch of coriander
   leaves
4 - 5 green chillies
5 - 6 dry red chillies
2 small onions
Juice of one lime

■ Grind together the garlic, cummin seeds and red chillies. Strain the water from the curd through fine muslin and tie up the remainder until it drips dry, for about 30 minutes. Add the already ground spices, finely chopped onions and green chillies to the curd. Wash the coriander leaves well and chop finely. Stir them with the ground green peas, salt and lime juice into the curd preparation and mix thoroughly.

HOT CHUTNEY

Makes 125 g/4 oz

1 bunch coriander leaves
1 bunch mint leaves (pudina)
6 - 7 green chillies
1 teaspoon chilli powder
½ teaspoon roasted cummin
   seeds

1 pinch asafoetida
2 teaspoons mango powder
Juice of 1 lemon
Salt to taste

■ Grind together all the ingredients except the lemon. Squeeze in the lemon juice. The chutney is then ready to serve.

SWEET CHUTNEY

Makes 225 g/8 oz

100 g/4 oz tamarind	*1 teaspoon coriander seeds*
100 g/4 oz jaggery	*1 teaspoon aniseeds*
Coriander leaves	*1 teaspoon roasted cummin seeds*
1 teaspoon chilli powder	*Salt to taste*

■ Soak the tamarind in 300 ml/½ pint hot water and strain out its pulp. Grind the jaggery with all other ingredients. Add water according to consistency required and decorate with chopped coriander leaves when serving.

FISH ROE PICKLE

Makes 900 g/2 lb

450 g/1 lb fresh fish roe	*3½ tablespoons ground mustard*
450 ml/¾ pint vinegar	*seeds*
4 tablespoons chilli powder	*300 ml/½ pint groundnut oil*
2 tablespoons turmeric powder	*2 tablespoons salt*

■ Clean the fish roes and sprinkle with 1 tablespoon chilli powder, ½ tablespoon turmeric and the salt. Mix well and keep aside for 30 minutes. Heat oil and fry the roes well on both sides. Cool and cut into 2.5 cms/1 inch pieces. Pack in layers in a pickling jar. Mix remaining spices with the vinegar and pour into the jar. Seal the jar tightly and shake the contents regularly. Allow the pickle to stand for a week before using.

PRAWN PICKLE

Makes 1.3 kg/3 lb

1 kg/2 lb shelled prawns
75 g/3 oz green ginger
2 pods garlic
4 onions
12 dry red chillies
1 teaspoon turmeric powder
½ teaspoon peppercorns
450 ml/¾ pint gingelly oil

450 ml/¾ pint vinegar
½ teaspoon mustard seeds
½ teaspoon cummin seeds
10 green chillies
1 sprig curry leaves
1 tablespoon sugar
Salt to taste

■ Grind the onions, red chillies, pepper, 4 cloves garlic to a smooth paste. Put in a saucepan to boil, together with the prawns and 300 ml/½ pint water and salt. Simmer until water has evaporated. Remove from heat.

■ Heat half the oil and fry the cooked prawns until well browned. Remove from oil and keep aside.

■ Grind with 2 tablespoons vinegar, 50 g/2 oz ginger, 12 cloves garlic and mustard seeds, turmeric powder and cummin seeds, to a paste. Slice remaining ginger, garlic and green chillies. Add remaining oil to the oil in which the prawns were fried and fry the sliced ingredients. Add the curry leaves and ground paste and fry stirring continuously. Pour in the vinegar, season with salt and bring to the boil. Add fried prawns and sugar and simmer, stirring occasionally, until the oil floats to the top. Cool and bottle in air-tight jars.

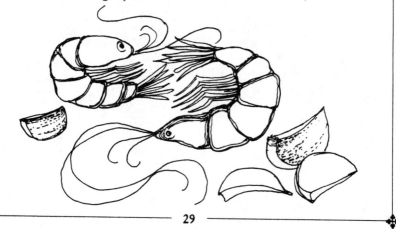

PICKLED FISH

Makes 1.8 kg/4 lb

1 kg/2 lb fish	*900 ml/1 ½ pints vinegar*
1.2 ltrs/2 pints gingelly oil	*2 pods garlic*
50 g/2 oz dry red chillies	*10 cms/4 inch piece ginger*
50 g/2 oz coriander seeds	*1 ½ teaspoons turmeric*
12 peppercorns	*powder*
1 teaspoon cummin seeds	*1 teaspoon salt*

■ Cut fish into 4 cms/1½ inch pieces and wash. Sprinkle with 1 teaspoon salt. Heat ½ pint oil and fry the fish pieces until crisp and dry. Remove and keep aside. Heat 1 tablespoon oil in a frying pan and fry chillies, coriander, pepper, and cummin seeds until brown. Grind together with garlic, ginger, turmeric and a little vinegar, to a fine paste.

■ Heat the remaining oil in a large saucepan, add paste and fry until dry. Add the vinegar and mix with a wooden spoon, cook until mixture thickens a little and remove from heat. Cool and put in the fish pieces. Mix well and preserve in air-tight jars.

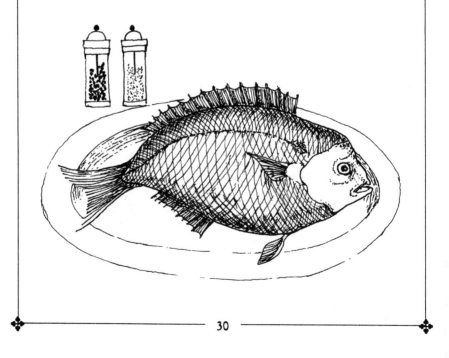

MUTTON PICKLE

Makes 3.1 kg/7 lb

1.8 - 2.3 kg/4 - 5 lb mutton
450 g/1 lb onions
450 g/1 lb ginger
2 pods garlic
900 ml/1½ pints vinegar
2 tablespoons chilli powder
2 tablespoons mango powder
2 teaspoons cummin seeds

12 cardamoms
15 cloves
¾ teaspoon nutmeg
1 teaspoon ground mace
4 tablespoons salt
Cut meat into 4 cms/1 ½ inch
    cubes.

■ Put in a large saucepan to simmer without adding any water, till all the liquid from the meat dries up. Keep on one side. Grind the onions, garlic and ginger to a paste. Heat oil and fry the paste till brown. Add meat pieces, mix well and fry. Add 300 ml/½ pint vinegar, all the remaining spices and cook for 5 minutes, stirring continuously. Remove from the heat, pour in remaining vinegar and cool. Put in air-tight jars and keep for a week before use.

BREADS

BREADS

In the punjab, in North India, climatic conditions favour the growth of the best quality wheat. The chappati, pulka, paratha, tandoori roti, nan and batura are varieties of bread or roti all originating in the punjab. Stuffed paratha (fried roti stuffed with chopped vegetables or meat) is a great favourite. Served with lassi or butter milk, it is the midday meal of the punjab farmer.

The chappati looks similar to the Mexican tortilla. It is a flat, round, pan-roasted pancake made of whole wheat flour. The paratha uses the same ingredients but is flaky and fried. Puris are pancakes fried in deep fat until they swell into round hollow balloons. Tandoori roti and nan are baked in a special clay oven called a tandoor. Every punjabi home has a tandoor in the garden or back yard and tandoori dishes are one of India's gifts to the world.

Indian breads can also be made from rice flour, maize, millet or lentils, but breads made from wheat flour are by far the best.

The preparation of a perfect pulka is an art that can be perfected only after long practice. The Sikhs, those stalwarts of the Punjab, are the best bakers in India. A busy day for bread-making is Gurpurb, the celebration of the birthday of Guru Nanak, the founder of Sikhism. Guru Nanak was a great religious reformer of the eighteenth century who, through his teachings, tried to liberalise the practices of both Hindu and Muslim religions. His activities were confined mostly to the Punjab where his followers banded together and formed a strong and militant Sikh community.

A prominent feature of Gurpurb celebrations is the mass feeding of worshippers at the Guru ka langar (the kitchen of the guru). More than fifty thousand are fed at some of the kitchens attached to the larger Gurudwaras (Sikh houses of worship). The common kitchens of the Gurudwaras have existed since the time of Guru Nanak Devji. Free food is served to anyone who wants it - even the rich accept it with gratitude. Kara Prashad, the sacred food, is made from whole wheat flour, sugar and ghee. The sugar is dissolved in water (the combined weight of the three other ingredients) and simmered. The impurities that rise to the top are removed with a flat spoon. When it forms into a thin clear syrup, it is taken off the fire. The ghee, in a large heavy iron pan (kerai) is then placed on the fire. Once the ghee is hot, the flour is gradually added and stirred continuously to prevent any lumps forming. When the flour is golden brown and rich in smell, the hot syrup is added and cooked until it reaches boiling point. The mixture is removed from the fire, poured into a large silver vessel and garnished with chopped nuts and poppy seeds. It is placed at the altar near the Granth Sahib (the Holy Book) and distributed, with hot puris, after the day's prayers.

CHAPPATI
or <u>PULKA</u>

450 g/1 lb whole wheat flour　　*Large pinch of salt*
300 ml/½ pint water　　　　　*1 teaspoon ghee*

■ For best results chappati should be cooked on a sigri but a gas or electric stove will do if a sigri is not available. Set aside a handful of flour for shaping the chappatis. Knead the remaining flour with your hands, adding water very gradually. Add salt to taste. Knead for at least 10 minutes, longer if possible. Make a thick roll about 20 cms/8 inches long and allow to stand for 1½ hours. Just before serving your meal, knead and roll the dough again.

■ Break off a small portion of the dough and roll it with a dash of ghee into a ball between the palms. Flatten the ball and with the help of a little dry flour, roll into a thin round pancake with a rolling-pin. Gently remove from the board and place on a hot tava, first cook one side, turn over and slightly cook the other.

■ Place on hot coals (or on a barbecue stove) and let the chappati rise like a balloon. This can be done by pressing down one side of the chappati on the tava with a spatula and then gently pressing all the sides of the chappati. Some people prefer a dry chappati, while others serve it with ghee sparingly spread on one side.

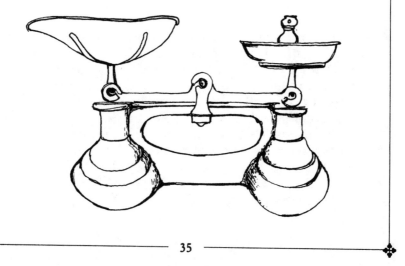

BESAN ROTI

GRAM FLOUR ROTI

450 g/1 lb gram flour
450 ml/ ³/4 pint warm water
2 green chillies

1 small onion
¹/2 teaspoon pomegranate seeds
Ghee

■ Chop the onion finely. Slice the chillies into very small pieces. Mix the flour, a little ghee, onion, chillies and pomegranate seeds. Knead with warm water into a stiff dough. Divide into equal portions and roll out as chappatis, but thick enough not to allow the onions to break up the bread. Heat a tava and cook on both sides, adding a little butter or ghee to the edges. Remove when brown on both sides.

SWEET ROTIS

225 g/8 oz toovar dhal
225 g/8 oz sugar
1 tablespoon ghee

Cardamoms as desired
Whole wheat flour (ata)

■ Soak the dhal in cold water overnight. Wash well and remove all course skins. Boil in enough water until well cooked and very tender. Drain off the water and mash the grain with a wooden spoon. Add sugar and ghee and cook over a medium heat until dry, stirring constantly. Add cardamoms and keep aside. Knead enough whole wheat dough for about 12 rotis.
■ Roll out a roti about the size of a puri (approximately 18 cm/ 7 inches in diameter) and put a small ball of the dhal filling in the centre. Close up the roti and seal well. Roll out roti taking care not to let the stuffing break through. Heat tava and cook the roti with a little ghee, like a paratha.

PYAZ
KI ROTI

ONION ROTI

450 g/1 lb whole wheat flour
   (ata)
6 green chillies
3 onions
1 tablespoon chopped
   coriander leaves

1 sprig curry leaves
Pinch bicarbonate of soda
Ghee
Salt to taste

■ Chop the onions, chillies and curry leaves finely. Sieve the flour into a bowl and add the chopped ingredients. Add bicarbonate of soda and salt and enough water to make a batter just thick enough to pour. Lightly grease a tava and pour in enough batter to cover it thinly. Spread with the back of a spoon, if necessary and pour a little ghee around the edge of the roti to prevent it from sticking. Flip over and brown on the other side.

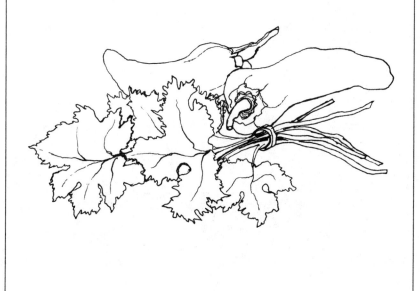

LAYERED MEAT PARATHAS

450 g/1 lb whole wheat flour
225 g/½ lb ground minced
   meat
1 onion
1 teaspoon coriander powder

½ teaspoon chilli powder
1 teaspoon garam masala
Salt to taste
Ghee or butter

■ Mince the onion. Heat 2 tablespoons ghee or butter and sauté the onion until it is cooked and well done, approximately 5 minutes. Add the coriander, chilli powder, garam masala and salt and fry until brown. Add 2 tablespoons water and simmer for a few minutes until the ingredients are tender and the liquid has evaporated.

■ Meanwhile, sieve the flour with the salt, rub in a little butter, add water and knead well into a stiff soft dough. Break off small portions and roll into 8 paper-thin, round, even chappatis. Smear one chappati with ghee and place another on it, smear again with ghee and place another until you have a layer of four. Sprinkle the surface with a little water and spread a thin layer of meat. Cover with four more chappatis in the same way. Roast on a tava until golden, adding a little ghee on the sides and fry, turning once, until brown and crisp.

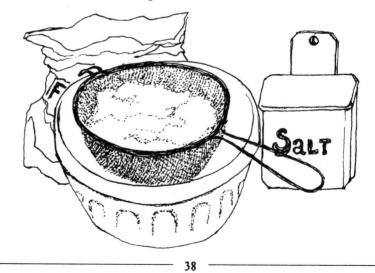

SWEET CHANA-DHAL PARATHA

SWEET LENTIL BREAD

450 g/1 lb flour
450 g/1 lb gram dhal (chana)
450 g/1 lb sugar
½ teaspoon ground cardamoms

3 cloves
2 teaspoons oil (sesame oil or olive oil)

■ Sieve the flour, add the oil and enough water, gradually, and knead to a thick dough. Roll lemon-sized balls from the dough and keep aside.

■ Meanwhile, boil the dhal in 600 ml/1 pint water for about an hour until tender. Drain off the water, add sugar, cardamoms and cloves and stir until a thread-like syrup is formed. Grind or mash the mixture to a paste. Roll into balls of the same number about double the size of the flour balls. Flatten out the flour balls. Place a ball of the gram mixture in the centre and cover completely with the flour dough. Roll into a smooth, large ball in the palm of your hand. Place on a rolling board and roll out with a rolling-pin into a round pancake about 0.5 cms/¼ inch thick. Bake on a tava until both sides are a crisp golden brown. Spread with butter or ghee and serve hot.

ALU
KI ROTI

1 kg/2 lb whole wheat flour
  (ata)
450 g/1 lb potatoes
2 onions
4 green chillies
1 clove garlic
½ bunch of coriander leaves

1 teaspoon roasted and ground
  coriander seeds
½ teaspoon freshly-ground
  black pepper
1 teaspoon pomegranate seeds
Salt to taste

■ Chop onions, green chillies, coriander and garlic finely. Boil potatoes, peel and chop. Heat a little ghee in a kerai and fry the onions until brown. Add the remaining ingredients, including potatoes and remove from the heat. Cool and mash with a fork.

■ Knead the flour with a little water and a pinch of salt as for plain rotis. Make eight equal portions from the dough. Also make eight equal portions of the potato stuffing. Roll out into the size of a puri, place stuffing in the centre of the dough and cover, bringing the edges over. Roll into a ball in the palm of the hand, flatten and roll out again as thin as possible (taking care not to break). Heat a tava and fry on both sides just like plain parathas.

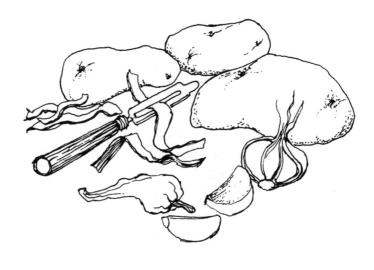

GOBI PARATHA

CAULIFLOWER PARATHA

450 g/1 lb wholewheat flour
450 g/1 lb cauliflower
2 onions
2 green chillies
1 tablespoon dried
    pomegranate seeds
    (anardhana)

1½ inch piece ginger
1 tablespoon chopped coriander
    leaves
½ teaspoon garam masala
Ghee
Salt to taste

■ Chop cauliflower finely or grate. Do not use the stalks. Sprinkle water with salt, put in the cauliflower and let stand for 30 minutes. Squeeze out the liquid and mix with finely-chopped onions, finely chopped ginger, chopped coriander leaves, finely chopped chillies, crushed pomegranate seeds and season.

■ Sieve flour, add 2 tablespoons ghee, a pinch of salt and enough water to knead to a stiff dough. Cover and keep aside for 10 minutes. Divide into 6 portions and roll out into round thick pancakes. Spread with a little ghee. Divide the cauliflower into 6 portions and put a helping of the mixture in the centre. Close up the mixture carefully. Roll into a ball and roll out as thin as possible without letting the mixture break through. Smear with ghee and fry on both sides on a heated tava until brown. Serve hot.

DHALBHARI PURIS

100 g/4 oz moong dhal	4 cloves
100 g/4oz gram dhal (chana)	3 cardamoms
575 g/1¼ lb whole wheat flour	½ teaspoon cummin seeds
(ata)	1½ teaspoons salt or to taste
8 peppercorns	Ghee

■ Soak both the dhals overnight. The next morning drain off the water and grind to a paste. Grind the cloves, peppercorns, cardamoms and cummin seeds. Heat 1 tablespoon ghee in a pan. Fry the dhal paste with the gound masala and salt. Knead the wheat flour to a stiff dough with 2 teaspoons ghee, water and salt. Divide the dough into small portions. Roll each portion into a ball. Flatten it in the palm of your hand and put in a little fried dhal. Close up the dough and roll out into a thickish puri. Deep fry in ghee.

SAVOURY PURIS

225 g/8 oz flour (maida)	1 tablespoon coriander leaves
5 green chillies	Ghee as required
1 teaspoon cummin seeds	1 clove garlic
1 teaspoon coarsely ground	Salt to taste
black pepper	

■ Sieve the flour and salt together and add the cummin seeds and pepper. Grind garlic, coriander leaves and chillies and add to flour. Rub a little ghee into the flour and adding warm water, gradually, knead into a stiff dough. Make small balls of the dough and roll out the puris. Fry in hot ghee until golden brown. Do not roll out too many puris at a time as then they will not puff up.

TIL
PURIS

450 g/1 lb flour (maida)
2 tablespoons sesame seeds (til)
2 teaspoons salt or to taste
2 teaspoons sugar or to taste
2 teaspoons celery seeds
2 teaspoons caraway seeds

2 teaspoons coarsely ground
   peppercorns
2 teaspoons onion seeds
   (kalonji)
Ghee

■ Sieve the flour and mix all the ingredients into it. Add enough warm water to knead to a stiff dough. Roll out into thin round puris. Heat the ghee in a kerai and deep fry on both sides until crisp and golden brown.

BANANA
PURIS

225 g/8 oz flour (maida)
100 g/4 oz gram flour (besan)
3 ripe bananas
¾ teaspoon cummin seeds
4 green chillies

¾ teaspoon chilli powder
¼ teaspoon sugar
Ghee
Salt to taste

■ Sieve the two varieties of flour. Mix the red chilli powder, turmeric, cummin seeds and salt into the flour.
■ Mash the bananas well with the sugar. Add 1 tablespoon of ghee to the flour and knead. Add the banana purée and continue to knead until soft. Divide into small balls and roll out into the shape of a puri. Heat the ghee and deep-fry the puris on both sides until crisp and brown, or fry with a little ghee on a tava on both sides until brown.

MASALA RICE BUNS

450 g/1 lb rice	1 marble-sized ball of tamarind
100 g/4 oz black gram dhal	2 onions
1 small coconut	1 tablespoon ghee
12 dry red chillies	Salt to taste

■ Clean the rice and dhal, then wash them and soak in enough water, in separate basins, overnight. Grate the coconut and grind with the chillies, tamarind and a cupful of water to a coarse paste. Drain rice and dhal and add to the paste. Grind again to a soft paste.Chop the onions finely and add to the paste. Add salt to taste. Grease the idli katoris with a little ghee. Fill up with the paste and steam in the idli steamer until done (about ¾ hour). Serve with curd.

COORGI PAPUTOO

RICE-MILK BREAD

450 g/1 lb coarsely crushed rice	6 tablespoons grated coconut
300 ml/½ pint milk	Pinch of salt

■ Wash the rice thoroughly, rinse and soak in 300 ml/½ pint fresh cold water for 15 minutes. Add the milk, coconut and a pinch of salt and mix well. Pour in equal amounts into three baking trays and steam for 30 - 35 minutes. When slightly cool, quarter bread and serve with curry or dhal. To prepare sweet paputoo, add 100 g/4 oz sugar instead of salt and serve with butter.

KADAMBUTTOO

RICE BALLS

675 g/1½ lb rice
4 tablespoons finely grated
    coconut

Butter or ghee
Salt to taste

■ Pound or crush the rice coarsely, wash well and drain off the water. Put 1½ pints water to boil in a saucepan, when boiling add ½ teaspoon salt and then the rice. Cook, stirring constantly, to avoid any lumps forming, for 8 - 10 minutes until the mixture is fairly solid. Remove from the heat and mix in the grated coconut.
■ Grease the palm of one hand and when the mixture is cool enough, form into lemon-size balls. Spread a damp muslin in the inner part of a steaming vessel and put in the rice balls. Steam for 30 - 40 minutes. Serve hot with pickles or curry. This recipe will provide enough for approximate 30 Kadambuttoos.

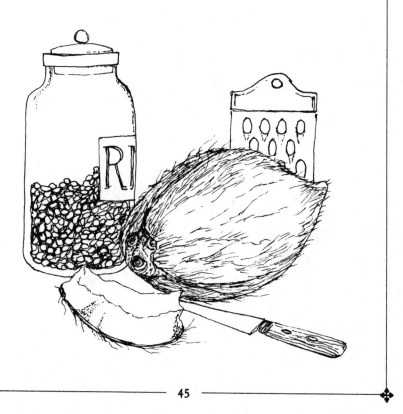

SOOJI
IDLE

450 g/1 lb sooji (semolina)
225 g/8 oz fine vermicelli
100 ml/3¹/₂ fl ozs ghee or oil
450 ml/³/₄ pint curd
4.0 cms/1¹/₂ inch piece ginger
4 green chillies
1 tablespoon mustard seeds

1 tablespoon black gram dhal
10 cashew nuts, chopped
2 dry red chillies
1 sprig curry leaves
Pinch of asofoetida (soak in a
little water)
Salt to taste

■ Heat half the ghee in a frying pan and fry the semolina and vermicelli lightly without letting it change colour. Keep aside and cool.

■ Heat the remaining ghee in a saucepan and fry the mustard, dhal, chillies, chopped cashew nuts and curry leaves. Chop the ginger and green chillies. Mix fried semolina and vermicelli into the curd. Add fried spices, ginger and chillies, asofoetida water and salt and mix well. Allow the mixture to stand for 30 minutes. Add enough water to the mixture to make a thick batter consistency and pour into a greased katoris or heat-resistant ramekin dishes. Cover and steam for 15 minutes. Test with a dry sharp knife to see if they are cooked throroughly. Serve immediately.

MYSORE IDLI

100 g/4 oz urad dhal   2 teaspoons salt
225 g/8 oz rice

■ Soak urad dhal and rice in separate basins in water overnight. The next day, grind the dhal to a paste. Grind the rice adding water to make a thick paste. Mix together and add the salt. Keep aside for 24 hours to rise. Pour 2 large spoonfuls of the paste into ovenproof dishes or katoris and steam the idlies for 30 - 35 minutes.

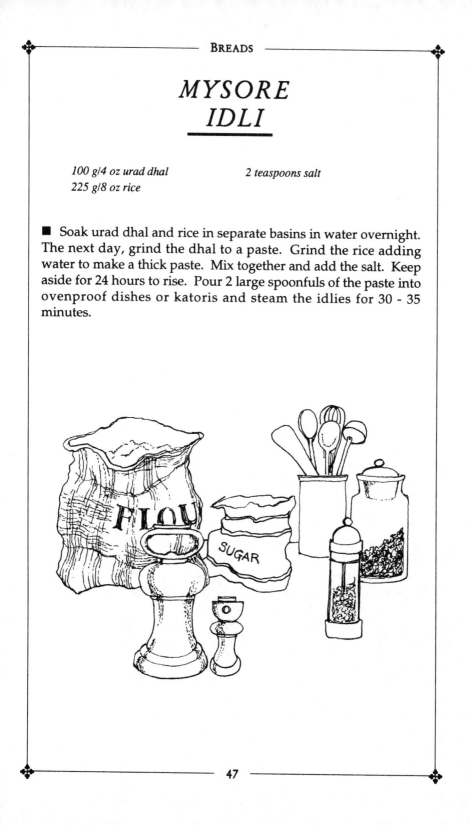

MASALA DOSAI

PANCAKES WITH POTATO FILLING

225 g/8 oz fine sooji (semolina)
2 teaspoons curd or yoghurt
450 ml/ ³/4 pint water

¹/2 teaspoon bicarbonate of soda
A pinch of salt

FOR THE FILLING:

4 potatoes
3 onions
2 green chillies
¹/4 teaspoon turmeric powder
¹/2 teaspoon mustard seeds

A sprig of curry leaves
A small piece of ginger
Salt to taste
2 tablespoons oil

■ Soak the sooji in water adding the curd and bicarbonate of soda. Beat well until a creamy batter is formed. Leave the batter in the mixing bowl overnight.

■ Next day, boil 2 onions together with the potatoes until soft. Peel and mash the potatoes and slice the onions. Mix together, adding salt. In a saucepan, heat 2 tablespoons oil and cook the mustard seeds until they begin to crackle. Add the sliced onions, chopped ginger and the remaining spices. Fry until the onion is brown. Add the potato mixture and blend thoroughly. Fry for 5 minutes and keep aside.

■ Heat a tava and spread with ghee. Pour 2 large spoonfuls of the batter in the centre of the tava and spread it in a circle with a spoon to cover the tava like a pancake. Cover with a large lid, cook for 1 minute. Remove the lid and place a spoonful of the potato mixture in the centre of the pancake (dosai). Fold over as for an omelette, put a little ghee on the sides of the tava, turn over once again and fry until crisp. Serve with coconut chutney (see page 22).

DAL DOSAI

450 g/1 lb rice	6 green chillies
225 g/8 oz toovar dhal	2.5 cms/1 inch piece ginger
100 g/4 oz black gram dhal	1 piece asafoetida
100 g/4 oz Bengal gram dhal	Small bunch of coriander leaves
4 onions	1 sprig curry leaves
8 dry red chillies	Ghee

■ Chop the onions, ginger, green chillies, coriander and curry leaves finely. Grind the dry red chillies coarsely.
■ Soak the rice and the dhals overnight in cold water. Next morning, drain and grind to a coarse paste. Add the chillies, salt and asafoetida. Add the chopped ingredients to the paste and salt to taste. Mix well. Heat a tava, grease it and spread a ladleful of paste evenly on it. Pour 2 teaspoons ghee or oil around the edge of the pancake (dosai). Turn over when cooked and serve with chutney.

OAT DOSAI

8 oz oats	0.5 cm/ ¼ inch piece ginger
100 ml/3½ fl oz curd	1 teaspoon salt
2 green chillies	Ghee or butter
1 onion	

■ Chop the onion, chillies and ginger finely. Put the oats in a mixing bowl, add the chopped spices, salt and curd and mix into a thick dough.
■ Heat a tava and grease the surface with a spoonful of ghee. Take a tablespoonful of the oats mixture and spread on the surface of the tava so as to make a thin pancake. Add a little more ghee, flip the pancake (dosai) over and fry on the other side until evenly brown. Serve hot with curry or pickles.

COCONUT DOSAI

1 kg/ 2 lb rice
2 fresh coconuts
4 green chillies (optional)
4.0 cms/1½ inch piece ginger
4 onions
1 heaped tablespoon chopped
   coriander leaves

½ tablespoon chopped curry
   leaves
2 tablespoons ghee
2 tablespoons oil
Salt to taste

■ Soak the rice overnight. Next day, drain the water and wash the rice thoroughly in fresh water. Grate the coconuts. Chop the ginger and chillies finely and grind the rice, coarsely. Add coconut, ginger and chillies and grind to a smooth paste. Slice the onions and sauté in a little ghee. Add to the rice paste, together with the coriander and curry leaves. Season with salt.

■ Take a frying pan with a lid and heat a little oil. Pour in a tablespoon of the batter and cook, covered, for a few seconds. Turn the pancake (dosai) over, add a teaspoon of ghee, cook for 1 more minute and remove. Prepare all the pancakes by similar method.

WHEAT-FLOUR DOSAI

450 g/1 lb whole wheat flour
3 onions
4 green chillies (optional)
1 teaspoon chopped coriander
   leaves

1 sprig curry leaves
Pinch of salt
Pinch of bicarbonate of soda

■ Chop the onions and chillies finely. Put the flour in a mixing bowl, add the onions, chillies and curry leaves. Stir in the salt and soda and mix with enough water to make a batter consistency. Lightly grease a frying pan or a tava and pour

on 2 tablespoons of the batter. Spread evenly with the back of a
wooden spoon or spatula. Pour a little ghee on the edges to
prevent sticking and cook, turning, until brown on both sides.
Serve hot with curry or chutney.

KHAMEERA
NAN

450 g/1 lb flour	*½ teaspoon fresh yeast*
1 egg	*Silver paper (varak)*
300 ml/½ pint milk	*Ghee*
3 tablespoons butter	*Salt to taste*
1 teaspoon aniseed	

■ Sieve the flour and add salt and aniseed. Rub in the butter
until the mixture is crumbly. Gradually add the lukewarm milk
and beaten egg. Finally, add the yeast and knead thoroughly.
Leave to rise for 2 - 3 hours until double in size. Make balls of the
dough and roll out to 1.9 cms/¾ inch thickness. Leave all nan to
rise further until again double in size. Deep fry in hot ghee until
brown on both sides. Remove and drain. Cover each nan with a
piece of silver paper before serving.

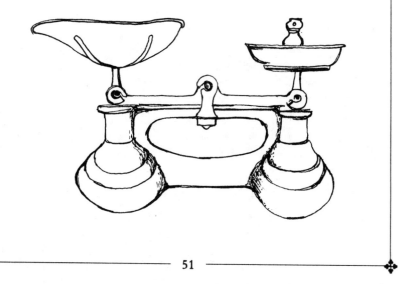

KHEEMA TANDOORI

*350 g/12 oz whole wheat flour
(ata)*
2 tablespoons fresh yeast

1 teaspoon salt
100 g/4 oz minced meat

■ Mix together the flour, yeast and salt with enough water to make a firm dough. Knead for 30 minutes and cover with a muslin cloth for 2 - 3 hours until the dough rises. Knead in the meat and a little salt if required. Divide into four parts. Roll in the hands and make flat round cakes about the size of a plate by slapping from one palm to the other. Bake in a tandoor or on a barbecue if possible.

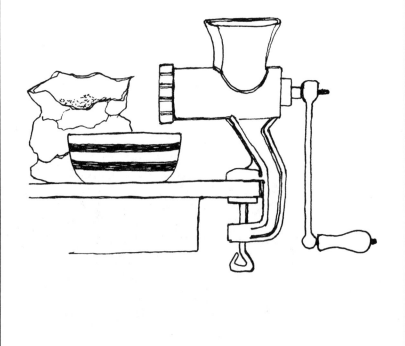

RICE AND
DHALS

RICE

Although rice is eaten all over India, it is the staple food of only South India and Bengal. Both the South Indian and the Bengali like plain, boiled rice. The curries in these areas are heavily spiced and so blend with the boiled rice. Although meat and rice dishes did originate in North India, the pulao is now a favourite dish in homes all over the country.

It has been said that the history of India could be written through her pulaos or pillafs. Fish and shell-fish, vegetables and lentils, chicken, meat and eggs, all cooked with rice, prove the influences of India's many peoples on her cuisine.

Many varieties of rice are available in India, but one of the best quality is a long grained rice grown in Dehra Dun, known as 'Basmati'. The rice grown and eaten in South India is of a much coarser texture but the flavour is far richer. The rice from Bengal has a very small grain. No Puja (or act of worship), is performed without sprinkling grains of rice, which symbolise health, wealth and fertility. The Hindu priest is always given a bag of rice as a token of gratitude after a religious ceremony.

An extremely colourful festival in South India is Pongal, which in Tamil means 'boiled rice'. This is the Tamilian New Year. The feast is in honour of Indra, the king of the heavens, the god of rain clouds, seasons, and all that is the source of happiness and bounty.

The Pongal festival lasts for three days, though the celebrations go on for a week. On the first day, the Sankranti - which is the last day of the Tamilian Calendar - brides collect their trousseau for the year: it consists of clothes, jewellery, household utensils and presents of oil, ghee and jaggery. All old and used earthenware pots are broken on this day and replace by new ones, for the Pongal rice sweet must be cooked in new utensils.

On Pongal New Year's Day, a large quantity of rice is cooked with milk and sugar (kheer) in every Hindu home. This delicious dish is prepared as an offering to Indra and served at breakfast after prayers. Children, in particular, delight in consuming large quantities of kheer, which has become a great favourite with children throughout the country. (A recipe for kheer is given in the chapter on sweet dishes). Many delicacies are prepared for the Pongal feast, extra sweet dishes are cooked in particular because they are supposed to please Indra. Young girls dress in the most vivid colour combinations, and spend the evening dancing and singing.

The third day of Pongal is a special day for cattle. All the animals are washed and decorated with colour and flowers. A thick soup is made from rice and sugar cane juice and fed to the cattle. In the evening there is much gaiety and the whole town or village turns up to watch the Pongal bull fights. Pouches of money are hung from the horns of fierce bulls who are then provoked by loud noises and the general excitement. All the young eligible bachelors of the village are dared to fight the bull by the girl judged the most attractive, and to retrieve the pouch of coins. The winner she will accept as her husband. There is heated speculation and the fields are crowded with fevered spectators.

The six months following Pongal are considered auspicious for marriage and mothers are kept busy searching for suitable brides for their sons and worthy lads for their daughters. Soon there will be much excitement in the homes again as elaborate preparations are made for wedding feasts. Here again rice is served - not only as a food but also as part of the dowry, for the bride is given barrels full of rice to take with her to her husband's home.

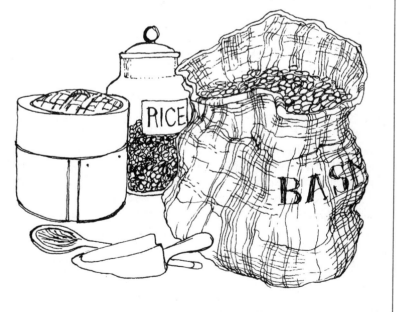

CHICKEN BIRYANI

1 medium sized chicken - or	25 g/1 oz almonds
4 chicken quarters	50 g/2 oz raisins
225 g/8 oz rice	4 eggs
600 ml/1 pint curd or yoghurt	1 teaspoon saffron
3 medium onions	Salt to taste
Ghee	

GRIND TOGETHER TO FORM A SMOOTH PASTE:

2 medium onions	2 blades mace
6 cloves garlic	4 cloves
10 cms/4 inch piece ginger	2 teaspoons poppy seeds
1 sprig coriander	1 inch stick cinnamon
1 sprig of mint	Green chillies to taste
4 small cardamoms	

■ Clean the chicken. Cut into 4 pieces. Add the ground spices to the curd and mix well. Marinate the chicken pieces in this mixture for about 2 hours. Fry the sliced onions in a pan containing a little fat, until they are golden and crisp. Add them to the chicken marinade and mix thoroughly.

■ Place the chicken in 600 ml/1 pint water over gentle heat and bring to the boil. Cook until tender. Now parboil the rice.

■ In a large ovenproof pan, put in a layer of rice, 2 pieces of the chicken with a proportionate amount of the marinade. Continue until all the chicken pieces and rice are finished. Place a generous quantity of ghee over the top layer of rice. Crush the saffron, dissolve in a little warm milk, and sprinkle over the surface. Cover the saucepan well with a tight fitting lid. Place it in a larger covered vessel containing water and set the whole to boil for about 30 minutes. Before serving blanch and slice the almonds, sort and wash the raisins, and fry in a little ghee. Garnish biryani with nuts and slices of hardboiled egg.

MASALA KHICHERI

450 g/1 lb rice	1 teaspoon garam masala
4 tablespoons green dhal	6 cloves garlic
2 large onions	2.5 cms/1 inch piece ginger
2 small potatoes	5 green chillies
2.5 cms/1 inch piece coconut	1/2 bunch coriander leaves
1 teaspoon turmeric powder	Oil
1 teaspoon red chilli powder	Ghee
1 teaspoon cummin seeds	Salt to taste

—— MEDIUM ——

■ Chop the onions and green chillies finely. Mince the coriander leaves, ginger and garlic. Peel the potatoes and cut into small cubes. Grind the coconut piece to a fine paste. Fry onions in a combination of 1 tablespoon ghee - 1 tablespoon oil. When the onions are light brown, stir in the minced garlic, ginger and green chillies. Add the garam masala together with the ground coconut. Fry for a 1 minute, put in the rice and dhal and fry both until crisp. Pour in warm water until it is about 5.0 cms/2 inches above the level of the rice.

■ If the water evaporates, more warm water may be added. Add potato cubes and salt. Bring to the boil, lower the heat and simmer until the rice is cooked. Sprinkle coriander leaves on the surface for a garnish.

MANGO
RICE

3 lb rice	1 tablespoon mustard seeds
6 medium sized green mangoes	1 tablespoon black gram dhal
2 - 3 green chillies	1 tablespoon cummin seeds
3 cups grated coconut	2 - 3 curry leaves
300 ml/½ pint gingelly oil or	A pinch turmeric powder
225g/ 8 oz ghee	Salt to taste

—— MILD ——

■ Clean the rice and put it in boiling water. Bring to the boil and cook for 15 minutes. When the rice is almost cooked, remove it from the heat. Drain the excess water and allow the rice to cool. Add the turmeric powder and half the quantity of gingelly oil (or ghee). Mix well.

■ Cut the mangoes into tiny pieces or grate them. Grind the cummin seeds, half the chillies, salt to taste, and the coconut gratings. Mix it with the mango pieces and add it to the cooked rice. Fry the mustard seeds, gram dhal, curry leaves and the remaining chillies in oil. Add to the rice. Mix well and serve.

NOOLPUTTU
PULAO

FOR NOOLPUTTU:

450 g/1 lb rice	300 ml/½ pint hot water
½ teaspoon salt	

FOR MEAT:

450 g/1 lb lamb	600 ml/1 pint coconut milk
2 medium onions	1 tablespoon black gram dhal
6 tablespoons ghee	50 g/2 oz nuts (almond, cashew
2 tablespoons garam masala	or pistachio)
Black pepper to taste	2 - 3 curry leaves

—— HOT ——

NOOLPUTTU:

■ Soak the rice for 2 hours. Wash, drain and grind. Roast on an ovenproof plate for 10 minutes taking care that it retains its white colour. Remove from the oven and cool. Add salt and make into a dough with the hot water. Squeeze this dough through the small holes of a *sevanazhi* or use a forcing bag, into a piece of wet muslin and steam for 10 minutes. (You can make 5 or 6 noodles.) When cold, cut into 2.5 cms/1 inch pieces which will look like vermicelli.

MEAT:

■ Wash and chop the meat. Slice one onion and fry in 2 tablespoons of ghee until brown. Add the garam masala, coconut milk, salt and pepper to taste. Add meat and cook until it is tender and the gravy is absorbed. Place another saucepan on the heat and pour in the remaining ghee. Slice the second onion and brown with dhal and a few curry leaves. Add the meat and the prepared noolputtu. Keep on a low heat for 5 minutes more. Garnish with fried nuts and serve hot. This dish can also be prepared with macaroni or spaghetti instead of the noolputtu.

ONION PULAO

450 g/1 lb Basmati rice
450 g/1 lb baby onions
4 cloves
2 sticks cinnamon
2 dry red chillies

1 heaped teaspoon cummin
    seeds
1 tablespoon chopped onion
2 tablespoons ghee
Salt to taste

—— *MILD* ——

■ Soak the rice in cold water for 10 minutes. drain off the water. Heat the ghee and fry the cummin seeds, chopped onion and red chillies for a few minutes. Add the cloves, cinnamon and rice and fry a little longer. Add enough water to cook the rice and salt to taste. Cook until the rice is halfway through cooking, approximately 8 minutes. Parboil the peeled small onions for 10 minutes. Drain and add to the half-cooked rice. Cover the pan and simmer gently until cooked through. For extra flavour add a cup of coconut milk (instead of water) to cook the rice.

VEGETABLE PULAO

450 g/1 lb rice	½ teaspoon turmeric powder
450 g/1 lb shelled peas	A small piece of ginger
450 g/1 lb string beans	4 green chillies
450 g/1 lb tomatoes	A sprig of mint leaves
3 medium onions	A bunch of coriander leaves
3 dessertspoons ghee	½ tablespoon garam masala
½ coconut	Salt to taste

—— MILD ——

■ Wash the rice and soak for 10 minutes. Cut the beans in half. Grind to a paste the turmeric powder, ginger chillies, mint and coriander leaves. Heat the ghee in a saucepan and fry the finely sliced onions and the garam masala. When the onions are golden brown, add all the vegetables except the tomatoes. Fry them for 10 minutes and stir in the coconut milk. Blend in the previously ground paste.

■ When almost cooked pour in the tomatoes, add the rice and 600 ml/1 pint water to cook the rice. Salt to taste and bring to the boil. Continue to cook on a very low heat. Garnish with crispy fried onions if desired and serve hot.

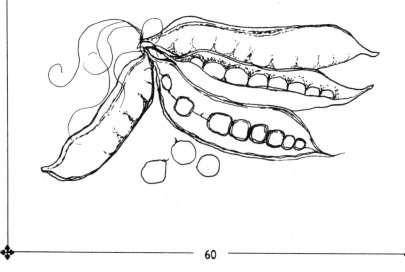

FISH PULAO

675 g/1½ lb rice
2 large pomfrets or plaice
3 large onions
1 coconut

½ lemon
7 tablespoons ghee
Salt to taste

GRIND TO A PASTE:

2½ teaspoons roasted
    coriander seeds
4 dry red chillies
1 teaspoon cummin seeds
1 small piece turmeric (or
    ½ teaspoon turmeric powder)

4 cloves
1 bunch coriander leaves
1 small piece ginger
100 g/4 oz dessicated coconut

—— *MILD* ——

■ Wash rice and soak for 1 hour. Clean the fish and cut into pieces of the desired size. Extract about 3 cups milk from the coconut. Heat 3 tablespoons ghee and fry the ground masala until it bubbles and becomes slightly red in colour. At this stage add the fish pieces and salt. Put in enough water and allow to cook, covered until tender. Remove the fish from the saucepan and keep warm, saving they gravy.

■ Heat 4 tablespoons ghee in another saucepan and fry the sliced onions until slightly browned. Add the rice and salt to taste. Mix well. Pour in the fish gravy, coconut milk, lemon juice and let the rice cook on a medium heat. When the rice is almost cooked and the water absorbed, arrange all the fish pieces on top. Cover and let it cook on a low heat. Serve hot.

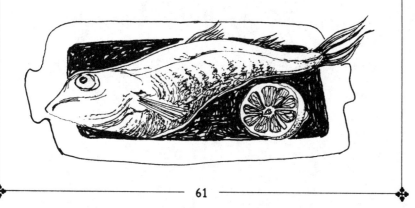

POMFRET KITCHEREE

450 g/1 lb rice
450 g/1 lb pomfret or any white fish
12 cloves
2 sticks cinnamon
4 cardamoms
1 teaspoon turmeric powder
2 large onions
1 tomato

4 cloves garlic
1 small piece ginger
½ teaspoon garam masala
½ teaspoon chilli powder
25 g/1 oz raisins
25 g/1 oz almonds
1 lemon
4 tablespoons ghee
Salt to taste

—— MILD ——

■ Clean the fish and cut into large cubes. Heat 2 tablespoons ghee and add the cinnamon, cardamoms, turmeric and one chopped onion. Add the rice and fry until the rice is a golden brown. Cover the rice with water until the water level is 2.5 cms/1 inch above the rice level. Leave to cook over a low heat.

■ At the same time, heat 2 tablespoons ghee and slice and fry the remaining onion until brown with the garlic, ginger, garam masala and sliced blanced almonds. Add the fish cubes and chopped tomato and sprinkle lemon juice over it. When the fish is cooked keep on one side, until the rice is nearly cooked. Add it to the rice and mix, together with the raisins and salt to taste. Keep on a low heat until the rice has cooked, taking care to see that it does not burn. This kitcheree should be served with curd and garnished with slices of hardboiled egg.

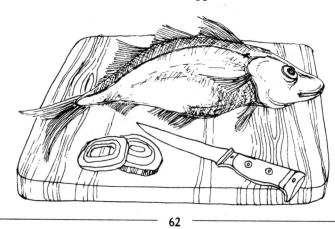

VANGI BAATH

BRINJAL RICE

SERVES 6

450 g/1 lb rice
1.2 ltrs/2 pints water
1 cinnamon stick
4 cardamoms
4 cloves
1 large onion

4 tablespoons ghee
450 g/1 lb brinjals (aubergines)
1 teaspoon mustard seeds
½ teaspoon turmeric powder
Salt to taste

FOR THE MASALA:

1 tablespoon grated coconut
A pinch of asafoetida
6-8 peppercorns
1 teaspoon coriander seeds

1 teaspoon gram dhal
1 teaspoon black gram dhal
6 dry red chillies

—— MEDIUM ——

■ Clean and wash the rice and put in water to soak. Meanwhile place a heavy bottomed saucepan on the heat, put in 2 tablespoons ghee, chopped onions, cloves, cardamoms, cinnamon and when the onion turn pale brown, mix in the drained rice. Fry the rice for 2 minutes, add 600 ml/1 pint water and salt. Cover with a lid and allow the rice to cook for 15 - 20 minutes. Remove from the heat.

■ Slice the brinjals lengthways into 6 sections each and soak them in water to prevent discoloration. Fry the masala ingredients in a little ghee and when they turn brown, grind to a coarse powder. Heat 1 tablespoon ghee in a saucepan and fry the mustard seeds until they splutter. Add the brinjals, sprinkle with salt and turmeric and cook until tender. Add the ground masala and stir well. Remove the pan from the heat. Replace the rice on the heat and add the brinjal curry and 1 tablespoon ghee. Mix well and allow to cook for a couple of minutes. Remove from the heat. Serve with slices of lemon and plain yoghurt.

MANGO PULAO

1 kg/2 lbs Basmati rice	1 teaspoon raisins
6 semi-ripe mangoes	2 - 3 curry leaves
2 cups coconut (grated)	4 tablespoons gingelly oil or
1 tablespoon mustard seeds	ghee
1 tablespoon black gram dhal	A pinch of saffron or 1 teaspoon
4 dry red chillies	turmeric
1½ dozen cashew nuts	Salt to taste

—— *MEDIUM* ——

■ Clean and wash the rice and cook with sufficient water. Peel the mangoes and grate coarsely. Grate the coconut.

■ Heat the oil or ghee and fry the mustard seeds, gram dhal and red chillies until they crackle. Add the coconut and when slightly brown, add grated mango and cook until soft. Add turmeric, chopped nuts, raisins, curry leaves and salt and cook for a few more minutes.

■ When the rice is almost done, add the mango mixture. Mix carefully with a fork. Level the top and place in a slow oven to complete cooking. Serve hot with a sweet chutney.

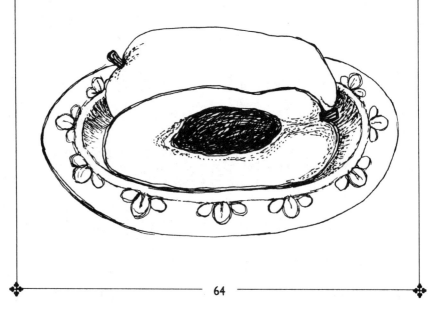

MEAT-BALL PULAO

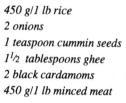

450 g/1 lb rice
2 onions
1 teaspoon cummin seeds
1½ tablespoons ghee
2 black cardamoms
450 g/1 lb minced meat

2 slices bread
2 eggs
150 ml/¼ pint milk
½ lemon
breadcrumbs

GRIND TOGETHER:

2 green chillies
1 teaspoon coriander seeds
4 cloves garlic

2.5 cms/1 inch piece ginger
1 teaspoon garam masala

FOR THE TOMATO SAUCE:

300 ml/ ½ pint coconut milk
450 g/1 lb tomatoes
25 g/1 oz flour
3 cloves

1 stick cinnamon
4 cloves garlic
2 teaspoons red chilli powder

—— MEDIUM ——

■ Soak the bread and milk together for 15 minutes. Squeeze out excess milk. Mince 1 onion. Mix together the meat, bread, minced onion, ground spices, juice of ½ a lemon and 1 raw egg. Shape the mixture into small balls, dip into beaten egg, roll in the breadcrumbs and deep-fry in hot ghee until reddish brown.

■ Wash and clean the rice. Heat 1 tablespoon ghee and slice and fry the remaining onion. Stir in the cummin seeds and cardamoms. Add the cleaned rice and fry for 5 minutes. Pour in 300 ml/½ pint and cook, covered until almost done. Gently put in the meat-balls covering them with rice. Place in the oven at 180°C/350°F/Gas mark 4 for 25 minutes.

■ Heat 1 tablespoon ghee, fry chopped garlic and cloves and cinnamon for 3 minutes. Add peeled tomatoes and cook until tender. Add the chilli powder and mash the tomatoes into a paste with the back of a wooden spoon. Bring to the boil, add the flour and coconut milk and cook until thick and creamy. Serve pulao on a flat dish with the sauce poured over it.

SAFFRON
RICE

450 g/1 lb Basmati rice
450 g/1 lb sugar
8 cardamoms
12 cloves
50 g/2 oz raisins

50 g/2 oz cashew nuts
1 tablespoon saffron colour
(pinch saffron, soaked in 1
    tablespoon hot water)
1 dessertspoon ghee

■ Wash the rice and boil in 300ml/½ pint water for 20 minutes. When half cooked add the sugar, stir well over a low heat. To prevent the rice from sticking, add a little ghee. Stir in the saffron colour, the remaining ghee, cloves, raisins and cashew nuts. Mix well, stirring gently until the rice is thoroughly permeated with the saffron colour.

■ Remove the saucepan from the heat, and put in the oven at 180°C/350°F/Gas mark 4 for 10 minutes. Sprinkle with the cardamom powder, mix well and serve hot.

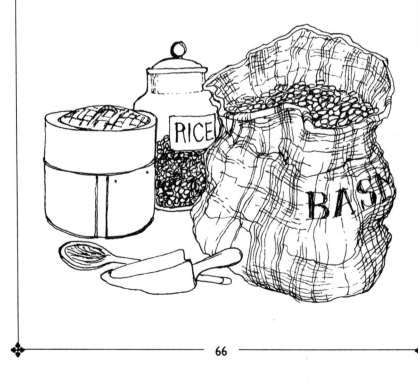

MOTI PULAO

PEARL PULAO

450 g/1 lb minced meat
450 g/1 lb rice
100 g/4 oz gram dhal
8 tablespoons ghee
2 onions
6 cloves garlic
2.5 cms/1 inch piece ginger
6 cardamoms
5.0 cms/2 inch piece cinnamon

4 cloves
6 peppercorns
1 dessertspoon chilli powder
Salt to taste
Silver paper for garnishing
(varak)
1 pinch saffron (kesar)
2 tablespoons milk
A few drops rosewater

■ Soak the rice in water and keep on one side. Mince garlic, ginger and 1 onion. Wash the dhal and put in a saucepan with the minced meat, 4 cardamoms, half the cinnamon, 2 cloves, 4 peppercorns, chilli powder, the minced garlic-ginger-onion and salt to taste. Add enough water to cover the minced meat and cook over low heat for 20 minutes. When the meat is tender and all the water absorbed take it off the heat and grind to a fine paste. Make the mixture into several small balls (the size of large beads approximately 2.5 cms/1 inch). Heat half the ghee in a frying pan and fry these meat balls until brown. When cooked, wrap them in the silver paper and set aside.

■ In another saucepan, heat the rest of the ghee, slice the onion into rings and fry with the remaining cardamoms, cinnamon and peppercorns. Pour in the rice and fry for 5 minutes. Salt to taste. Pour in enough water so that its level is 4.0 cms/1 ½ inches above the level of the rice. Leave to boil over a low heat. When all the water is absorbed, remove from the heat. Blend the saffron (kesar) in the milk and pour it over the rice.

■ Just before serving, put the rice in a dish with the meat balls as decoration on the top. Sprinkle with a few drops of rosewater. This will give the meat balls the appearance of pearls on the coloured rice.

SOUTHERN YELLOW RICE

450 g/1 lb Basmati rice
3 large onions
1 teaspoon peppercorns
8 cloves
1 teaspoon cardamom powder
Few sprigs fennel

4-5 curry leaves
1 teaspoon turmeric powder
Milk of 2 coconuts
2 tablespoons ghee
Nuts for garnishing
Salt to taste

—— MILD ——

■ Slice 2½ onions. Wash the rice. Heat the ghee in a saucepan and fry the sliced onions and curry leaves untill the onions are golden brown. Add the rice and fry for 2 minutes. Mix all the spices except the cardamom powder into the coconut milk and pour into the rice. Boil rapidly for 15 minutes. When the rice is nearly cooked add the cardamom powder. Slice and fry the remaining onions until crisp. Fry some sliced almonds and chopped cashew nuts and garnish the rice before serving. Serve with chicken or meat curry.

PRAWN PULAO

450 g/1 lb rice
450 g/1 lb prawns (cleaned)
1 large onion
¼ coconut
3 cloves garlic
4 cloves
6 peppercorns
2 sticks cinnamon

175 g/6 oz peas
1 teaspoon chilli powder
1 teaspoon turmeric powder
A little thick tamarind juice
2 tablespoons ghee
Salt to taste
1 egg

—— MILD ——

■ Slice the onion finely and chop the garlic. Wash the rice. Heat 1 tablespoon ghee in a large saucepan and fry the onion, garlic, grated coconut until just brown. Add the cloves, peppercorns, and cinnamon and fry for 2 minutes. Stir in the rice and fry until dry.

■ Pour in enough water to cover the ingredients and leave to cook, on medium heat adding a little salt if required. Mix the peas, prawns, tamarind juice, chilli powder and turmeric and keep to one side for 30 minutes. In a separate saucepan heat the remaining ghee and fry the mixture until almost tender.

■ When the rice is three-quarters cooked, gently stir in the cooked prawn mixture. Place in the oven at 180°C/350°F/Gas mark 4 for 15 - 20 minutes. Serve garnished with fried onions and slices of hardboiled egg.

MUSSEL PULAO

450 g/1 lb rice	2 onions
450 g/1 lb fresh mussels	6 cloves garlic
1 coconut	4 dry red chillies
12 peppercorns	Ghee
2 sticks cinnamon	Salt to taste
1 teaspoon coriander seeds	

—— MILD ——

■ Wash and clean the mussels well and carefully remove the meat from the shells. Grate half the coconut and fry in a tablespoon of ghee and grind. Fry peppercorns and cinnamon in a teaspoon of ghee and grind. Repeat this with the coriander seeds. Chop onions and garlic. Heat 2 tablespoons ghee and fry the onions and garlic until brown. Add the fried spices and cleaned rice. Extract the milk from half the coconut and add to the rice with enough water 300 ml/½ pint to cook the rice. Stir in the salt.

■ In a frying pan fry the mussels in a little ghee, season with salt and powdered chillies and keep aside. When the rice is almost cooked add the mussels and grated coconut. Mix well and place in the oven at 180°C/350°F/Gas mark 4 for 15 - 20 minutes. Serve with tomato chutney.

APPLE PULAO

225 g/8 oz rice
3 tablespoons ghee
2 bay leaves
2 sticks cinnamon
10 cloves

5 cardamoms
50 g/2 oz almonds
50 g/2 oz raisins
2 - 3 pinches saffron
900 ml/1½ pints water

FOR THE SYRUP:

3 apples
350 g/12 oz sugar

450 ml/¾ pint water
A pinch of saffron

■ Peel, core, and cut the apples into 8 pieces each. Put the apple in a covered saucepan with the 450 ml/¾ pint water and heat for 5 minutes. Drain.

■ Put the sugar and 450 ml/¾ pint water in another saucepan and stir well. Add the apple pieces and heat for 30 minutes until about one third of the syrup remains. Add the pinch of saffron just when the mixture begins to boil.

■ Heat 3 tablespoons ghee in a saucepan and stir in the bay leaves, cinnamon, cloves and cardamoms. Fry for a minute or two then add the rice. Stir in the sliced almonds and raisins and fry for 2 - 3 minutes. Pour over 900ml/1½ pints water. Bring to the boil and stir in 2 - 3 pinches of saffron. Cook for 15 minutes. When the rice is almost cooked, remove from the heat.

■ Make a hole in the centre of the rice and place the apple pieces and a little syrup in the centre. Cover with rice and pour the rest of the syrup on top. Cook on a low heat for a further 15 minutes and serve.

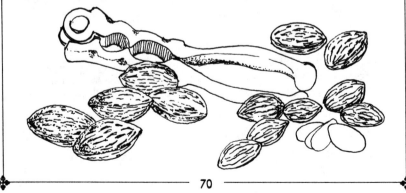

FISH
BIRYANI

450 g/1 lb fish
450 g/1 lb Basmati rice
4 eggs
4 potatoes
3 tomatoes
1 coconut
1 teaspoon cummin seeds

4 green chillies
1 medium onion
4 cloves garlic
A small piece of turmeric
4 tablespoons ghee
Salt to taste

—— MILD ——

■ Wash the fish and cut into pieces. Place in a saucepan and pour in a cup of salted water. Bring to the boil, remove the fish and take out the bones. Keep aside. Wash the rice.

■ Peel tomatoes and squeeze out the pulp and juice. Hardboil the eggs and shell. Boil the potatoes, peel and cut into cubes. Grind the turmeric, cummin seeds, chillies, garlic and ½ the onion to a paste.

■ Extract 3 cups of coconut milk from the coconut. Heat the ghee in a saucepan, slice and fry the remaining ½ onion. Stir in the rice and mix well. Continue to cook until slightly brown and pour in the coconut milk. Add water if necessary so that the liquid will be 2 fingers above rice level. When the rice is almost cooked, add the ground paste, fish and salt. Mix gently and reduce the heat. Cover the saucepan and bake at 180°C/350°F/Gas mark 4 until the rice is sufficiently dry. Serve garnished with slices of hardboiled egg and potatoes.

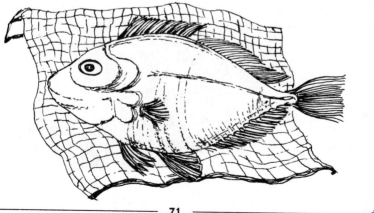

GULABI PULAO

PINK PULAO

225 g/8 oz rice	¾ teaspoon turmeric powder
3 brinjals (aubergines)	1 tablespoon gram dhal
1 large beetroot	1 tablespoon urad dhal
2 medium onions	Salt to taste
½ coconut	1 handful cashew nuts
6 green chillies	1 sprig curry leaf
1 teaspoon mustard seeds	3 - 4 tablespoons ghee
1 teaspoon black pepper	1 lemon
½ teaspoon cummin seeds	

—— MEDIUM HOT ——

■ Cook the rice. Boil the beetroot until tender, then scrape off the outer skin. Heat 1 tablespoon ghee, fry the mustard seeds, pepper, cummin seeds, gram dhal, urad dhal and chopped green chillies. When the ingredients turn brown, cut the brinjals into small cubes and add to the mixture. Chop the onions and stir into the mixture with the curry leaves. Cook until soft. Add the boiled beetroot to these vegetables. Salt to taste, stir in the turmeric powder and grated coconut and fry for 1 minute.

■ Blend this mixture with the cooked rice. Fry the cashew nuts in the remaining ghee. Season with the lemon juice and stir into the pulao. Cover and keep on a low heat for a few minutes. Serve hot with plain yoghurt.

SINDHI PULAO

PULAO FROM SIND

450 g/1 lb rice	4 - 5 bay leaves
225 g/8 oz onions	8 cardamoms
8 tablespoons ghee	2 tablespoons cummin seeds
450 g/1 lb lamb chopped	50 g/2 oz almonds (soaked and
1 tablespoon ground coriander	blanched)
1 tablespoon peppercorns	50 g/2 oz pistachios
2 black cardamoms (whole)	150 ml/¼ pint curd or yoghurt
1 tablespoon red chilli powder	Salt to taste

—— HOT ——

■ Wash and soak the rice in water for 2 hours. Heat 4 tablespoons ghee in a saucepan. Add the finely chopped onions to hot ghee and fry until brown. Sprinkle a few drops of water over the onions and stir until soft. Take out half the onions and keep on one side. Put the lamb in the saucepan and stir until the meat is golden brown. Grind together the coriander, 1 black cardamom, cardamoms and cummin seeds. Add the curd and cook, stirring for 5 minutes. Blend in the ground spices with salt and the chilli powder and cover the saucepan with a lid. Continue to cook adding more water if necessary. Simmer until the meat is soft and the gravy has thickened.

■ Put 3 tablespoons ghee in another saucepan, add the bay leaves, peppercorns, rice (the water from the rice should be preserved), ¼ teaspoon cummin seeds, 1 whole black cardamom and 1 level teaspoon salt. Stir for 3 minutes, then add the remaining brown onions.

■ Remove saucepan from the heat and put three-quarters of the rice on a platter. In the saucepan, first put in a layer of rice, then the cooked lamb, sprinkle with chopped onions and pistachios and repeat this process until the rice and meat are finished. Pour in the water (in which the rice was cooked) evenly so as not to break the layers, to 1.9 cms/¾ inch above the rice level. Cook and remove when the rice is almost cooked and there is no water left. Sprinkle with more almonds and pistachios, cover with a tight lid and keep in a warm oven until serving time.

DHALS

A favourite legend about the creation of Ganesh, the elephant god of Hindu mythology, tells about the time when Lord Shiva went hunting and left Parvati, his wife, alone at home. Parvati decided to have a luxurious oil and turmeric bath. She took handfuls of gram flour and rubbed the oil from her body. With the scrapings she modelled the figure of a child. Her delight in her creation was so great that she placed the figure in front of the door to protect her while she finished her bath. She named him Ganesh or Ganapati which means, 'Head of the people'.

Meanwhile, Shiva returned, but Ganesh refused to let him enter the house without the permission of his mistress. This so angered Shiva that he slashed off the head of the doll. When Parvati discovered this, she wept and would not let Shiva touch her till he had found and replaced Ganesh's head. Shiva looked everywhere but could not find the head so he stuck on the head of a cow-elephant and the doll came to life. Ganesh was given the position of headman. Later, he was elevated to be the god of knowledge and success because of his good deeds.

Ganesh, who is also known as the Lord of the Harvest, is often pictured riding a rat, his mode of transport. This symbolizes the rats he destroyed to protect the harvest. Around his fat belly, which represents a full barn, is coiled a hooded cobra, the greatest killer of the field rat.

Harvest time is a happy time for the people of India. 'Rice and dhal' is the mainspring of the working-man's diet. In every Indian home a dish made of dhal is prepared at least once a day. Sweets and savouries made from dhal flour are served on all occasions. It is the cheapest source of rich protein, and many delicious Indian dhal recipes exist.

In August or September is the Ganapati festival. It is one of the most important festivals of Maharashtra, and the beaches of Bombay attract crowds of devotees. Clay images of the harvest god are kept in the house and worshipped for nine days. Dhal ladoo (sweetmeats made of lentil flour) are offered to Ganesh. Other foods prepared from the harvest crop are also offered. On the tenth day, the image is dressed in colourful robes and garlands, his rat is also saddled and decorated and placed on a cart. Amid the rejoicing shouts of men, women and children of

'Ganapati Bappa Moria' ('Lord Ganapati, we wish you a speedy return'), the image is taken to the river or sea and immersed in the water. A handful of sand is brought back from the river and ceremoniously sprinkled in the barnyard and rooms where the year's grain is stored.

SABAT MAANH

PUNJABI BLACK DHAL

350 g/12 oz whole black lentils (maanh)	4 green chillies
1 onion	1 teaspoon garam masala
1.2 ltrs/2 pints water	2 dry red chillies
600 ml/1 pint milk	2 tablespoons ghee
50 g/2 oz ginger	1 tablespoon cream or white butter
1 small pod garlic	Salt to taste

—— MILD ——

■ Wash the dhal well under running water. Add the water and boil with the finely sliced ginger and garlic, red chillies and salt. Reduce heat and simmer till nearly cooked. Add milk and cook gently. This will take about 4 hours. Add a little more water if necessary. Mash the dhal with a wooden spoon and simmer till a creamy consistency.

■ Heat ghee and fry finely chopped onion and green chillies, add garam masala and pour into the dhal. Just before serving, mix in the cream or butter. Serve with chappatis.

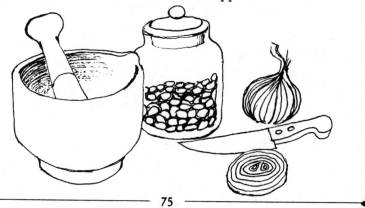

MIXED LENTIL NASHTA

BREAKFAST DISH

50 g/2 oz moong dhal	100 g/4 oz rice
50 g/2 oz channa dhal	3 tomatoes
50 g/2oz whole masoor dhal	3 onions
50 g/2 oz toova dhal	Ghee
50 g/2 oz millet	Salt to taste
50 g/2 oz wheat	

GRIND TO A FINE PASTE:

2 teaspoons coriander seeds	4 cloves
1 teaspoon cummin seeds	1 stick cinnamon
A piece of dry coconut	2 cloves garlic
A piece of dry turmeric	A few mint leaves
2 red dry chillies	

—— MILD ——

■ Cook all the dhals, wheat and millet in water. Heat the ghee and fry the chopped onions. When they are browned add the ground spices and stir in the chopped tomatoes. Put in the rice and enough water, and cook until tender. Mix in the cooked dhals, millet, wheat and salt. Blend well and serve hot with yoghurt.

DHAL KABABS

450 g/1 lb moong dhal	2 green chillies
50 g/2 oz gram flour	Salt to taste
2 teaspoons garam masala	Powdered breadcrumbs
1 onion	1 tablespoon curd or yoghurt
4 eggs	

—— MILD ——

■ Wash and soak the moong dhal overnight. Drain water and grind to a fine paste. Fry finely sliced onion until crisp and brown. Remove, grind coarsely and keep aside. In the same ghee, fry gram flour and garam masala for 1 minute. Mix ground dhal, gram flour mixture, beaten eggs, curd, finely-chopped chillies, fried onion and salt until well blended. Form into flat cutlets, roll in breadcrumbs and fry in ghee until evenly brown. Serve immediately.

DAHI VADAS

225 g/8 oz black dhal (urad)
600 ml/1 pint oil or 450 g/1 lb
    ghee
6 green chillies
1 teaspoon mustard seeds

4 dry red chillies
1 cup grated coconut
1 sprig curry leaves
1.2 ltrs/2 pints buttermilk
Salt to taste

—— MEDIUM ——

■ Grind the grated coconut to a fine paste with 4 green chillies and some salt, and mix with the buttermilk. Put a pan on the heat containing about a tablespoon of oil. When hot, add the mustard seeds and red chillies. When the mustard begins to splutter remove the pan from the heat. add the buttermilk and keep on one side. Remove the black skin of the gram dhal if necessary and soak in water for about 2 hours. Drain. Add salt to taste and grind dhal to a fine paste without too much water. Chop the remaining green chillies and curry leaves and mix with the dhal paste. Put a pan on the heat with the remaining oil. When hot make the paste into small balls, each about the size of a lemon and fry. Remove and put them in the prepared buttermilk. Keep for about 2 - 3 hours until they are well soaked and soft.

DAHI BARAS

LENTIL CAKES IN YOGHURT

1 kg/2 lb gram dhal	A small piece of ginger
1 teaspoon garam masala	A small piece of asafoetida
2 teaspoons chilli powder	Ghee or oil
1.2 ltrs/2 pints curd or yoghurt	Salt to taste

■ Soak dhal overnight. Next morning drain and grind it, adding asafoetida and ginger. Use a little hot water, if necessary, when grinding.

■ Place a fine textured wet muslin cloth over a saucepan, make small balls of the mixture and flatten them out on the muslin. In a kerai, heat ghee or oil, pick up the baras one by one from the muslin cloth and fry them until golden brown. Remove and put to soak in salt water. After about 10 minutes take them out, squeeze them slightly without changing their shape, and leave aside.

■ Prepare curd by beating well and mixing in salt, chilli powder and garam masala. Arrange the baras on a plate and pour on prepared curd. Sprinkle with a little chilli powder and some mustard seeds fried in ghee or oil.

AAM DHAL

225 g/8 oz toovar dhal	1 teaspoon mustard seeds
2 unripe mangoes	2 dry red chillies
1 onion	A sprig of curry leaves
3 cloves garlic	1 tablespoon gheee
1 teaspoon turmeric powder	Salt to taste

—— MILD ——

■ Wash and soak the dhal for an hour. Change the water, add salt and set to boil on a medium heat. Peel the mangoes, cut into three pieces each and add to the half-cooked dhal. Cook till dhal is tender and the magoes are cooked to a pulp.

■ Heat the ghee in a frying pan and add the spices. Add chopped onion and garlic and fry till brown. Add to the cooked dhal. Aam dhal should be of a watery consistency. Serve with rice.

DHAL AND GREENS MAATVADA

100 g/4 oz toovar dhal
100 g/4 oz gram dhal
A small piece of asafoetida
¼ coconut
3 - 4 dry red chillies
¼ teaspoon cummin seeds
1 teaspoon mustard seeds

¼ teaspoon black dhal
3 tablespoons gingelly oil (or any cooking oil)
2 large bunches of fenugreek (methi)
Salt to taste

—— MILD ——

■ Soak the toovar dhal and gram dhal together in water for 30 minutes. Clean and chop the tender fenugreek. Drain the dhals and grind them to a rough paste together with the grated coconut, asafoetida, red chillies and cummin seeds, adding no water. Add the chopped fenugreek and salt to this.

■ Place a kerai on the heat, put in the gingelly oil and when it is hot fry the mustard seeds until they start to splutter. Add the black dhal. When the dhal turns golden brown add the coarsely ground spices and continue stirring until the mixture turns a golden brown and becomes crisp. Serve hot as a side dish with curry and rice.

ONION SAMBAR

350 g/12 oz very small onions	2 teaspoons salt or to taste
225 g/8 oz green dhal (moong)	2 teaspoons ghee
1 lemon-sized lump tamarind	A handful of grated coconut
½ teaspoon mustard seeds	A sprig of curry leaves
1 teaspoon turmeric powder	½ bunch coriander leaves

FRY THE FOLLOWING IN 1 TEASPOON GHEE OR OIL:

9 dry red chillies	2 teaspoons gram dhal
2 teaspoons coriander seeds	A small piece of asafoetida
1 teaspoon fenugreek	

—— HOT ——

■ Wash the green dhal, cook it well in 2 pints water and keep aside. Grind all the fried ingredients with the grated coconut into a paste. Pour 600 ml/1 pint water into a saucepan. Add the peeled onion whole. Add the turmeric powder and salt. Allow to boil for 3 - 4 minutes. Soak tamarind in ½ cup water for 2 - 3 minutes. Remove as much juice as possible from it and add to the boiling onions. When the onions are well cooked, add the cooked dhal and ground paste. Stir well and leave to boil for a minute or two, then add the curry leaves. Remove from the heat and keep covered.

■ Heat 1 teaspoon ghee and fry the mustard seeds until they splutter. Remove seeds and add to the sambar.

DAHI WADA KUDI

450 g/1 lb black gram dhal (urad)	4 green chillies
	Pinch of bicarbonate of soda
1.2 ltrs/2 pints curd or yoghurt	25 g/1 oz raisins
1 teaspoon mustard seeds	3 limda leaves (lemon leaves)
½ teaspoon asafoetida	Coriander leaves
¼ pint oil	Salt to taste

—— MILD ——

■ Soak the dhal in water overnight. Next morning drain and grind to a paste. Add the salt and bicarbonate. Chop the green chillies. Soak the raisins in hot water.

■ Heat the oil, make small balls of the dhal paste and fry until golden brown. Remove and add to the curd. (First prepare the curd by adding 1 cup water to it and mixing with a beater. Add the chopped green chillies, soaked raisins and salt to taste). Let the wadas soak in the curd for 2 hours. Before serving, heat 1 tablespoon oil in a saucepan, fry the mustard seeds and asafoetida until the seeds splutter and add the limda leaves. Pour into the curd mixture. Remove the limda leaves, garnish with chopped coriander leaves and serve.

PINEAPPLE RASAM

1 medium pineapple	$\frac{1}{2}$ teaspoon turmeric powder
100 g/4 oz arad dhal	$\frac{1}{4}$ teaspoon asafoetida
1 teaspoon gram dhal	$\frac{1}{2}$ teaspoon mustard seeds
1 teaspoon black dhal	A sprig of curry leaves
2 teaspoons oil	A small bunch of coriander
1 teaspoon black pepper	leaves
2 dry red chillies	Salt to taste

■ Cook the arad dhal in water. Peel pineapple, squeeze out 6 cups of juice, adding water if necessary. Fry the gram and black dhal, pepper, red chillies and asafoetida in a teaspoon of oil and grind to a paste. Mix the paste with a cup of water and add turmeric powder and salt. Pour the mixture into the pineapple juice and then pour this juice into the cooked dhal. Now add the coriander and curry leaves. Leave the dhal to cook for 15 minutes. Fry the mustard in a teaspoon of oil and pour it into the pineapple rasam when the seeds start spluttering. Serve with boiled rice.

DHAL SOUP

100 g/4 oz dhal	½ turnip
½ carrot	600 ml/1 pint water or stock
1 dessertspoon ghee	1 - 2 onions
1 potato	2 teaspoons flour
150 ml/¼ pint milk	Salt and pepper to taste

■ Clean and wash the dhal and soak for a few hours. Clean the vegetables and chop into fine pieces. Put the ghee into a saucepan and fry the drained dhal and vegetables without browning. Add water and seasoning and bring slowly to boiling point. Simmer until the vegetables are cooked. Remove the vegetables, rub through a sieve and return to the soup. Allow to boil for 10 minutes. Mix the flour with milk, pour into the soup and allow to boil for 5 minutes. Remove from the heat and serve with slices of fried bread.

MYSORE RASAM

MYSORE SOUP

225 g/8 oz dhal	A bunch of coriander leaves
225 g/8 oz tomatoes	Salt to taste
1 small ball of tamarind	1 teaspoon mustard seeds
A sprig of curry leaves	Ghee

FRY THE FOLLOWING INGREDIENTS SEPARATELY:

4 dry red chillies	¼ teaspoon fenugreek
1 teaspoon coriander seeds	A small pinch of asafoetida
1 teaspoon cummin seeds	¼ teaspoon turmeric powder
¼ teaspoon black peppercorns	

—— MILD ——

■ Soak the tamarind in 150 ml/¼ pint boiling water for 10 minutes. Boil dhal in 1.2 ltrs/2 pints water and when cooked, add chopped tomatoes. Grind all the fried ingredients to a powder and add to the dhal tomato mixture. Strain the juice from the tamarind and add it to this, together with salt. Let simmer for about 15 minutes. Season with curry and coriander leaves.

■ Fry the mustard seeds in a little ghee and when they splutter, remove and add to the rasam. Serve hot with boiled rice.

SOUTH INDIAN KUTU

225 g/8 oz dhal
1 kg/2 lb french beans
½ coconut
½ teaspoon mustard seeds
½ teaspoon turmeric powder

1 teaspoon rice
1 tablespoon coriander seeds
A small piece of asafoetida
5 - 6 dry red chillies
Salt to taste

—— MEDIUM HOT ——

■ Clean dhal, salt to taste and boil with enough water to cover, until soft. When cooked, strain but keep the water. Wash the beans and cut into tiny pieces, then cook them in the dhal water. Add salt. Grind all the other ingredients to a smooth paste and when the beans are tender add cooked dhal and the ground masala to them. Add a little water and stir well until the curry thickens. Remove and serve hot with cooked rice or chappatis.

■ Any remaining dhal could be made into a chutney by grinding it with 4 - 5 chillies, a little grated coconut and a pinch of salt, coriander leaves and asafoetida. This is particularly delicious with puris.

CHANA
KA GHUGNI

450 g/1 lb gram dhal

1/2 coconut

2 teaspoons turmeric powder

1 1/2 teaspoons cummin seed
    powder

1 small piece ginger

A sprig of bay leaves

8 green chillies

225 g/8 oz raisins

4 sticks cinnamon

6 cardamoms

4 cloves

2 large onions

50 g/2 oz sugar or to taste

4 tablespoons ghee

4 tablespoons mustard oil

Salt to taste

—— MEDIUM HOT ——

■ Clean dhal, salt to taste and boil with enough water to cover, until soft. Strain and keep aside. Heat the mustard oil in a saucepan and add 2 tablespoons of ghee. Cut coconut into small pieces and fry them in the ghee. Remove and keep aside. Fry the chopped onions until brown.

■ Make a smooth paste of turmeric, cummin seeds and ground ginger. Fry it with the browned onions to remove the raw smell, and add it to the dhal. Mix in the bay leaves, chillies, raisins, coconut pieces and sugar. Stir well. Grind cinnamon, cardamoms and cloves together, and a few minutes before removing the dhal mixture from the heat add them to it with the remaining ghee. Leave to simmer for a further 2 minutes. Serve hot with puris or parathas.

SUKHA
DHAL

450 g/1 lb whole moong dhal

100 g/4 oz grated coconut

2 medium onions

3 green chillies

1/4 teaspoon asafoetida

2 tablespoons ghee

1/4 teaspoon turmeric powder

1/2 teaspoon mustard seeds

1 lemon

1/2 teaspoon red chilli powder

Salt to taste

—— MILD ——

■ Soak the dhal overnight. Wash and remove skin the next day. Heat the ghee and fry the mustard seeds and asafoetida, adding the moong dhal and the remaining spices. Stir in 300 ml/½ pint hot water and cook on a low heat until the dhal is tender and the water has evaporated. Squeeze lemon juice into it and sprinkle with chilli powder. Garnish with chopped coriander leaves.

MOONG DHAL HALWA

225 g/8 oz moong dhal	8 almonds
225 g/8 oz sugar	4 cardamoms
450 ml/ ¾ pint milk	½ teaspoon saffron
300 ml/½ pint water	A pinch of yellow colouring
4 tablespoons ghee	10 raisins (washed)

■ Soak the dhal overnight. Grind coarsely, using very little water. Put ghee in a kerai, add dhal and fry until golden brown on a low heat. Add raisins, milk, water and sugar. Stir in the saffron and yellow colouring. Stir over a low heat until all liquid is absorbed and ghee separates. Remove from the heat and add crushed cardamoms and blanched finely-sliced almonds.

JOSHE BRENJ

225 g/8 oz dry red or white
beans
225 g/8 oz moong dhal
225 g/8 oz gram dhal
3 large onions
450 g/1 lb chopped meat

225 g/8 oz rice
1 bunch coriander leaves
1 teaspoon cummin seeds
Salt and black pepper to taste
1 bunch dill leaves
Salt to taste

■ Soak the beans for an hour before cooking. Fry the sliced onions in a little ghee in a large saucepan. Add the meat, beans, moon and gram dhals, salt and enough water to cook the dhals. When the meat is tender, add the rice, salt and enough water for it to cook properly. Add the chopped dill, coriander leaves, cummin seeds and freshly ground pepper. Leave to boil until the rice is cooked, then remove from the heat and serve hot. This is a favourite dish amongst Iranis in India.

PADAVAL SAMBAR

1 medium snake-gourd
600 ml/1 pint curd or yoghurt
225 g/8 oz gram flour
50 g/2 oz gram dhal
1 teaspoon cummin seeds
2 teaspoons mustard seeds
1 pinch asafoetida
1 teaspoon turmeric powder

2 teaspoons sugar
6 green chillies
2 tablespoons ghee
A bunch of coriander leaves
A sprig of curry leaves
½ coconut
Salt to taste

FOR SAVOURY BALLS:

225 g/8 oz gram dhal
225 g/8 oz black dhal (urad)
3 - 4 green chillies
1 teaspoon cummin seeds
1 teaspoon turmeric powder

1 pinch asafoetida
600 ml/1 pint oil or 450 g/1 lb
ghee
Salt to taste

—— MEDIUM HOT ——

■ Soak gram dhal and black dhal in water for 2 hours, then grind coarsely. Mix in cummin seeds, turmeric, asafoetida, finely chopped green chillies and salt. Shape into firm marble-sized balls. Fry them in hot ghee until golden brown. Drain and keep aside. Slice the snake-gourd into 1.3 cms/½ inch thick rings and boil with a little water until soft.

■ Add a little water to the curd and churn to form thick buttermilk. Blend gram flour with buttermilk until all lumps have disappeared. Add 1 teaspoon each of powdered cummin seeds and mustard seeds, finely chopped green chillies, salt and sugar and soaked gram dhal. Cook, stirring, on a low heat until the mixture boils. Remove from the heat. Heat 2 tablespoons ghee in a saucepan and cook the remaining mustard seeds. When the seeds splutter add turmeric, asafoetida and curry leaves. Pour this into the prepared sambar.

■ Place each fried savoury ball in a snake-gourd ring and arrange in a shallow dish. Pour sambar over these. Garnish with coriander leaves, curry leaves and grated coconut. Serve hot or cold with rice.

GRAM-DHAL TIFFIN

8 oz gram dhal
2 dry red chillies
½ teaspoon mustard seeds
½ teaspoon black dhal
2 green chillies
A piece of ginger

A bunch of coriander leaves
50 g/2 oz grated coconut
2 teaspoons coconut oil
Salt to taste
Lemon juice

—— *MILD* ——

■ Cook the dhal in enough water until tender. Pour the coconut oil in a saucepan and add salt, mustard seeds, black dhal and red chillies. Chop finely the green chillies, ginger, coriander leaves and when the mustard splutters stir these in, together with the cooked dhal. Mix in the grated coconut and sprinkle with lemon juice to taste.

AAMBAT
SPROUTED LENTIL CURRY

225 g/8 oz lentil seeds
    (sprouted whole moong)
½ coconut
3 dry red chillies
1 marble sized ball of tamarind
¼ teaspoon fenugreek

Salt to taste
1 teaspoon coconut oil
2 small onions
1 tablespoon ghee
Few cashew nuts

—— MILD ——

■ Soak the lentil seeds overnight. Next morning, drain and remove them from the bowl. Put them in a pan with a tight fitting lid and place in a warm place with a fairly heavy weight on the lid. By evening they will have sprouted. Put the sprouted lentils in plenty of water and leave again overnight. Next morning drain the water and remove the outer skins.

■ Put a saucepan containing 1.2 ltrs/2 pints water to boil and add the lentil seeds. Bring to the boil and cook for 10 minutes or until half cooked, drop in a few cashew nuts and cook until the mix is tender. Add the salt. Grind the coconut with red chillies and tamarind to a smooth paste. Fry the fenugreek in the coconut oil until it turns red and grind it with the paste. Pour all the ground spices into the lentils, bring to the boil and cook for 5 minutes. Remove from the heat. Chop the onions, fry in ghee to a golden brown and stir into the curry.

MASSOOR DHAL WITH VEGETABLES

225 g/8 oz lentils (masoor dhal)
6 tablespoons ghee
2 medium potatoes
3 medium ripe tomatoes
1 medium brinjal (aubergine)
1 onion
4 cloves garlic

½ teaspoon turmeric powder
½ bunch coriander leaves
6 green chillies
1 teaspoon cummin seeds
1 teaspoon garam masala
Salt to taste

—— HOT ——

■ Scrub and chop potatoes, tomatoes and brinjal, slice the onion and set all vegetables aside. Wash the dhal thoroughly and boil in 1.2 ltrs/2 pints water, adding turmeric powder for 25 minutes. When the dhal is halfway through cooking add the chopped vegetables, together with the ground cummin seeds and salt. Cook until the potatoes are soft, adding chopped coriander leaves and whole green chillies, cover and set aside.

■ Heat ghee and fry the spices and garlic. Add to the dhal and keep covered. The consistency of the dhal should not be too thick. Serve hot with plain white rice.

CABBAGE UTTAPPAM

100 g/4 oz toovar dhal	10 dry red chillies
225 g/8 oz rice	Salt to taste
450 g/1 lb cabbage	1 teaspoon tamarind
1 small coconut	Oil
2 onions	

—— HOT ——

■ Clean the cabbage and onions, cut into small pieces and keep on one side. Soak the dhal and rice together in water for about 3 hours. Fry red chillies in a little oil and scrape the coconut. Grind the coconut, fried chillies and tamarind together and when half ground add the rice and dhal. Grind to a thick paste, adding water as required. Next add the chopped cabbage and onions to the paste and mix well. Add salt.

■ Spread this paste to about the size of a saucer on a hot, greased tava. Fry well on both sides, over a low heat. Serve hot.

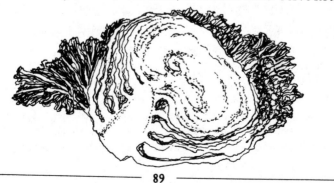

LEMON RASAM

100 g/4 oz arad dhal	Pinch of asafoetida
1 teaspoon cummin seeds	1/4 teaspoon mustard seeds
1/2 teaspoon black pepper	1 teaspoon salt
2 green chillies	2 medium lemons
Small piece of ginger	Coriander leaves

—— MILD ——

■ Wash the dhal and cook it in a little water. Dilute with about 1.2 ltrs/2 pints water. Grind the cummin seeds and black pepper and add to the dhal with the salt. Blend in the juice of the lemons. Heat a little ghee and fry the mustard seeds until they splutter. Stir in the chopped ginger and chillies. Add to the dhal, lower the heat and when the dhal curry comes to the boil, remove from the heat. Add the chopped coriander leaves and serve in cups.

SHAHJAHANI DHAL

450 g/1 lb split peas or gram dhal	2 medium onions
	1 coconut
3 tablespoons ghee	1/2 pint cream
4 cardamoms	Salt and sugar to taste
6 cloves	4 green chillies
2 - 2.5 cms/1 inch sticks cinnamon	

—— MILD ——

■ Bring the peas or dhal to boil in a little water. When parboiled, remove from the heat.

■ Heat the ghee in a saucepan. Fry the garam masala (cardamoms, cloves, cinnamon) for 1/2 minute. Add the thinly-sliced onions and fry until golden brown. Stir in the dhal, cover and cook for about 10 minutes. Meanwhile, grate half the coconut and extract the milk by boiling it in a little water. Strain this milk and mix with the dhal. When the coconut milk has almost evaporated add the cream, sugar and salt. Chop the other half of the coconut into small cubes, fry slightly and add to the dhal. Add the sliced green chillies and stir until the dhal has a dry thickish consistency. Serve hot.

CHANA BATURA

CURRIED WHOLE GRAM

FOR BATURA:

100 g/4 oz flour	*Salt to taste*
1 egg	*Curd or yoghurt*
A pinch of baking powder	*Ghee for frying*

FOR CHANA:

450 g/1 lb boiled gram	*Chilli powder to taste*
2 tablespoons curd or yoghurt	*A large piece of ginger*
3 tablespoons ghee	*Garam masala*
2 large onions	*Amchoor (powdered dry mango)*

■ Knead all the batura ingredients into a dough the day before. Set aside in a warm place to rise. The next day, shape into thick puris and deep-fry in hot ghee.

■ Grind the onions to a fine paste. Heat ghee in a dekchi and brown the onions and chopped ginger. Add the chilli powder, curd and gram. Cook for about 5 minutes. Take off the heat and sprinkle with garam masala and amchoor. Garnish with slices of tomato, chopped coriander and green chillies. Serve with baturas.

VEGETABLES

VEGETABLES

Some time in August or September, the people of the Malabar Coast of South India celebrate the country's oldest traditional festival - the twelve day celebration of Onam. This festival commemorates the reign of Mahabali, the mythological king who is said to have ruled at Mahabalipuram, the ancient city near Madras. His reign brought peace and prosperity and his people worshipped him as a god. The gods in heaven, however, were angered by the power exercised by a mere mortal. They sent the god Vishnu, in the form of a Brahmin youth named Vamana (deceiver), to beg a favour of the king. Mahabali, whose generosity was well known, offered Vamana all his lush vegetable gardens (it is believed that vegetables have never grown as well in India as during Mahabali's reign). The youth refused the offer but asked that he be given all that he could cover in three strides. This meagre request was readily granted, whereby Vamana grew to gigantic proportions and in three strides covered the whole kingdom. Thus did King Mahabali lose his power and his kingdom and was banished to the underworld. In answer to his last request his spirit was allowed to return to his realm once a year.

Some poeple believe that Mahabali returns to earth during Onam to see if his people will enjoy life as they did during his reign. Streets and shops are stacked with vegetables, fruit and flowers and the people do all they can to please their revered king. It was Mahabali's special plea that his subjects should celebrate Onam with great pomp and joy and the whole festival is supposed to signify the atmosphere of Mahabali's reign. Little children run through the streets, twanging bowstrings to announce the commencement of the festival. The sound of bowstrings is a predominant feature during this holiday. Homes are cleaned and freshly painted and housewives proudly decorate their floors and walls with designs made of coloured powdered chalk and flowers. Images of clay, brightly painted, with a sprig of holy bass stuck on top are prominently displayed in the home. During the festival a small prayer-offering is made to the images before each meal. A beautifully fashioned clay image of Vishnu is worshipped in almost every home. On the twelfth and last day of the festival, the image is placed on a decorated stool or stand and amidst much singing, dancing and fireworks, is carried to the sea or river where it is immersed.

A great attraction at the Onam festival is the boat race. Over a hundred oarsmen row long graceful boats built in the shape of snakes and painted in bright hues. They sing to the rhythm of drum and cymbals and the banks are crowded with enthusiastic spectators. Nobody does any work during this happy festival.

The Nendran (a variety of cooking banana) is eaten at every meal during Onam. Any variety of semi-ripe banana can be substituted and is delicious cooked with mixed vegetables. A popular vegetable dish with Nendran is Aviyal, for which we must thank Mahabali's vegetable gardens.

The variety of Indian vegetable dishes expresses the generosity of the country's hospitality. Boiled vegetables are unheard of, for boiling is considered a sure way to kill their rich goodness. In most of the recipes that follow, the vegetables are allowed to cook in their own juices to preserve their subtle flavours. There are many rich Indian vegetables that are difficult to find elsewhere but suitable substitutes have been suggested.

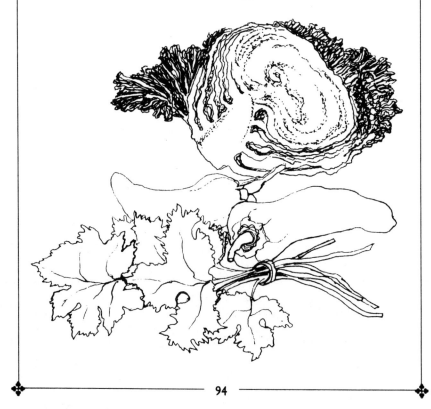

AVIYAL

2 brinjals i.e. aubergines (long thin variety)	100 g/4 oz ash-gourd
2 cooking bananas	8 green chillies
2 large potatoes	½ coconut
100 g/4 oz marrow	½ pint sour curd or yoghurt
100 g/4 oz french beans	1 teaspoon turmeric powder
100 g/4 oz bitter beans	1 teaspoon cummin seeds
3 thick long drumsticks or celery sticks	A sprig of curry leaves
	2 tablespoons fresh coconut oil
	Salt to taste

—— MEDIUM ——

■ Wash and clean the vegetables. Remove stringy edges from the beans and drumsticks. Peel the potatoes and ash-gourd. Scrape the skin off the marrow. Cut up all the vegetables into 5.0 cms/2 inch pieces, do not remove the skin from the bananas. Put enough water in a saucepan to cover all the vegetables and bring to the boil. Add turmeric and 2 curry leaves and boil until tender. Add salt and turn the vegetables carefully so as not to break the pieces.

■ Grate the coconut. Take the green chillies, grated coconut, cummin seeds and grind to a thick paste. Add a little water to this masala and pour into the vegetables. Cook gently for 2 minutes. Add 1 cup of water to the curd and whip until smooth. Stir this buttermilk into the vegetables. Dip a small bunch of curry leaves in the oil and add to the vegetables. Bring to the boil and remove from the heat. Pour the remaining oil on top and mix gently.

OLAN

1 green banana	*450 ml/ ³/4 pint coconut milk*
100 g/4 oz beans	*A small piece of pumpkin*
100 g/4 oz carrots	*A sprig of curry leaves*
100 g/4 oz potatoes	*A small piece of cucumber*
100 g/4 oz peas (shelled)	*Salt to taste*
8 green chillies	

—— MEDIUM ——

■ Cut the vegetables into thin slices 2.5 cms/1 inch in length and cook in sufficient water, to which the green chillies have been added, until tender. When well cooked and when the water has evaporated, add the coconut milk and curry leaves. Boil and remove from the heat. Serve with rice.

DRUMSTICK DOROO

1 dozen drumsticks or celery sticks	*1 large onion*
¹/2 pint tamarind water	*¹/2 teaspoon turmeric powder*
600 ml/1 pint coconut milk	*¹/2 teaspoon garam masala*
1 tablespoon chopped coriander leaves	*1 teaspoon jaggery*
	Salt to taste
	1 tablespoon ghee

FOR THE MASALA:

¹/2 teaspoon cummin seeds	*1.4 cms/¹/2 inch piece ginger*
9 dry red chillies	*1 tablespoon grated coconut*
6 cloves garlic	

—— MEDIUM ——

■ Grind the masala ingredients finely. Wash and clean the drumsticks. Peel the hard skin off the drumsticks and cut into 10 cms/4 inch pieces. Take 4 pieces and tie together with a piece of string or the peeled skin from the drumsticks. Continue until you have tied all into bundles. Boil in enough water until tender.

■ Heat the ghee and fry the onion until brown. Add the masala paste and fry for 1 minute. Add the garam masala, jaggery, salt, tamarind and coconut milk. Bring to the boil, lower heat and cook for 15 minutes. Add drumsticks and simmer for 10 minutes. Serve with rice or dosai.

LIME CURRY

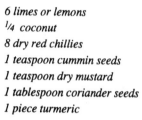

SERVES 4

6 limes or lemons	2 green chillies
¼ coconut	1 clove garlic
8 dry red chillies	1 piece ginger
1 teaspoon cummin seeds	2 onions
1 teaspoon dry mustard	1 sprig curry leaves
1 tablespoon coriander seeds	1 tablespoon ghee or oil
1 piece turmeric	

—— MEDIUM ——

■ Wash the limes and cut into small pieces. Bring to the boil in 600 ml/1 pint water and boil for 5 minutes. This will remove the bitterness from the fruit. Drain off the water.

■ Heat the ghee in a saucepan, fry the dry spices and coconut. Remove and grind them finely. Grind the fresh masala (i.e. the onions, chillies, ginger and garlic) into a paste. Add to the ground spices. Mix all the ingredients with the lime pieces, curry leaves, adding salt to taste. Cook gently for 45 minutes when the curry will be ready for serving.

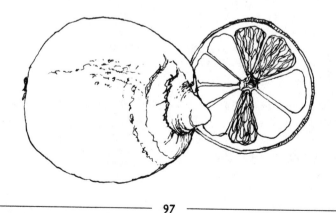

LOTUS STEM CURRY

450 g/1 lb lotus stems (bhein)	1 teaspoon cummin seeds
1 large tomato	1 fresh coconut
1 onion	1 tablespoon ghee
4 green chillies	Salt to taste
2 dry red chillies	
1 teaspoon chopped coriander leaves	

—— MILD ——

■ Grate the coconut, add 3 cups hot water and extract the milk. Make a paste from the green chillies, onion, cummin seeds, coriander leaves and tomato. Wash and clean the lotus stems and cut into 1.4 cms/½ inch thick slices.

■ Heat the ghee and fry the red chillies, then add the masala paste and cook well. Stir in the coconut milk and boil for 15 minutes. Add sliced lotus stems and salt. Lower heat and simmer for 30 minutes or until tender. This vegetable may have a sticky consistency but the flavour is delightful.

BANANA AND YAM PATIYA

450 g/1 lb yam (suran)	2 teaspoons turmeric powder
225 g/8 oz cooking plantains	1 sprig curry leaves
1 fresh coconut	1 tablespoon ghee
2 teaspoons black peppercorns	Salt to taste
2 teaspoons mustard seeds	

■ Wash and peel the yam and cut into 2.5 cms/1 inch cubes. Soak in salted water for about an hour to neutralise the sharp flavour. Peel and cut the plantains into cubes of the same size. Powder the peppercorns. Boil about 900 ml/1½ pints water adding the turmeric, salt and pepper. Add the yam pieces. When yam is half cooked, add plaintain pieces and if necessary, a little warm water.

■ Grate the coconut and grind to a fine paste. Keep aside 1 tablespoon of the coconut paste for seasoning. When the vegetables are tender, add the bulk of the coconut paste and cook for 10 minutes. Heat the ghee and fry the curry leaves and mustard seeds until they splutter. Add remaining coconut paste and cook until brown. Stir in the cooked vegetables.

CURRIED STUFFED RADISH

450 g/1 lb white radish	1 teaspoon coriander seeds
2 onions	2 dry red chillies
½ coconut	½ tablespoon ghee
1 teaspoon garam masala	4 cloves
1 teaspoon turmeric powder	4 peppercorns
1 teaspoon fresh chilli powder	Salt to taste

—— MILD ——

■ Grate the coconut. Wash and scrape the radishes and slice them into quarters lengthways, leaving the stem intact. Heat the ghee in a frying pan and fry the onions and red chillies until golden brown. Add the grated coconut, coriander seeds, pepper and cloves and fry for 5 minutes. Remove from the heat and grind to a paste, adding a little water. Add the remaining spices and salt to the paste and mix well. Stuff the radishes with the masala.

■ Take a saucepan and lay the stuffed radishes at the bottom. Cover with remaining masala and a cupful of water. Cook over a low heat until the radishes are tender and serve with rotis.

PIAZ BHAJI

225 g/8 oz onions
225 g/8 oz tomatoes
1 small piece ginger
2 cloves garlic
2 green chillies

½ teaspoon turmeric powder
½ teaspoon garam masala
Salt to taste
1½ tablespoons ghee

■ Heat the ghee in a saucepan and fry the sliced ginger, chopped garlic and chopped chillies for a few minutes. Add sliced onions and chopped tomatoes to the ghee. Stir in the turmeric, garam masala and salt and cook on a low heat until the onions are golden brown. Pour in a little water if necessary.

PEA KOFTA CURRY

6 cloves garlic
2 tomatoes
¼ teaspoon browned cummin
    seeds
1 medium onion

½ teaspoon turmeric powder
2 teaspoons coriander powder
6 dry red chillies
1 teaspoon garam masala
Ghee

GRIND TOGETHER TO FORM A PASTE:

450 g/1 lb green peas (shelled
    and boiled)
3 potatoes (boiled and peeled)

1 teaspoon poppy seeds.
little gram flour
Salt to taste

—— MEDIUM ——

■ Shape the pea paste into balls and deep-fry immediately in hot ghee. Set these koftas aside.
■ Mince the onion finely. Heat some ghee in a saucepan and fry the onion until brown. Stir in the rest of the spices with the chopped tomatoes. Cook in a little water until the raw masala smell disappears. Add the koftas and simmer for 2 minutes.

DRUM GOBI

1 large cauliflower
2 large onions
4 cloves garlic
1 piece ginger
3 dry red chillies
1 stick cinnamon
1 bay leaf
2 green chillies

4 cloves
1/2 teaspoon cummin seeds
3 black cardamoms
300 ml/1/2 pint curd, yoghurt or
    tomatoe purée
Ghee
Salt to taste

■ Heat the ghee in a saucepan and brown the whole cauliflower slightly. Chop the onions finely. Chop the ginger and garlic. Cover the cauliflower with the chopped ingredients and sprinkle with all the spices. Pour the curds (or tomato pureé) and 1 cup of water over the cauliflower. Add a little more ghee. Cover and bake at 160°C/325°F/Gas mark 3 for 40 minutes until tender. A little more water can be added from time to time to prevent sticking.

RIPE MANGO CURRY

4 large ripe mangoes	2 teaspoons turmeric powder
¹/₂ coconut	1 heaped teaspoon mustard
50 g/2 oz raisins	seeds
25 g/1 oz sugar	5 dry red chillies
3 cloves	Salt to taste
1 sprig curry leaves	

—— *MEDIUM* ——

■ Peel and slice the mangoes into 2.5 cms/1 inch cubes. Heat 1½ teaspoons ghee and fry the mustard seeds and chillies until they begin to crackle. Stir in the grated coconut and turmeric and fry until brown. Add the mangoes, 600 ml/1 pint water, raisins, cloves, sugar and salt to taste. Simmer for about 12 minutes. Serve hot with plain boiled rice and garnish with curry leaves.

SABATH ALOO

WHOLE SMALL POTATOES

450 g/1 lb very small potatoes	¹/₂ teaspoon ground cummin
1 onion	seeds
1 teaspoon mustard seeds	1 sprig curry leaves
3 green chillies	1¹/₂ tablespoons oil or ghee
1 teaspoon turmeric powder	Salt to taste

■ Boil the washed potatoes in their jackets until tender. Remove the skins. (This dish may also be prepared without removing the skins if the potatoes are very tender.) Heat the oil in a kerai (if available) and stir in the mustard seeds. Cook until they begin to crackle and add the chopped onion and remaining spices. Add the potatoes, salt and 150 ml/¼ pint water. Cook until dry and the potatoes are nicely browned.

TOMATO MAHASHAS

STUFFED TOMATOES

1 kg/2 lb red tomatoes
1 stick cinnamon
225 g/8 oz fine (Basmati) rice
2 onions
225 g/8 oz peas
½ grated coconut
1 teaspoon turmeric powder

1 teaspoon chilli powder
4 cardamoms
4 cloves
Chopped coriander leaves
Ghee
Salt to taste

■ Slice the tops off the tomatoes and scoop out the inside pulp without damaging the outside. (Save the tomato lids).

■ Clean and wash the rice. Slice the onions. Heat 1 tablespoon of ghee and fry cloves, cardamoms and cinnamon. Add the onions and fry until tender. Stir in the turmeric, chilli powder, rice and peas. Pour in 300 ml/½ pint water. Salt to taste and cook for 15 minutes. Remove from the heat and cool.

■ Stuff the tomatoes with the pulao and cover with the tomato lids. Brush with a little melted fat and bake in a medium oven for 15 minutes. Arrange on a large plate or tray and garnish with coriander leaves and coconut.

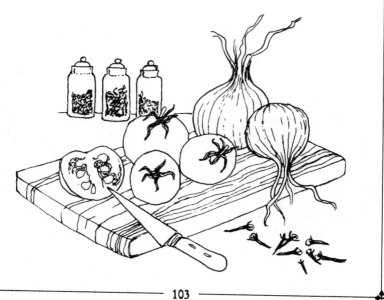

CAPSICUMS
WITH CURRANTS

450 g/1 lb capsicums (sweet
    peppcrs)
100 g/4 oz currants or raisins
225 g/8 oz ground-nuts
50 g/2 oz gram dhal
1 cup grated coconut

1 lemon-sized lump tamarind
2 teaspoons sesame seeds
A pinch of asafoetida
3 tablespoons ghee
Salt and jaggery to taste

■ Cut each capsicum into 6 - 8 pieces. Grind the tamarind, coconut, roasted gram dhal and sesame seeds to a fine paste with a little water. Heat ghee and fry the pieces of capsicums. Add coarsely-powdered ground-nuts, currants, jaggery, 600 ml/1pint water and salt. Mix in the masala paste, cover the saucepan and simmer on a medium heat for about 1 hour. When the gravy is thick, remove and serve hot.

PATREL
or PATHRAVADE

1 dozen tender colocacia leaves
1 ball tamarind (2.5 cm/1 inch
    diameter)
1 dozen dry red chillies

½ coconut
25 g/1 oz sugar (optional)
Salt to taste

—— HOT ——

■ Soak the gram in water overnight. Next day, drain the gram and grate the coconut. Grind together with the chillies, tamarind, asafoetida, salt and sugar to a fine paste. Clean the leaves thoroughly, remove the hard veins with a sharp knife but take care not to tear them. Spread a thin layer of the paste on the back of the leaf and then place another leaf on top of this. Repeat process until you have used all the paste and leaves.
■ Turn in the edges of the leaves on both sides and roll tightly and neatly. Tie the roll with string and place to steam for about ½ hour or until tender. Remove and cut off the string without

damaging the roll. Cut slices with a sharp, thin knife and serve hot. Another way of serving Patrel is to cut it into slices and deep-fry until very crisp.

BAGARU BAIGAN

8 small brinjals (aubergines)	1 lemon-sized lump tamarind
3 tablespoons coriander seeds	1/2 teaspoon turmeric
8 dry red chillies	1 small piece of jaggery
2 large onions	1 teaspoon mustard seeds
1/4 coconut	1 sprig curry leaves
2 cloves garlic	Gingelly oil
2 tablespoons gingelly seeds	2 green chillies

—— MEDIUM ——

■ Clean and cut the brinjals lengthwise without breaking the stems. Fry in gingelly oil until the skins turn light brown. Remove and keep aside. In 1 tablespoon oil, fry the coriander, red chillies, chopped onions, turmeric and grind them together with coconut and garlic. Fry the gingelly seeds separately without oil and powder them. Soak the tamarind in 1.2 ltrs/2 pints warm water. Strain the pulp and keep the tamarind water on the heat with the ground spices.

■ When it has boiled for 5 minutes, add the brinjals and gingelly seeds. Cover and cook until the gravy is thick, then add the jaggery. In a saucepan heat 2 tablespoons ghee, add mustard seeds, 2 slit green chillies and curry leaves. When the mustard splutters, add it to the curry. Stir well and serve hot with chappatis.

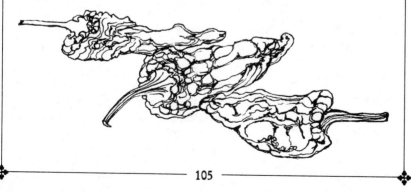

CURRIED BANANAS

6 green bananas
6 cloves garlic
2 onions
3 dry red chillies
2 teaspoons coriander seeds
1 teaspoon garam masala

1 teaspoon mango powder
   (amchoor)
3 tablespoons ghee
Coriander leaves
Salt to taste

■ Chop the onions and grind to a paste with the garlic, salt, chillies and the remaining spices. Peel the bananas and split lengthways. Remove the seeds. Fill the bananas with the masala paste and tie with a piece of thread or pin together with cocktail sticks or toothpicks so that the masala does not leak out. Heat ghee in a kerai and fry the bananas. When they are nicely browned, add the curd and cook until they are soft and tender. Add 1 cup hot water if necessary. Garnish with chopped coriander leaves and serve as a side-dish.

KOFTA CURRY

450 g/1 lb white gourd or
   marrow
2 red tomatoes
3 green chillies
50 g/2 oz gram flour
1 onion
3 cloves garlic
1 stick cinnamon

2 cardamoms
1 teaspoon turmeric powder
1 teaspoon garam masala
$\frac{1}{2}$ teaspoon coriander-cummin
   seeds powder
Coriander leaves
Ghee

—— MILD ——

■ Grate the gourd without peeling it and cook in sufficient water. Slice the green chillies and 1 onion very finely and mix into the vegetables. Put in the gram flour and salt and knead the mixture. Heat ghee in a kerai. Shape white gourd mixture into small balls and deep-fry until brown. Remove and keep aside.

■ Heat 2 tablespoons ghee in a saucepan and fry the cinnamon and cardamoms. Add chopped onion and tomatoes and fry. Stir in all the remaining spices, salt and 600 ml/1 pint of hot water and cook. Blend in 1 teaspoon chilli powder if desired. Lastly, add the koftas and garnish with chopped coriander leaves before serving.

JACKFRUIT BHARTHA

1 tender jackfruit (or breadfruit)	8 green chillies
½ coconut	3 curry leaves
1 teaspoon chilli powder	Coriander leaves
1 teaspoon mustard seeds	2 tablespoons oil or ghee
1 teaspoon turmeric powder	Salt to taste

■ Peel the fruit and cut into pieces. Put the fruit in a saucepan, add turmeric and salt and enough water to cover the fruit. Place on a medium heat to cook. When the fruit is tender, remove from the heat and mash with a fork. Do not remove the seeds as they too have a special flavour. Mix the grated coconut and chilli powder into this mixture. In a kerai, heat the oil, add the mustard seeds, chopped green chillies and curry leaves. When the mustard seeds begin to splutter, add the mashed jackfruit. Cook for 10 - 15 minutes and remove from the heat. Garnish with chopped coriander leaves.

MATTAR PANEER

PEAS WITH INDIAN CHEESE

1.2 ltrs/2 pints milk	1½ teaspoons coriander seeds
450 g/1 lb peas	1 teaspoon garam masala
2 large onions	1 piece ginger
1 large lemon	Ghee
1 teaspoon turmeric powder	Salt to taste
½ teaspoon chilli powder	

■ Boil up the milk twice on a high heat and squeeze the juice of the lemon into it. The whey will separate from the curd. Separate the curd and tie it in a muslin cloth. Hang up all day to allow the water to drain. When dry, place the muslin with the curd under a heavy weight to ensure that all the moisture is squeezed out. This will flatten the curd into a flat round cake when removed from the muslin. Cut the cheese into strips or cubes and deep fry in hot ghee. Remove and keep aside.

■ In a saucepan, heat 2 tablespoons ghee and add chopped onions and ginger. Add the spices, salt and peas and cook, adding a little water, until the peas are tender and a little gravy remains. Stir in the fried cheese and boil for 5 minutes. Serve hot with chappatis.

STUFFED CAPSICUMS

6 - 8 large capsicums (sweet peppers)	½ teaspoon mango powder (amchoor)
50 g/2 oz shelled peas	1½ teaspoons garam masala
3 potatoes	A few pomegranate seeds
1 small onion	Ghee
½ teaspoon turmeric powder	Salt to taste
½ teaspoon chilli powder	

■ Wash the capsicums and boil them whole on a medium heat until they are tender but still crisp, and lighter in shade. Remove, drain and allow to cool. Peel the potatoes and boil with peas in a little salted water. When cooked, remove from heat and mash with a fork. Chop the onion very finely. Heat 2 teaspoons of ghee in a frying-pan and brown the onions. Add the mashed mixture and the spices and fry together.

■ With a very sharp knife, gently cut out the stem and seeds of the capsicums. Fill the potato mixture into the capsicums and tie them carefully with a string. Heat the ghee in a kerai and fry the stuffed capsicums on all sides. Snip off the threads before serving.

BHARTHA KA RAITHA

2 large seedless brinjals
　　(aubergines)
4 finely-chopped green chillies
275 g/10 oz chopped walnuts
1 teaspoon roasted cummin
　　seeds

300 ml/½ pint curd or yoghourt
1 finely-chopped stick celery
Salt to taste

■ Rub a little ghee or butter on the skin of the brinjals and bake them on an open sigri until tender. Wash off the burnt skin and mash the vegetables to a pulp with a fork. Mix in the curd. Another cupful of curd may be added if wished. Mix in all the remaining ingredients and add salt to taste. Serve as a side-dish at a barbecue party.

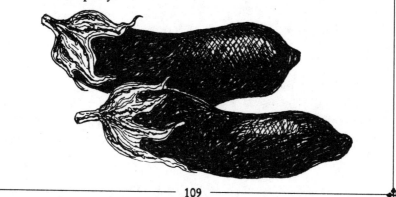

POTATO KABABS

450 g/1 lb potatoes	8 tablespoons ghee
4 green chillies	1 small piece coconut
4 cloves garlic	1/4 teaspoon cummin seeds
2 eggs	1 dessertspoon vinegar
1/4 teaspoon turmeric powder	1 dessertspoon gram flour
2 onions	Breadcrumbs

■ Wash and quarter the potatoes. Add salt and boil until tender. Remove and wash off any salt. Grind the coconut coarsely. Add the rest of the ingredients (except eggs, potato and breadcrumbs) and grind to a paste, using the vinegar to bring it to a fairly thick consistency. Peel the potatoes, chop into tiny pieces and mix with the paste. Beat the eggs and stir into the mixture. Shape the mixture into kababs, roll in the breadcrumbs and fry on both sides in hot ghee.

'SPONGE CURRY'

600 ml/1 pint milk	6 cloves
1 kg/2 lb potatoes	1 lemon
4 cardamoms	6 tablespoons ghee
1 stick cinnamon	Salt to taste

GRIND TO A FINE PASTE:

1 large onion	1/2 teaspoon turmeric powder
6 cloves garlic	1 tablespoon chilli powder
5 cms/2 inch piece ginger	

—— MILD ——

■ Peel the potatoes. Prick them thoroughly with a knitting needle until they are very soft (almost like sponge). Soak them in cold water for a few minutes, then drain off the water. Mix the masala paste, salt, milk and lemon juice and add to the potatoes. Set the mixture aside for 1 hour. In a saucepan, heat ghee and fry cinnamon, cardamoms and cloves. Put in the potatoes and salt. Cover with a lid and cook over a low heat. When the potatoes are cooked and the gravy has thickened, remove the pan from the heat and add a little ghee and lemon juice. Serve immediately.

COORG PINEAPPLE CURRY

1 large ripe pineapple
600 ml/1 pint water
1 tablespoon ghee
1 large onion
¹/₂ teaspoon mustard seeds

1 teaspoon coriander seeds
8 dry red chillies
1 egg-sized piece of jaggery
Salt to taste

—— *MEDIUM* ——

■ Grind coriander and chillies to a paste. Heat some ghee in a saucepan. When it is very hot, add the sliced onion and the mustard seeds and fry until the onions are slightly brown. Add the pineapple, chopped into cubes and the coriander-and-chillies paste. Add the jaggery, water and salt to taste. Simmer slowly on a very low heat until the gravy thickens. Serve hot with rice or puris.

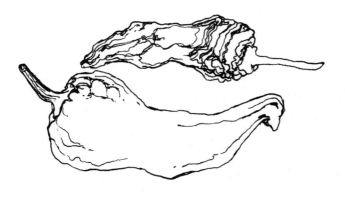

STUFFED BRINJALS

1 lb. small brinjals, i.e. aubergines (long variety)

2 large onions

½ teaspoon mustard seeds

1 lump tamarind (size of a small lemon)

GRIND TOGETHER
(ALL EXCEPT SALT TO BE FIRST FRIED IN GHEE OR OIL):

A few curry leaves

8 dry red chillies

1 tablespoon coriander seeds

½ teaspoon cummin seeds

1 teaspoon fenugreek

1 teaspoon turmeric powder

Salt to taste

—— *MEDIUM HOT* ——

■ Slice the brinjals into fours, keeping the stem intact, and leave to soak in water. Grind together all the fried ingredients with a little water, adding salt and tamarind. The grated coconut should be added last. Fill the brinjals with three-quarters of this mixture, keeping the remaining quarter for the gravy.

■ Heat 3 teaspoons ghee in a shallow saucepan. Fry the mustard seeds and curry leaves in the ghee until the mustard splutters. Add finely chopped onions and fry to a golden brown. Place the brinjals carefully in the same pan and add the remaining ground spices, mixed with a little water. Cover and cook on a low heat. Turn the brinjals every few minutes so that they are cooked evenly. By the time they are cooked the gravy will have thickened.

GUJARATI BATATASAG

450 g/1 lb potatoes

2 teaspoons coriander powder

½ teaspoon turmeric powder

½ teaspoon chilli powder

1 small lump tamarind

½ coconut

A small bunch fresh coriander

1 tablespoon jaggery

1 green chilli

1 teaspoon mustard seeds

2 tablespoons ghee

—— *MILD* ——

■ Quarter the potatoes. Mix the turmeric, coriander and chilli powder. Make half a cup of tamarind juice and dissolve the jaggery in it. Grate the coconut and chop the coriander. Slice the chilli. Fry the mustard seeds in ghee until they splutter. Add salt, the powdered spices and potatoes and fry for a few minutes. Cover with water and cook until the potatoes are tender. Blend in the tamarind juice, coconut, chopped coriander and chillies. Cook until the gravy has thickened. Serve hot.

ONION THIYYAL

8 dry red chillies

1 dessertspoon coriander seeds

1 small lump tamarind

½ coconut

3 large onions

½ teaspoon turmeric powder

1 teaspoon mustard seeds

A sprig of curry leaves

Ghee or oil

—— *MEDIUM HOT* ——

■ Place a kerai on the heat and roast the coriander seeds and 7 red chillies lightly, then grind them to a paste. Keep on one side. Fry the grated coconut and half a sliced onion in a little oil over a low heat, stirring constantly, until the coconut turns brown in colour. Remove and grind to a paste with the turmeric. Slice and fry the remaining 2½ onions in oil or ghee to a golden brown.

■ Put 600 ml/1 pint of tamarind water in a saucepan, add salt and mix in the coriander and chilli paste. When it begins to boil, pour a little water in the coconut-onion-turmeric paste and add this to it. Stir in the fried onions and cook over a low heat. Remove when the curry thickens. Heat the oil in a frying-pan and fry the curry leaves, remaining red chilli and mustard seeds, until the seeds splutter. Blend into the curry.

LADY'S FINGERS PACHNADI

1 kg/2 lb Lady's fingers (okra)
6 green chillies
1/2 teaspoon cummin seeds
2 cloves garlic

75 g/3 oz grated coconut
3 teaspoons coconut oil
150 ml/1/4 pint thick curd or
    yoghurt

SEASONING:

1 tablespoon coconut oil
1/2 teaspoon mustard seeds

2 small chopped onions
A sprig of curry leaves

—— MEDIUM ——

■ Wash and cut the lady's fingers (okra) and green chillies into thin round pieces. Pour oil into a heavy-bottomed frying-pan and roast the vegetable and chillies until golden brown. Grind the cummin seeds and garlic with the coconut.

■ Heat a saucepan containing 600 ml/1 pint water and the ground spices and cook to a thick gravy. Add salt and the roasted lady's fingers then immediately remove it from the heat. While still hot, add the curd and mix well.

■ Pour oil into a frying-pan and when hot add mustard seeds, chopped onions and curry leaves. When brown, pour the mixture over the prepared curry. Serve cold.

POTATO-STUFFED KARELA

8 medium bitter-gourds
    (karelas)
2 large potatoes
1 ripe tomato
1 onion

1/4 teaspoon turmeric powder
1/2 teaspoon chilli powder
3/4 teaspoon garam masala
7 - 9 tablespoons ghee or oil
Salt to taste

—— MEDIUM ——

■ Scrape gourds well, cut into halves lengthways, smear with plenty of salt and leave for 1 hour. Wash them out well several times so as to remove the bitterness. Squeeze out all the water. Scoop out and discard the central pulp. Boil the potatoes until very soft, peel and mash well. Heat 1 tablespoon ghee in a pan and fry the chopped onion in it until golden brown. Chop and add the tomato and when very soft stir in the salt, garam masala, chilli powder and turmeric. Add potato and stir well. Remove from heat.

■ Stuff this mixture into the bitter-gourds and tie each with a piece of string or thread. Heat 6 - 8 tablespoons of ghee or oil, in a deep frying-pan, put the filled gourds in, one by one, and when brown, remove and drain. (Be sure to lower the heat when frying the gourds.) Before serving, remove thread.

LADY'S FINGERS WITH GRAVY

450 g/1 lb tender lady's fingers	*Salt and red chillies to taste*
4 medium onions	*150 ml/¼ pint curd or yoghurt*
6 cloves garlic	*8 tablespoons ghee*
¼ teaspoon turmeric powder	*1 teaspoon garam masai*

■ Wash the lady's fingers (okra) and dry on a clean towel. Cut off the top part with a sharp knife. Heat some ghee in a frying-pan and fry the lady's fingers to a light brown and set aside.

■ Grind onions and garlic to a thin paste. Heat the rest of the ghee in a heavy-bottomed saucepan and fry this paste. Add salt, turmeric powder, garam masala and chilli powder. Keep adding a little water from time to time to prevent the spices from sticking to the bottom of the saucepan. Finally, add the curd and stir continuously. When ghee separates from the spices put in 900 ml/1½ pints water and allow to simmer for about 30 minutes. Put the fried lady's fingers in this gravy and simmer for another 15 minutes. Just before serving, sprinkle with garam masala and garnish with coriander leaves.

SNAKE-GOURD KOOTU

1 snake-gourd (alternatives: 450 g/1 lb brinjal, cabbage, cauliflower etc.)	1 dry red chilli (broken into small pieces)
	4 green chillies
100 g/4 oz moong dhal	1 teaspoon mustard seeds
1/2 grated coconut	1 teaspoon ghee or oil
1 teaspoon cummin seeds	1 pinch turmeric powder
1 sprig bay leaf or curry patta	Salt to taste

—— MILD ——

■ Boil the dhal with the turmeric in 600 ml/1 pint water until very soft. Cut snake-gourd into 4 cms/ ½ inch squares and bring to the boil in a little water, adding a pinch of turmeric. When half cooked, approximately 5 - 8 minutes, add the salt. Mix in the cooked dhal and leave to simmer.

■ Grind the coconut, cummin seeds and green chillies to a fine paste and mix with the dhal and vegetables. Boil for 5 - 10 minutes, remove from heat and add the bay leaves.

■ Heat 1 teaspoon ghee or oil in a frying-pan, and when smoking hot, add the red chilli pieces and mustard seeds and fry until the mustard starts to splutter. Remove and pour it over the vegetable. Serve with rice or chappatis.

STUFFED CABBAGE

1 cabbage	1 teaspoon turmeric powder
1.5 kg/3 lb potatoes	A bunch of coriander leaves
2 onions	1 lemon
8 green chillies	A small piece of ginger
1 teaspoon red chilli powder	Ghee or oil
1/2 teaspoon garam masala	Salt to taste

—— MEDIUM HOT ——

■ Boil the potatoes, peel and cut into small cubes. Fry sliced onions, chopped green chillies, ginger and coriander leaves in ghee and when half-fried, add turmeric powder. Fry until the onions are golden brown. Add the potatoes, chilli powder, garam masala and salt. Fry for 3 - 4 minutes, stirring well. Allow the stuffing to cool. Sprinkle with lemon juice and blend again.

■ Separate the cabbage leaves and boil them for 5 minutes. Remove from the water and dry. Put a little of the mixture on each leaf and roll it to any shape desired, bind with a piece of thread and fry in ghee until golden brown. Remove, drain, cut off thread and serve.

VEGETABLE 'YOGIRATHNA'

450 g/1 lb potatoes	450 g/1 lb peas
450 g/ 1 lb tender white pumpkin	450 g/1 lb cashew nuts (broken into pieces)
450 g/1 lb french beans	1 large coconut
450 g/1 lb lentils	5 green chillies (sliced in two)
450 g/1 lb yam	Salt to taste
450 g/1 lb ash-gourd	

FOR SEASONING:

1 teaspoon mustard seeds	Bay leaves
1 teaspoon cummin seeds	Ghee

—— MEDIUM ——

■ Wash and chop all the vegetables finely, and boil them in sufficient water for 10 minutes. Stir in the salt, green chillies and cashew nuts and continue cooking until tender. Grate the coconut and grind with a little water. Extract the milk, and strain it through a fine muslin cloth. Set aside. Grind the coconut again and extract the thinner milk. Add this second milk to the cooked vegetables and stir well. Lower the heat and allow to simmer for 2 minutes. Remove from the heat, pour in the thick coconut milk and blend. Fry the mustard seeds, cummin seeds and bay leaves in a little ghee and stir them into the vegetables. Serve hot with puris or chappatis.

WATANA PATTIES

PEA CUTLETS

450 g/1 1b potatoes
450 g/1 lb shelled green peas
8 dry red chillies
1 teaspoon coriander seeds
6 cloves
5 cms/2-inch stick cinnamon
2 medium onions

¼ teaspoon mustard seeds
½ teaspoon turmeric powder
100 g/4 oz grated coconut
100 g/4 oz rice flour
Ghee or oil
Salt to taste

—— MEDIUM ——

■ Boil the potatoes, peel and mash them thoroughly, adding some salt. Fry the chillies, coriander seeds, cloves and cinnamon together in 1 teaspoon ghee or oil. Grind them, with the turmeric powder, to a thick paste. Fry the grated coconut and sliced onions together in 2 teaspoons oil or ghee. Heat 1 tablespoon of oil or ghee in a saucepan and fry the mustard seeds, when they splutter put in the peas. Simmer for 2 minutes and add 300 ml/½ pint water and cook for 12 minutes. Stir in the paste and salt and cook until dry.

■ In another bowl, make a very thin paste of rice flour adding a little salt. Take a little of the mashed potato, shape it in the hollow of your hand, put in the centre some of the pea mixture and seal the sides to form a round shape. Dip this ball into the rice-flour paste and keep aside. Continue in this manner until all the pea mixture and potato are used. Heat the ghee in a pan and fry patties until they are brown, remove and drain. Serve with green chilli chutney or tomato sauce.

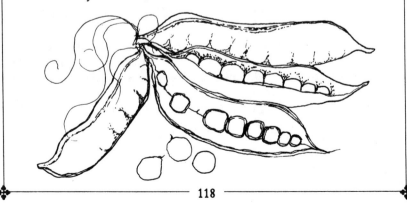

STUFFED BITTER-GOURDS

2 large bitter-gourds   2 tablespoons ghee

TO BE FRIED, THEN POWDERED:

3 teaspoons black gram dhal $\frac{1}{2}$ teaspoon cummin seeds

5 teaspoons coriander seeds $\frac{1}{2}$ teaspoon fenugreek seeds

GRIND TO A FINE PASTE:

8 dry red chillies   A little asafoetida (size of a

1 small ball tamarind (size of a   tamarind seed)

  small lemon)   Salt to taste

—— *MEDIUM HOT* ——

■ Wash the bitter-gourds and cut into even round pieces. Remove only the seeds from the pulp then fill these pieces with the thick paste made by mixing the fine paste with the powdered ingredients. Cook over steam until tender.

■ Place a saucepan over a low heat and heat 1 tablespoon ghee. Transfer the cooked bitter-gourd pieces to the saucepan and pour the remaining ghee over them. Fry them on both sides until they become crisp and brown in colour. Serve with idlis, rice or chappatis, as preferred.

GROUND-NUT CURRY

225 g/8 oz ground-nuts (raw)　　1 teaspoon jaggery
2 onions　　　　　　　　　　　　1 teaspoon coriander leaves
1 ripe tomato　　　　　　　　　　Ghee

GRIND TO A PASTE:

1 teaspoon poppy seeds　　　　　1 teaspoon mango powder
1 teaspoon coriander seeds　　　　　(amchoor)
1 teaspoon cummin seeds　　　　　¼ coconut
1 teaspoon gingelly seeds　　　　　½ teaspoon turmeric powder
2 dry red chillies

—— MILD ——

■ Chop the onions and fry until brown in a little ghee. Add the masala paste and cook until it separates from the ghee. Add nuts, chopped tomato, jaggery, salt to taste and 600 ml/1 pint water. Cook gently until the nuts are tender. Serve hot, garnished with finely chopped coriander leaves and accompanied by hot puris.

RASAM
PEPPER-WATER

600 ml/1 pint water　　　　　　2 teaspoons chopped coriander
1 teaspoon crushed black　　　　　leaves
peppercorns　　　　　　　　　　1 teaspoon mustard seeds
6 cloves garlic　　　　　　　　　½ small onion
1 teaspoon cummin seeds　　　　2 teaspoons ghee or oil
1 small ball of tamarind　　　　　Salt to taste
　(size of a marble)

■ Crush together the pepper, cummin seeds and garlic. Mix these spices with the tamarind juice, water, coriander leaves and salt to taste. Keep aside. (To prepare the tamarind juice, soak the tamarind in ½ cup boiling water and pass through a sieve when cool.)
■ Take another pan, heat the ghee or oil and fry the mustard

seeds, add the onion (finely chopped) and continue frying until brown. Add the pepper-water mixture to this and simmer for 5 minutes. Serve hot in small coffee cups. Rasam is served during or after a meal as a digestive.

SOUTH INDIAN TOMATO RASAM

4 large red tomatoes

1.75 ltrs/3 pints water

2 teaspoons salt, or to taste

1 large onion

1 teaspoon cummin seed powder

½ teaspoon black pepper powder

10 cloves garlic

2 dry red chillies

1 bunch coriander leaves

1 tablespoon gingelly oil

¼ teaspoon mustard seeds

6 fenugreek seeds

—— *MILD* ——

■ Wash the tomatoes, boil them with the water and salt until soft, then mash. Grind the cummin seeds, pepper and garlic coarsely, without any water and add to the tomato mixture.

■ Slice the onion and break the red chillies into 1.4 cms/¼ inch pieces. Put a saucepan over a low heat, pour in the oil and when hot, add the mustard and fenugreek seeds. Cook until the mustard seeds splutter, add the onions and red chillies, fry for 1 minute and pour into the tomato mixture. Bring to boiling-point, add the chopped coriander leaves and remove from heat. Serve in cups after a heavy meal, or with rice as a soup.

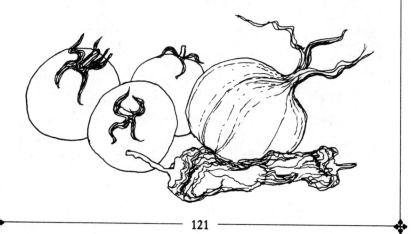

FISH

FISH

The fisherfolk along the coasts of India are amongst its happiest and most carefree inhabitants, for the riches of the sea are abundant and except during the monsoon months, fish and shell-fish are plentiful.

A festive time of the year for the fisherfolk is Barani or the cock festival, when the beaches are crowded with people on a pilgrimage to the temple. The cock festival originated in the tiny port town of Craganore, where there is a little temple dedicated to Kali, the bloodthirsty goddess of death and destruction whose appetite must be appeased. At Barani, cocks are sacrificed to the goddess Kali. Elaborate preparations are made for the journey and rice, spices and other foods are carried along. Every fisherman's family takes part in this sacred pilgrimage. People start off in little groups at an auspicious time and set off along the beach, carrying lamps, crowded chicken coops and their rations. This journey could last for several days, depending on the distance to the nearest Kali temple.

Throughout the journey the fisherfolk sing, dance, eat and drink gallons of toddy, the local palm wine. They catch fish on the way and barbecue them over open fires under coconut palms. They arrive at the temple, rowdy and drunk, and there takes place a boisterous cock-butchering ceremony on a marble slab at the feet of Kali. People arrive from near and far at the appointed hour and thousands of cocks are sacrificed. The ceremony leaves everybody subdued after the exhausting experience and they quietly wend their way home.

Many varieties of the fish to be found in the Arabian Sea are not available elsewhere, but there are substitutes for all of them. Pomfret which is the king of the fishes of India, is now being exported. Beckti, a rich succulent variety of white fish, and Hilsa, a member of the kipper family are specialities of Bengal. The Bombay bhangra is similar to herring and Bombay duck, a small strong-flavoured fish, is dried in the sun and cooked with vegetables in a curry or served crisply fried. Bombay duck is exported and is available in speciality stores.

PICKLED FISH

3 medium sized pomfrets or plaice	1 small pod garlic
4 tablespoons chilli powder	1.2 ltrs/2 pints vinegar
2 tablespoons turmeric powder	1 pint pure mustard oil
4.0 cms/1½ inch piece ginger	A little wheat flour
	Salt to taste

—— *HOT*——

■ Wash the fish thoroughly, cut into small pieces and remove the bones. Coat with a little wheat flour. Apply the turmeric, salt and a little vinegar to the fish and marinate for an hour. Fry the pieces of fish in smoking oil. Dry the pieces of fish for 4 hours in a warm oven.

■ Grind the chilli powder, garlic and ginger in a little vinegar. Heat the oil in a saucepan. When it begins to smoke put in the ground spices and fry, stirring continuously, for a few minutes.

■ Put the prepared fish into the hot oil, add the rest of the vinegar. Let it boil for 5 minutes. Cool and preserve in an airtight jar.

JHAL OF CRAB

8 large live female crabs with roe	4 large tomatoes
	Sugar and salt to taste
4 medium onions	2 - 3 medium potatoes
6 green chillies	A pinch of turmeric powder
1 clove garlic	Mustard oil

—— *MEDIUM HOT* ——

■ Pour boiling water on the crabs and separate the legs from the body, discarding the outer shell, eyes and apron. Wash well.

■ Heat the mustard oil in a saucepan and when smoking hot, put in the crab meat and fry well. Remove and keep aside. Slice the onions and fry to a light brown in the same oil. Slice and add the chillies, garlic and crab meat. Cover the saucepan and leave to simmer for a few minutes. Add the quartered tomatoes and potatoes which have already been boiled, peeled and cubed, and simmer until tender. Season with salt and sugar. Serve hot.

PUI SAG CHORCHORI

450 g/1 lb pui sag or spinach
225 g/8 oz shrimps
2 tablespoons mustard seeds
8 dry red chillies

Mustard oil
1 teaspoon turmeric powder
Salt to taste

—— MEDIUM HOT ——

■ Peel off all but the tails of the shrimps then wash thoroughly. Fry in hot mustard oil until brown. Remove and keep aside.

■ Wash the pui sag and separate the leaves from the stems. Cut the stems into 5 cms/2 inch pieces and fry in the mustard oil for about 2 minutes. Drain and discard the oil.

■ Grind to a paste the mustard seeds and red chillies. Heat some oil in a saucepan and when smoking hot, put in the leaves and stems of pui sag. Fry for 1 minute, add the paste and turmeric and continue frying until water oozes out from the sag. Finally, add the shrimps and salt. Cook for a further 5 minutes. Remove from the heat and serve hot. This is a favourite Bengali dish.

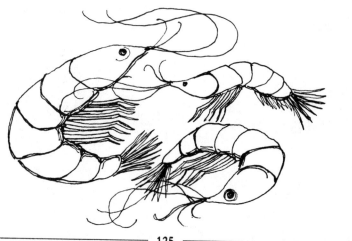

MASALA STUFFED FISH

1 large salmon or haddock
   (1.8 - 2.3 kg/4 - 5 lb)
6 spring onions
6 - 7 green chillies
100 g/4 oz peas
100 g/4 oz mashed potatoes
3 tablespoons chopped mint
3 tablespoons chopped
   coriander
25 g/1 oz raisins
3 eggs

4 lemons
1/2 teaspoon freshly ground
   black pepper
1 teaspoon turmeric powder
1 teaspoon garam masala
3 teaspoons juice of fresh ginger
3 teaspoons salt
3 tablespoons ghee
25 g/1 oz almonds
Red pepper

—— *MEDIUM HOT* ——

■ Clean the fish thoroughly. Trim off the head if necessary. Rub the juice of one lemon, pepper and salt all over the fish and inside. Let stand in a cool place for an hour.

■ Heat the ghee in a kerai. Fry the almonds and raisins. Remove from the pan and set aside. Put the onions in the ghee and fry lightly until tender. Add the peas, potatoes, salt, pepper, garam masala and turmeric. Remove from the heat and allow to cool. Add lemon juice, ginger juice, fried almonds and raisins, finely sliced green chillies, mint and coriander. Blend well. Pack the mixture into the fish and using string, tie up. Fry in mustard oil or steam whole, taking care not to break the fish. Serve on a large platter, garnished with fried tomatoes, chipped potatoes and slices of sour lime.

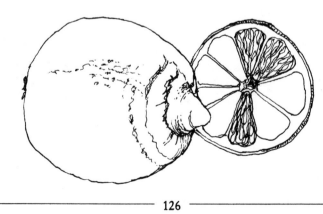

PRAWN PATURI IN COCONUT

SERVES 2

8 medium prawns	¼ teaspoon turmeric powder
4 green chillies	Salt to taste
4 slices green mango	6 dry red chillies
(or 1 teaspoon lemon juice)	1 large coconut
2 tablespoons mustard seeds	2 tablespoons mustard oil

—— *VERY HOT* ——

■ Cut the top off the coconut, make many incisions in the kernel and keep aside. Parboil the prawns and drain. Make a paste of the red chillies and the mustard seeds. Heat the oil and when smoking, take off the heat and cool. Pour the oil into the coconut and put in the prawns, blended with the mustard-and-chillie paste and salt to taste. Add sliced green chillies, the green mango or lemon juice, and the turmeric powder.

■ Seal the top of the coconut with its own cover and cover it tightly with foil. Bake in a low oven at 150°C/300°F/Gas mark 2 for 2 - 3 hours. Remove and serve in the shell.

■ In parts of India where a fire is still in use the top of the coconut would be sealed with its own cover and the edge lined with some flour paste or a bit of pastry mixture to secure it. The coconut would then be placed in the hot embers of a dying fire, the top covered with ashes and allowed to remain in the heat for 2 - 3 hours before serving in the shell.

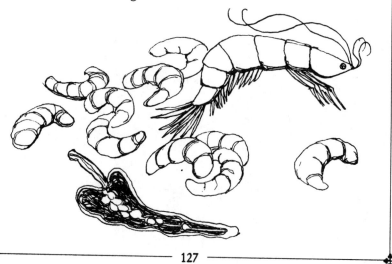

WHOLE FISH IN BANANA LEAF

1 beckti, rohu or similar fish
such as haddock (approx
450 g/1 lb)
450 g/1 lb fresh coriander
leaves

600 ml/1 pint sour curd or
yoghurt
10 green chillies
1 large banana leaf

—— *VERY HOT* ——

■ Clean the fish by slitting lengthwise along the top and belly, removing the bone between the base of the head and the tail, leaving these intact. Scrape off the scales carefully. Grind and make a paste of the green chillies and coriander leaves. Whip the curd slightly and mix with this paste. Add the salt. Meanwhile, in a large pan heat some water and allow it to boil. Cover the fish carefully, inside and out, with the paste.

■ Wrap the fish securely in the banana leaf or, if not available, use foil. Put in a smaller pan than the one in which the water is boiling. Place the smaller pan in the larger, making sure that the water will not seep into the fish. Cover tightly and put a weight on the lid. Steam for about 20 minutes. Test with a knife and when the skin becomes flaky, the fish is ready. Serve garnished with lemon slices and sprigs of coriander.

STUFFED POMFRETS

2 large pomfrets or plaice
2 dozen prawns
1 dessertspoon tomato purée
1 large onion
1 dessertspoon ghee
3 green chillies

2 hardboiled eggs
1 egg
A little garlic
Salt to taste

—— MILD ——

■ Clean and wash the pomfrets but keep them whole. Make slits in the sides for the stuffing and remove the centre bone if possible.

■ Boil the prawns and keep aside ½ cup of the water (if prawns are large, chop roughly). Heat the ghee in a saucepan and brown the onion. Add to it the chopped chillies, garlic and boiled eggs, the prawns, tomato purée and stock in which the prawns were boiled. Cook slowly until the mixture thickens.

■ Remove from the heat and allow to cool completely. Break the egg into the mixture and blend well. Divide the mixture in half and stuff each pomfret with it. Rub a little ghee on greaseproof paper, sprinkle with salt and pepper and wrap around each pomfret. Bake in a hot oven 220°C/425°F/Gas mark 7 for 45 minutes. Garnish with potatoes, fried crisp and brown.

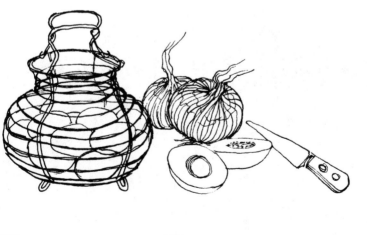

PRAWN
PATIA

3 dozen large prawns

1 tablespoon vinegar

$^1\!/_2$ teaspoon coriander powder

$^1\!/_2$ teaspoon cummin powder

$1^1\!/_2$ teaspoons turmeric powder

$^1\!/_2$ teaspoon salt

$^1\!/_4$ pint cold water

$^1\!/_4$ pint sweet oil (til)

2 very large onions

A small green mango, sliced
  (optional)

Juice of 1 lemon

$^1\!/_2$ teaspoon jaggery

GRIND TO A FINE PASTE:

11 green chillies

7 dry red chillies

2 cloves garlic

Small bunch coriander leaves

Salt to taste

—— *VERY VERY HOT* ——

■ Clean and wash the prawns. Boil them in water for about 4 minutes, to which the vinegar, coriander powder and salt have been added. Slice the onions. Heat the oil and fry the onions until brown. Remove the onions and fry the ground spices in the same oil. Add the cummin powder, the turmeric, jaggery, lemon juice and mango. Stir for about 2 minutes. Stir in the browned onions and continue stirring. Add the prawns and fish stock. Cook, stirring from time to time, until the mixture is quite dry. Add salt if necessary.

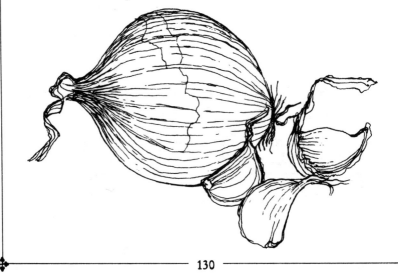

FISH VINDALOO

1 large fish
225 g/8 oz onions
6 dry red chillies
10 - 12 cloves garlic
1 large piece ginger
½ tablespoon cummin seeds
300 ml/½ pint vinegar

3 tablespoons ghee
1 piece cinnamon
Salt to taste
25 g/1 oz sugar
1 teaspoon garam masala
6 green chillies

—— *VERY HOT* ——

■ Cut the fish into small pieces. Rub with salt and leave for 10 minutes, then wash a second time. Chop the onions. Grind the red chillies, garlic, onions, ginger and cummin seeds with a little vinegar to a fine paste. Melt ghee in a saucepan and fry the ground spices in the ghee for a few minutes. Add the cinnamon and fish. Add salt and fry for 5 minutes on a high flame. Lower the heat and simmer for 10 minutes. Stir in the vinegar, sugar, green chillies and garam masala and cook uncovered until the gravy thickens. Serve immediately.

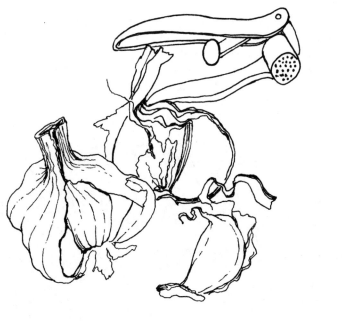

FISH
KORMA

450 g/1 lb haddock	*100 g/4 oz breadcrumbs*
100 g/4 oz onions	*2 sticks cinnamon*
5 cms/2 inch piece ginger	*2 cardamoms*
1 small pod garlic	*¹/₄ lime*
2 dry red chillies	*8 teaspoons ghee*
¹/₂ teaspoon turmeric powder	*Salt to taste*
1 egg	

—— *MILD* ——

■ Clean the fish and cut into pieces 2.5 x 5 cms/1 inch x 2 inches approximately. Grind the onions, garlic, ginger and red chillies to a smooth paste. Smear the fish pieces with half the amount of paste, lime juice and salt. Allow to stand in a cool place for 30 minutes.

■ Grate the coconut and pour 600 ml/1 pint hot water over it. Allow to cool, then squeeze out the coconut milk and keep aside in a bowl. Dip each piece of fish in beaten egg and roll in the breadcrumbs. Heat 6 tablespoons ghee and fry the fish pieces until a pale brown.

■ Heat the remaining ghee in a saucepan and fry the cinnamon, cardamom and other half of the masala paste. Add turmeric and gradually pour in the coconut milk. Season to taste and simmer for 15 minutes. Spoon in the fish pieces and green chillies and cook for a further 10 minutes. Serve with rice, chappatis or other kind of bread.

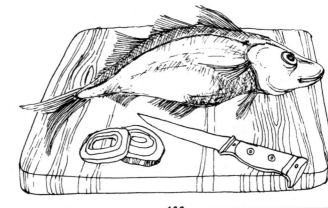

CABBAGE DALNA WITH SHRIMPS

1 medium cabbage	2 small cardamoms
225 g/8 oz shrimps	3 cloves
2 onions	2.5 cms/1 inch stick cinnamon
1 teaspoon coriander seeds	1 teaspoon turmeric powder
1 teaspoon cummin seeds	Salt and sugar to taste
3 cloves garlic	300 ml/1/2 pint curd or yoghurt
6 dry red chillies	Mustard oil or ghee
1 piece ginger	

—— MEDIUM ——

■ Make a smooth paste of the coriander, cummin seeds, garlic, 1 onion, chopped, chillies and ginger. Slice the other onion. Shred the cabbage finely and set aside. Heat some oil in a frying pan and fry the cleaned shrimps for 5 minutes. Remove and drain. In the same oil fry the sliced onion until crispy. Stir in the spices and paste and cook until well browned.

■ Add shredded cabbage and fry for 5 minutes stirring constantly. Stir in the beaten curd, cover and cook until the water is almost absorbed. Blend in the cardamoms, cloves, cinnamon and turmeric and fold in the shrimps. Season to taste with the sugar and salt and continue cooking until the mixture thickens.

PRAWN AND KARELA

450 g/1 lb bitter-gourd
  (karelas)
450 g/1 lb prawns
225 g/8 oz onions
6 dry red chillies
½ teaspoon cummin seeds
A small piece of turmeric
3 green chillies
1 piece of ginger

1 clove of garlic
1 tablespoon ghee
2 tablespoons coconut oil
100 g/4 oz jaggery
2 tablespoons vinegar
Tamarind to taste (soaked in a
  little hot water)
Salt to taste

—— MEDIUM ——

■ Cut the gourd into round slices. Wash thoroughly. Remove all the seeds and pith. Grind the dry spices with tamarind water. Cut up all the green spices. Heat the oil and ghee and fry them for a few minutes. Add the ground spices, vinegar and salt to taste. Shell and wash the prawns. Bring the mixture to the boil, pour in the vegetables and cook over a low heat until tender. Stir in the prawns and allow to simmer for 5 minutes. Stir in the jaggery before removing from the heat.

FISH CURRY WITH LADY'S FINGERS

450 g/1 lb fish
225 g/8 oz lady's fingers (okra)
225 g/8 oz onions
4 dry red chillies
150 ml/¼ pint curd or yoghurt
4 whole cardamoms

1 small piece ginger
1 teaspoon sugar
1 ½ tablespoons ghee
1 ½ tablespoons mustard oil
Salt to taste

—— MILD ——

■ Cut the fish into large pieces and keep aside. Slice the onions. Chop the lady's fingers (okra). Remove the seeds from the chillies and grind the skins. Grind the ginger. Fry the cardamoms in ghee and oil. Add the sugar and stir until it turns brown. Cook the sliced onions in this mixture until they are brown.

■ Beat the curd to a smooth paste and add to the onions. Put in the fish, lady's fingers, chillies, ginger and salt. Cover the pan and cook for 10 minutes, or until tender. Serve hot or cold with rice.

PRAWN MANGO CURRY

225 g/8 oz shelled prawns
2 large green mangoes
1 coconut
8 green chillies
6 small onions

4 cloves garlic
Sprig curry leaves
1 tablespoon cooking oil
Salt to taste

—— MEDIUM ——

■ Peel the mangoes, chop into small pieces and leave in a bowl of cold water to avoid discolouration. Grate the coconut and grind to a coarse paste with the green chillies, garlic and onions. Put prawns, mango pieces, ground paste and curry leaves in a saucepan, pour in the oil and mix ingredients well. Add 300 ml/½ pint water and salt to taste and cook on a low heat. Simmer gently, stirring occasionally until the prawns are tender and the oil floats to the top. Serve hot with boiled rice.

STEAMED FISH

BENGALI STYLE

1 kg/2 lb fish	1 heaped teaspoon mustard
1 level dessertspoon turmeric	seeds
powder	2 tablespoons mustard oil
3 dry red chillies	Salt to taste
6 green chillies	

—— MEDIUM HOT ——

■ Wash and slice the fish or cut into large pieces. Add the salt and set aside. Grind the turmeric, red chillies and mustard seeds with a tablespoon of water to make a paste. Slit the green chillies. Mix together the fish, ground paste, oil and green chillies in a double boiler and steam for 10 minutes. Uncover, turn the pieces of fish and steam again for 10 more minutes. Serve with boiled rice.

HIMALAYA FISH CURRY

1 kg/2lb fish (river trout)	1/2 teaspoon ginger powder
2 large white radishes (mouli)	4 cloves
1/2 teaspoon turmeric powder	2 sticks cinnamon
1/2 teaspoon chilli powder	2 cardamoms
4 tomatoes	6 tablespoons mustard oil
Pinch of asafoetida	Salt to taste

—— VERY MILD ——

■ Cut fish into 5 cms/2 inch cubes and wash in salt water. Dry with a clean kitchen towel. Slice the radishes. Heat 4 tablespoons oil and fry the fish and radishes until golden brown. Keep on one side.

■ Heat the remaining oil in a saucepan, add the chopped tomatoes, turmeric, chilli powder, asafoetida, ginger and remaining spices. Simmer gently for 10 minutes, adding a little water if necessary. Add the fish, season with salt and cook until the fish is tender. Keep aside for 2 hours before serving. Re-heat thoroughly or serve cold with boiled rice.

TANDOORI FISH

1 whole fish (1 kg - 1.25 kg/ 2 - 2½ lb)

1 tablespoon garam masala
3 tablespoons cooking oil

GRIND TO A FINE PASTE:

4 cms/1½ inch piece ginger
8 cloves garlic
5 cms/2 inch cube green papaya
1 teaspoon turmeric powder

½ teaspoon cummin seeds
1 tablespoon red chilli powder
Juice of 2 lemons
Salt to taste

—— *HOT* ——

■ Clean and scale the fish and wash well. Wipe dry, apply the ground paste all over including inside the stomach. Make four slits on either side of the fish with a sharp knife to allow the spices to permeate. Allow to stand in a cool place for 1 hour.

■ Pierce the fish lengthways with a skewer (seekh) using two skewers if one is not long enough and cook in a tandoor or on a charcoal barbecue. If these methods of cooking are not available, cook under a grill or bake in the oven.

■ Turn the fish every 10 minutes and cook until light brown. Heat the oil and brush on the fish with a pastry brush while cooking. When the fish is almost cooked sprinkle with garam masala and cook until a dark golden brown. Serve garnished with slices of lemon.

LOBSTER
MAHARASHTRIAN STYLE

1 kg/2 lb large lobsters	*Salt and sugar to taste*
6 cloves garlic	*1 tablespoon ghee*
1 lemon	*1 tablespoon chopped coriander*
1 teaspoon chilli powder	*leaves*
1 teaspoon turmeric powder	

—— MILD ——

■ Carefully remove the meat from the lobster shells and wash well. Heat the ghee in a saucepan and fry the crushed garlic until a pale gold. Add the lobster meat and fry for about 5 minutes. Blend in the lemon juice, chilli powder, turmeric, sugar and salt. Cover and simmer gently on a low heat until tender, adding a little water if necessary. Serve garnished with coriander leaves.

PARSI FISH SAUCE

1 large pomfret (or plaice)	*50 ml/2 fl oz vinegar*
2 onions	*2 eggs*
4 cloves garlic	*2 tablespoons ghee*
4 green chillies	*Salt to taste*
½ teaspoon cummin seeds	*1 tablespoon chopped coriander*
1 tablespoon sugar	*leaves*
1 tablespoon flour	

—— MILD ——

■ Clean the fish and slice into 6 pieces. Slice the onions. Grind the garlic, chillies and cummin seeds together to a smooth paste.
■ Heat the ghee and fry the onions until translucent in colour. Stir in the ground mixture and fry for a few minutes. Pour in 450 ml/¾ pint water, bring to the boil and cook for 10 minutes. Blend the flour with 2 tablespoons water to a smooth paste and add it to the onion mixture.
■ Cook until the sauce thickens, add the fish slices and simmer for 8 - 10 minutes until the fish is tender. Blend sugar, eggs and

vinegar together. Take the fish sauce off the heat and pour into the fish mixture, stirring gently. Carefully fold in the coriander leaves. Serve with kitcheree or yellow rice.

FISH KOFTA CURRY

450 g/1 lb fish	4 sticks cinnamon
3 onions	1 teaspoon cummin seeds
8 green chillies	2 tomatoes
Small bunch coriander leaves	2 teaspoons coriander powder
4 cloves	1 small piece ginger
1 teaspoon peppercorns	6 tablespoons ghee
6 cardamoms	Salt to taste

—— MEDIUM ——

■ Bake or grill the fish slowly. Remove all flesh from the bones. Finely slice 1 onion, 4 green chillies and coriander leaves and mix them with the fish. Grind together the peppercorns, cummin seeds, 3 cardamoms, cloves and cinnamon and add to the fish. Mix well and mash to a paste. Make small round balls from the paste.

■ Heat half the ghee in a frying pan and fry the fish balls until they are brown. If the fish balls tend to break apart, dip in beaten egg before frying.

■ Heat the remaining ghee in a saucepan, add 2 sliced onions and 4 sliced chillies and fry until brown. Stir in the chopped tomatoes and 600 ml/1 pint water and simmer gently on a low heat. When the liquid has evaporated, add chopped ginger, 3 cardamoms, coriander powder and salt to taste. Pour in a further 600 ml/1 pint water. Bring to the boil and carefully add the fish balls. Simmer gently for 15 minutes and serve hot with boiled rice.

PRAWN MUSTARD CURRY

3 dozen large shelled prawns	1 dessertspoon mustard seeds
6 dry red chillies	4 large onions
⅛ teaspoon turmeric powder	Sprig curry leaves
3 teaspoons cummin seeds	½ lemon
1 large pod garlic	3 tablespoons ghee

—— MEDIUM HOT ——

■ Grind together the chillies, turmeric, cummin seeds, garlic, mustards seeds and onions. Mix the ground paste with the prawns.

■ Heat the ghee in a saucepan and add the prawn mixture. Stir in 900 ml/1½ pints water, curry leaves and salt to taste. Bring to the boil, lower the heat and simmer until the prawns are cooked and the gravy thickens. Just before serving add the lemon juice and serve with rice or chappatis.

PRAWNS IN SPINACH

450 g/1 lb large prawns	4 large onions
3 bunches fresh coriander	Bunch fresh green garlic
1 teaspoon cummin seeds	450 g/1 lb spinach
6 cloves garlic	1 teaspoon turmeric powder
5 green chillies	2 tablespoons ghee
2 dry red chillies	5 tablespoons sweet oil (til oil)
Bunch spring onions	Salt to taste

—— MEDIUM HOT ——

■ Clean the prawns and wash thoroughly. Apply a little salt and keep on one side. Chop the coriander leaves finely, grinding the stalks with the cummin seeds, garlic and chillies. Chop the spinach, onions and fresh garlic.

■ Combine a little of the ground spices with the cleaned prawns and fry in a little ghee and oil. Fry the onions in the remaining ghee and oil and when browned, add the remaining ground spices, turmeric and fresh garlic. Stir well and add the fried spices and prawns, spinach, coriander and salt. Stir occasionally, cooking until the mixture is well browned. Pour in 600 ml/1 pint water and cook on a low heat until the prawns are cooked and the ghee floats on top of the liquid.

PRAWNS WITH SPINACH

SERVES 2

225 g/8 oz shelled prawns	1/2 teaspoon chilli powder
225 g/8 oz spinach	1 slit green chilli
2 onions	1/2 teaspoon garam masala
4 cloves garlic	2 tablespoons ghee
4 tomatoes	Salt to taste

—— MILD ——

■ In a saucepan, heat ghee and fry the chopped tomatoes, garlic and chopped onions until slightly brown. Stir in the spices and salt.

■ Cook for 5 minutes adding the spinach. Continue cooking on a low heat for 15 minutes. Put in the prawns and cook for about 8 minutes until they are tender.

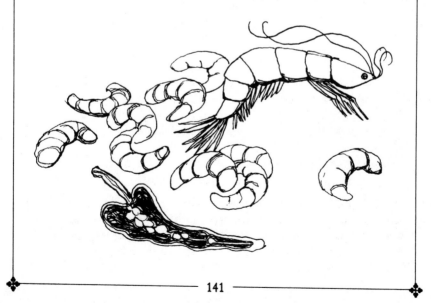

PRAWN AND DRUMSTICK SOUP

225 g/8 oz prawns	5 cms/2 inch piece ginger
1 large onion	1 teaspoon sugar
1 green chilli	1½ tablespoons ghee
4 drumsticks (or stick celery)	Rice water from cooked rice
cut into 7.5 cms/3 inch	½ teaspoon turmeric powder
pieces	Salt to taste

—— MILD ——

■ Heat the oil and ghee in a dekchi, add the sliced onion, sliced ginger and the green chillies, slit lengthways. Allow to cook until the onion is translucent but not brown. Pour in 1.2 ltrs/2 pints of rice water, the cleaned prawns and the drumsticks. Cook on a low heat until the drumsticks are cooked, approximately 30 minutes.

■ Add the prawns and cook for a further 10 minutes. Stir in the turmeric powder, sugar and salt to taste. Serve with boiled rice and slices of lemon.

PATRA NI MACHI

FISH IN BANANA LEAVES

2 pomfrets or any white fish	1 large onion
½ coconut - grated	2 tablespoons cummin seeds
Bunch mint leaves (pudina)	2 lemons
Bunch coriander leaves	2 tablespoons ghee
10 green chillies	Banana leaves
10 cloves garlic	Salt to taste
1 teaspoon sugar	

—— HOT ——

■ Grind the mint, coriander leaves, grated coconut, chillies, garlic, sugar, onion, cummin seeds and salt to a fine paste. Clean the fish and slice each pomfret into 4 pieces. Cut banana leaves (or use foil if banana leaves are not available) into wrappers large enough to wrap each fish piece. Heat both sides of the banana leaf before wrapping the fish.

■ Apply the ground chutney to the fish pieces and sprinkle a little lemon juice on them. Place each piece on a separate bit of a leaf, wrap and tie firmly with string. Grease a baking tin and place fish parcels in it carefully. Put a little ghee on the banana leaves and bake on both sides for 15 minutes, or until cooked. This dish may also be steamed if preferred.

GOA CURRY

450 g/1 lb fish or any sea food	*5 cloves*
1 coconut - grated	*5 peppercorns*
1 tablespoon coriander seeds	*1 small stick cinnamon*
1 tablespoon turmeric powder	*½ teaspoon fenugreek seeds*
1 teaspoon mustard seeds	*1 tablespoon tamarind*
7 dry red chillies	*6 tablespoon oil or ghee*

—— *MEDIUM* ——

■ Grind half the coconut, add 2 cups hot water and squeeze out the milk. Soak the tamarind in the milk for an hour. Strain before use. Grind all the spices to a very fine paste with the remaining half a coconut. Fry this masala paste in oil or ghee. Put in the fish and pour in the coconut milk. Lower the heat and cook for 15 minutes until the fish is tender. This curry can also be made with chicken, lamb or pork.

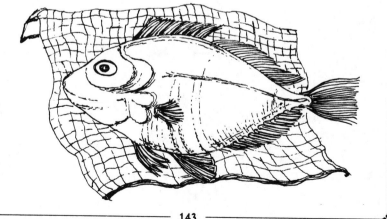

FISH IN COCONUT CREAM

1 kg/2 lb fish	2 curry leaves (cassia leaf)
1 coconut	4 green chillies
4 medium onions	4 tablespoons ghee
12 cloves garlic	A pinch of salt
4 cms/1½ inch piece ginger	A few coriander leaves

—— MILD ——

■ To make the coconut cream, grate the coconut and grind it. Pour in 300 ml/½ pint water and leave for 10 minutes. Extract the milk and grind the coconut once again, extracting more milk. Strain the milk through a fine sieve (including any coconut water, if any). Grind the onions, garlic and ginger to a fine paste. Clean and cut the fish into fairly large, flat pieces.

■ Warm the ghee in a frying pan. Add the curry leaves and fry until brown. Put in the ground spices and fry, stirring occasionally. Add the fish and turn the pieces after a few minutes to blend in the spices. Stir in the coconut milk. The gravy should cover the fish completely. Put in the green chillies and coriander. Cover with a tight-fitting lid and put a weight on it. After 5 minutes cooking, uncover, add salt to taste and turn the fish. Leave to cook for a further 10 minutes. The fish will be cooked and the gravy thickened. Remove the curry leaves before serving and garnish with coriander leaves.

FRIED PRAWNS

450 g/1 lb prawns	1 onion
1 coconut	A few curry leaves
1 teaspoon chilli powder	Ghee
1 teaspoon turmeric powder	

—— MILD ——

■ Clean and wash the prawns. Grate the coconut and add it

with the chilli powder, turmeric and curry leaves to the cleaned prawns. Mix well, add 300 ml/½ pint water and boil until the prawns are tender. Slice the onion and brown in the ghee. Stir in the cooked prawn mixture and fry to a golden brown.

PRAWN VINDALOO

450 g/1 lb shelled prawns	2 small pieces ginger
3 large onions	1 marble-sized piece tamarind
8 dry red chillies (remove seeds)	4 tablespoons vinegar
	¼ teaspoon mustard seeds
1 pod garlic	1 tablespoon chopped coriander
¼ teaspoon cummin seeds	2 tablespoons ghee or oil
1 tablespoon turmeric powder	Salt to taste

—— HOT ——

■ Grind all the spices except for half the ginger, to a fine paste, moistened with a little of the vinegar. Chop and fry the onions in 1 tablespoon of oil or ghee to a golden brown. Stir in the ground spices and fry for 2 - 3 minutes. Add the prawns and salt to taste. Mix well. Stir in the remaining ginger (chopped) and vinegar.

■ Cook on a low heat for about 30 minutes taking care the prawns do not disintegrate. When the gravy begins to thicken, remove from the heat.

■ In another saucepan, heat 1 tablespoon oil or ghee. Put in the mustard seeds and coriander leaves. Cook until the leaves turn almost brown, remove from the heat and pour over the gravy. Serve hot or cold.

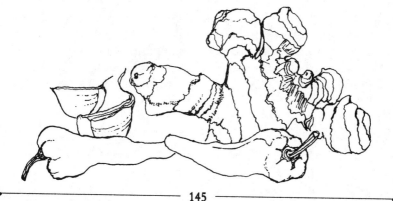

PRAWN
WITH MUSTARD

450 g/1 lb prawns
½ coconut, finely grated
1 tablespoon mustard seeds
3 green chillies
2 teaspoons turmeric powder

1 teaspoon chilli powder
Small bunch of coriander leaves
4 tablespoons mustard oil or
    ghee
Salt to taste

—— MILD ——

■ Shell and wash the prawns. Grind the finely-grated coconut, mustard seeds and green chillies to a fine paste and mix it with the prawns, turmeric, chilli powder, salt and coriander. Heat the oil or ghee in a dekchi and put in the prawn mixture. Steam slowly until the prawns are cooked.

PRAWN
KOFTA CURRY

450 g/1 lb small prawns or
    shrimps
2 large onions
4 green chillies, finely chopped
50 g/2 oz breadcrumbs
1 egg
2 tablespoons ghee

2 tablespoons mustard oil
½ coconut (milk)
Bay leaves
1 tablespoon chopped coriander
    leaves
Salt to taste

—— MEDIUM ——

■ Shell and wash the prawns. Boil them for 5 minutes. Grind or pass them through a mincer to make a smooth paste. Stir in the salt, 2 onions and green chillies. Blend the mixture well and form into 12 balls, or koftas, dip in egg and breadcrumbs. Fry in hot mustard oil or ghee. Keep these on one side and prepare the curry as follows:

GRIND TO A FINE PASTE:

1 large onion
2 teaspoons garam masala

5 cms/2 inch piece turmeric
2.5 cms/1 inch piece ginger

■ Heat ghee and oil in a dekchi until smoking hot. Fry the bay leaves and ground spices for 5 minutes, stirring all the time and adding a little water to keep the spices from burning. Gradually stir in the coconut milk extract and a little salt. Add the koftas and allow the curry to simmer for about 10 minutes until the gravy becomes rich and thick. Serve hot, garnished with chopped coriander leaves.

PRAWN CUTLETS

1 cup cooked prawns (mashed
    to a paste)
½ cup grated coconut
6 green chillies
Small bunch fresh coriander

1 clove garlic
1 teaspoon cummin seeds
A little turmeric powder
Ghee

—— MEDIUM ——

■ Slice the chillies, coriander and garlic finely. Mix all the ingredients, add salt to taste and form into flat cutlets. Dip into beaten egg, roll in breadcrumbs and fry until brown.

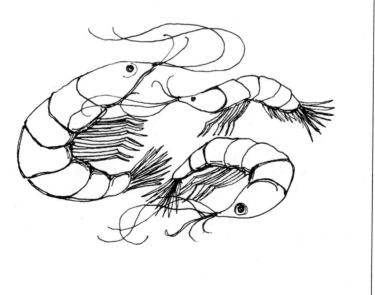

PRAWN SAMBOL

450 g/1 lb prawns	2 onions
1/2 coconut	Salt to taste
Large bunch drumstick leaves or spinach	Oil or ghee

GRIND TO A PASTE:

3 green chillies	1 large piece of turmeric (or 1
4 - 6 cloves of garlic	teaspoon turmeric powder)
1 teaspoon cummin seeds	

—— MILD ——

■ Boil the shelled prawns in a little water. If the prawns are large, chop them after they are cooked. Mix the prawns, masala paste, coarsely-ground coconut and salt to taste. Slice the onions and brown in a little oil or ghee. Put in the chopped drumstick leaves and the prawn mixture. Fry until the mixture is cooked thoroughly (approximately 8 - 10 minutes) and add 300 ml/$\frac{1}{2}$ pint water. Simmer until the fish and vegetable are tender and there is very little gravy left in the pan. Serve hot with boiled rice.

HOT MALAYALEE FRIED PRAWNS

40 large prawns	10 green chillies
30 dry red chillies	13 small onions
1 teaspoon peppercorns	2.5 cms/1 inch piece ginger
1 teaspoon mustard seeds	1 sprig curry leaves
1 1/2 teaspoons fenugreek	Tamarind (1 dessertspoon
2 dessertspoons coriander powder	soaked in a little hot water)
2.5 cms/1 inch piece turmeric	Oil
14 cloves garlic	Salt to taste

—— VERY VERY HOT ——

■ Fry and grind the pepper, mustard, fenugreek, coriander and turmeric and set aside. Grind the red chillies to a paste. Heat enough oil in a pan and fry a few curry leaves and tamarind, add the finely chopped onions, crushed garlic and ginger. Stir in the red chilli paste and the green chillies cut into small pieces.

■ Place the prawns into the mixture, add the ground spices and salt to taste and enough water to cover the prawns. Cook until the water is absorbed and the prawns are tender.

MALARBARI FISH MOLEE

1 kg/2 lb fish	100 g/4 oz flour (maida)
1 coconut	1 teaspoon turmeric powder
3 onions	2 small tomatoes
12 cloves garlic	3 tablespoons oil
5 cms/2 inch piece ginger	100 ml/ 3½ fl oz vinegar
8 green chillies	Salt to taste

—— HOT ——

■ Grate the coconut, add 300ml/½ pint hot water and extract thick milk. Add 1.2 ltrs/2 pints hot water to the grated coconut and extract the second milk. Be careful to strain it well and keep the thick and thin milks separate.

■ Slice the onions finely and chop the tomatoes. Finely chop the ginger and garlic and slit the chillies lengthways. Wash the fish and cut into slices (pomfret, salmon or any variety available may be used).

■ Heat the oil in a large saucepan and fry the onions, garlic and ginger for 2 minutes. While this is frying put in the green chillies. Add the flour and turmeric powder, stirring well so that the flour does not form into lumps. Pour in the tomatoes and thin coconut milk and boil for 10 minutes. Add the fish and vinegar and cook for 15 minutes. Stir in the thick coconut milk and salt and cook for a further 5 minutes. Tamarind water may be used instead of vinegar. Serve with plain boiled rice or idlis.

SHELL PRAWN CURRY

48 large fresh prawns
2 onions
12 dry red chillies
1½ teaspoons turmeric powder

3 tablespoon coconut oil
Coriander leaves
Salt to taste

—— VERY HOT ——

■ Chop the onions coarsely. Grind the dry red chillies to a powder. Add the onions to the chilli powder and grind together to a paste.

■ Clean and wash the prawns; remove head, tail and the back thread (intestines) but do not remove the shells. Put them in a saucepan with 600 ml/1 pint water, turmeric powder and salt and bring to the boil. Cook over a low heat for 30 minutes or until nearly all the liquid has evaporated.

■ In another saucepan, heat the oil and fry the paste until the onions are translucent. Add the prawn mixture and simmer over a low heat until there is a thick gravy. Garnish with chopped coriander leaves.

SHRIMP PATIA

450 g/1 lb shelled shrimps
3 large onions
8 green chillies
4 cloves garlic
1 teaspoon cummin seeds
1 teaspoon turmeric powder
1 teaspoon coriander powder

1 teaspoon chilli powder
1 tablespoon vinegar
1 teaspoon sugar
1 green mango
Sweet oil (til)
Salt to taste

—— MEDIUM ——

■ Wash the shrimps in water to which 1 teaspoon vinegar has been added. Grind the green chillies, garlic and cummin seeds. Wash the spices off the grinding stone with a cupful of water and keep this water on one side. Chop the onions finely and fry in hot oil until light gold in colour. Add the ground spices. Cook until they begin to bubble and stir in the turmeric, coriander powder, and chilli powder. Fry for 3 minutes.

■ Stir in the shrimps, spicy water and salt and continue to cook until the shrimps are tender, approximately 10 minutes. A little extra water can be added if necessary. Pour in the chopped mango, remaining vinegar and sugar to taste. Cook until the oil floats to the top. Serve with kitcheree.

KARELAS STUFFED WITH SHRIMPS

1 dozen karelas (bitter-gourd)	*1 lemon*
225 g/8 oz shrimps.	*Salt to taste*
1 tomato	*Ghee*

GRIND TO A PASTE:

1 onion	*$\frac{1}{2}$ teaspoon coriander seeds*
3 dry red chillies	*3 cloves garlic*
$\frac{1}{2}$ teaspoon turmeric powder	

—— *MILD* ——

■ Lightly scrape the karela skins. Make a split lengthwise and remove all the seeds. Soak karelas in salt and water for an hour as this will help lessen the bitter flavour. Drain and wipe dry. Heat a little ghee in a saucepan and fry masala paste until well cooked.

■ Add cleaned shrimps and chopped tomatoes and cook until tender and dry. Stir in the juice of lemon and leave to cool. Fill the karelas with shrimp mixture and tie with string. Heat ghee in a frying pan or kerai and when it smokes, fry karelas, 3-4 at a time. Cook until the skins turn brown and crisp. Serve hot with chappatis. Use cucumber if bitter-gourd is not available, preferably a bitter variety.

MUSTARD
CURRY

1 pomfret or plaice	6 cloves garlic
2 tablespoons mustard seeds	Milk of 1 coconut
1 large piece turmeric	3 tablespoons oil
2 onions	Salt and vinegar to taste
6 green chillies	Few coriander leaves
1 piece ginger	

—— MEDIUM ——

■ Clean and cut the pomfret. Grind the mustard seeds and turmeric. Slice the onions finely. Grind the ginger and garlic. Slit the chillies. In a saucepan, heat the oil and fry the ground mustard seeds and turmeric for 1 minute. Add the ground ginger and garlic and cook for a few seconds. Stir in the green chillies and fry until brown. Add the onions and cook until tender and translucent. A little water can be sprinkled into the mixture to mellow the mustard smell.

■ Pour in the thin coconut milk (second extractions) and stir constantly to prevent curdling. Blend in the vinegar and salt. Boil for 2 minutes. Add fish and blend in the thick coconut milk. Cook until the fish is tender, stirring to prevent curdling. Remove from the heat and garnish with chopped coriander leaves. Serve with boiled rice.

FISH
SHASLIK

1.8 - 2.3 kg/4 - 5 lb fish	1 piece ginger
300 ml/½ pint curd or yoghurt	8 cloves garlic
225 g/8 oz onions	Ghee
8 dry red chillies	Salt to taste

FOR GARAM MASALA - GRIND:

12 cloves	2 black cardamoms
12 peppercorns	1 stick cinnamon

—— MEDIUM ——

■ Clean the fish well and, with a sharp knife, chop into cubes. Grind the chillies and ginger together. Grind the garlic and add it to a saucepan of water. Wash the fish pieces in this water to get rid of the strong fishy smell. Mix the masala paste and the fish cubes together. Mix in the curd and salt to taste.

■ Fix alternate fish and onion cubes securely onto skewers. Roast over a barbecue or under a low grill. Brush every few minutes with a little ghee. When browned, remove from the skewers and serve very hot, sprinkled with garam masala.

FISH SHIFTA

3 cups minced fish	1 piece ginger
4 large onions	2 teaspoons turmeric powder
1 sprig coriander	Oil
Small sprig mint	Salt and pepper to taste
2 - 3 cloves garlic	

■ Mince the onions, coriander and mint. Grind the ginger and garlic together. Blend all the ingredients together and pour in 2 tablespoons oil. Shape into a number of sausage shapes and fry them in hot oil in a frying-pan. Serve hot, with chutney or tomato sauce.

BAKED
MASALA POMFRET

1 large pomfret or plaice	*2 ripe tomatoes*

FOR STUFFING:

2 large onions	*A pinch of turmeric powder*
1 green chilli	*1 teaspoon melted jaggery*
Small bunch of coriander	*300 ml/½ pint water*
leaves	*Salt and lemon juice to taste*
1 large ripe tomato	*Ghee*

—— *VERY MILD* ——

■ Clean the pomfret and make a slit in one side. Wash thoroughly and rub all over with salt.

■ Prepare the stuffing by chopping the onions, chilli, fresh coriander and tomato. Heat the ghee in a pan, put in the turmeric. Add the chopped chilli and coriander and fry for 2 minutes. Put in onions, frying them until they are brown. Stir in the chopped tomato, jaggery, water, salt and lemon juice to taste. Cook until the mixture thickens and all the liquid is absorbed.

■ Wipe the fish dry and pack the cavity with the stuffing. Place fish in a greased pie-dish or baking tin and arrange slices of tomato on and around it. Bake at 180°C/350°F/Gas mark 4 allowing 12 minutes cooking time for each lb of fish.

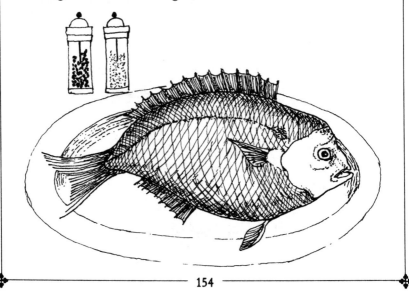

PRAWN AND PUMPKIN CURRY

450 g/1 lb prawns (cleaned and
    shelled if wished, though
    they have more flavour
    with their shells left on)
450 g/1 lb white pumpkin
8 dry red chillies
1 teaspoon fenugreek
1 tablespoon coriander seeds

1 medium onion
3 cloves garlic
1 teaspoon turmeric powder
A small piece of tamarind (size
    of a small lemon)
½ coconut
Salt to taste

—— *MEDIUM* ——

■ Grate the coconut and fry with all the spices. Grind them together to a smooth paste. Chop the pumpkin into cubes and cook with the prawns in 300 ml/½ pint water, adding salt to taste. Cook for 20 minutes, add the ground spices and let the mixture boil. This curry can be seasoned with 2 tablespoons chopped onion fried in 1 tablespoon ghee. This makes a delicious dish and goes well with rice.

CHICKEN AND EGGS

CHICKEN AND EGGS

The varied and distinctive flavours of Indian cooking result from a combination of the food of many nationalities. All those countries that have played a part in the history of India have added subtle influences to Indian cuisine. Centuries ago the Parsis, followers of the prophet Zorastra, came to India from Persia (Iran), and imprinted their own culinary taste and genius on the cooking of the country. A distinctive use of spices characterises many Parsi dishes and imparts an exotic flavour. There are literally hundreds of Parsi egg recipes.

The highlight of any Parsi festival or ceremony is the food served specially for the occasion. One has yet to meet a person who has had so little appetite as to refuse an invitation to a Parsi dinner - unless he is very ill! There is a now famous legend of a student in Bombay who looked up the marriage columns of the daily newspapers for any Parsi weddings, and gate-crashed every one of them. It was rumoured that he attended no less than a hundred and fifty marriage feasts during his three years at university!

Of all the festivals observed by the Parsis, Nowroz Pateti is the most important. This is the Parsi New Year (the 1st of Farradin), and a day when social and moral virtues are practised to the fullest extent. All ties of friendship are drawn closer, offences are pardoned and every heart is filled with gladness.

On New Year's Day, the Parsis rise earlier than usual, dress themselves in new clothes and attend prayers at the fire temples. Later, they visit friends and relatives and perform a small ceremony called Hamma-i-join (hand-joining) to wish each other a happy New Year. They invite each other to the traditional New Year breakfast of 'Rava' (a milky sweet made with semolina or vermicelli and garnished with chopped nuts and rose petals), harboiled eggs, sweetmeats and chilled Falooda. Later in the day, an elaborate lunch of rice, eggs, chicken, meat and fish dishes is served. The Parsi Akoori on Toast (savoury scrambled eggs), Chicken Dhansak (a brown pulao-like rice with meat or chicken, served with a lentil 'curry') and Patra ni Machi (chutney fish baked in banana leaves) have taken their place among the national dishes of India.

DHANSAK

225 g/8 oz toovar dhal

225 g/8 oz mixed dhals (gram,
    moong and val dhals)

675 g/1½ lb meat or chicken

1 large potato

1 small brinjal (aubergine)

2 onions

Large bunch fenugreek greens
    (methi)

Small slice red pumpkin

Small slice white pumpkin

3 red tomatoes

Ghee

Salt to taste

GRIND TOGETHER,
WITH 1 TABLESPOON TAMARIND WATER:

½ teaspoon cummin seeds

½ teaspon turmeric powder

½ teaspoon fenugreek seeds

½ teaspoon mustard seeds

½ teaspoon ground black
    pepper

1 teaspoon chilli powder

1 teaspoon coriander powder

1 teaspoon cummin powder

A few mint leaves

2.5 cms/1 inch piece ginger

8 cloves garlic

4 cms/1½ inch piece cinnamon

8 green chillies

A few coriander leaves

—— MEDIUM HOT ——

■ Wash and clean the dhals and soak in a saucepan of water. Clean and cut the meat into large pieces. Bring to the boil with the dhals, chopped-up vegetables and 1 sliced onion.

■ Grind all the spices to a fine paste with the tamarind water. In another saucepan, heat a little ghee and fry 1 chopped onion adding the ground spices. Chop tomatoes, mint and coriander leaves finely and fry with the onion. When the meat, dhal and vegetables are well cooked, remove the meat pieces carefully and keep on one side. Grind the dhal mixture to a thick paste. Put the dhal paste and meat in with the fried onions etc., in the second saucepan. Add salt to taste and more water according to the thickness required for the gravy. Cook for 5 minutes and serve with brown rice and Shami Kababs.

CHICKEN GARUDA

SHREDDED CHICKEN

1 medium chicken	*8 green chillies*
½ teaspoon cummin seeds	*1 tablespoon tomato purée*
½ teaspoon coriander powder	*½ teaspoon vinegar*
2.5 cms/1 inch stick cinnamon	*4 tablespoons ghee*
4 cloves	*Salt*
3 large onions	

GRIND TOGETHER:

1 large onion	*5 cms/2 inch piece ginger*
½ teaspoon aniseed	*2 cloves garlic*
¼ teaspoon cummin seeds	

—— *MEDIUM* ——

■ Boil the chicken with 1.2 ltrs/2 pints water, cummin seeds, coriander, cinnamon, cloves and ½ teaspoon salt in a saucepan until tender. Separate the meat from the bones, shred coarsely and keep aside. Finely slice the onions and green chillies. Heat the ghee in a frying pan and sauté the vegetables until well browned.

■ Strain and keep aside. In the same ghee fry the shredded chicken. Add the ground paste and fried onions and chillies. Blend until well mixed. Stir in the tomato purée, vinegar and salt as desired and simmer gently until dry. Serve with bread or puris.

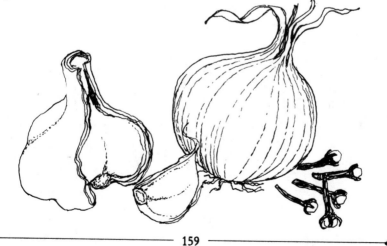

MAI VHALLAN

PARSI CREAMED CHICKEN

1 large chicken	*225 g/8 oz almonds*
1.2 ltrs/2 pints milk	*225 g/8 oz raisins*
6 cloves garlic	*4 eggs*
6 green chillies	*1 teaspoon butter*
2.5 cms/1 inch piece ginger	*2 tablespoons ghee*
5 onions	*Salt to taste*

—— *MEDIUM* ——

■ Joint the chicken and cut into medium sized pieces. Grind the chillies, garlic and ginger to a paste. Heat a little ghee in a saucepan and fry 1 sliced onion until golden brown. Add the chicken pieces, the ground paste, 1 tablespoon ghee and salt. When the chicken turns light brown, pour in 1.2 ltrs/2 pints water and simmer until the meat is tender and a little gravy remains. Blanch and slice the almonds and the remaining onions. Fry the almonds, raisins and onions together, and set aside.

■ Remove the chicken meat from the bones and shred it. Cook the shredded chicken in the milk on a medium heat until the milk is reduced to half its original volume. Butter a baking dish and pour in the remaining chicken gravy. Spread a layer of the milk-cooked chicken meat, then a layer of the fried onion mixture, then a layer of cream. Repeat these layers and finally break the eggs on top of the last layer, taking care that the yolks stay whole. Put the dish in a moderately hot oven and bake until the eggs are well set. This dish goes well with hot buttered toast.

PICKLED CHICKEN or CHICKEN VINDALOO

1 medium chicken
3 dozen red chillies (Goa chillies)
100 g/4 oz jaggery or molasses
100 g/4 oz cummin seeds

4 pods garlic
1.2 ltrs/2 pints vinegar
900 ml/ 1½ pints gingelly oil
Salt to taste

—— *VERY VERY HOT* ——

■ Joint the chicken, leaving the skin on, and boil it in vinegar. Wash the chillies in vinegar and grind them with the cummin seeds and garlic to a fine paste, using a little vinegar in the paste itself.

■ Heat the oil in a saucepan, stir in the ground paste and fry for a few minutes on a low heat. Add the chicken, and 600 ml/1 pint vinegar. Scrape the jaggery and blend it with the molasses into the chicken. Cook until the sauce thickens, remove from the heat and allow the mixture to cool. Store in a large air-tight jar.

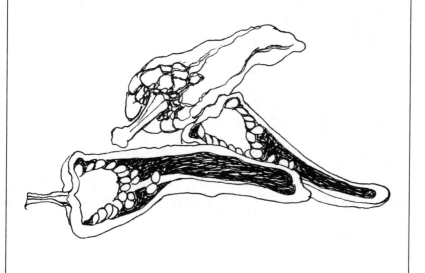

KHOBANI MURGHA

1 medium chicken	2 medium tomatoes
100 g/4 oz dried apricots	1 stick cinnamon
2 medium onions	2 small cardamoms
1 clove garlic	15 g/½ oz saffron
1.5 cms/½ inch piece ginger	Ghee
3 green chillies	

—— MILD ——

■ Clean and joint the chicken. Slice the onions finely. In a large pan, heat 2 tablespoons ghee and fry the onions until they are a light golden colour. Make a smooth paste of the garlic, ginger and chillies and sauté this in the same pan until well-cooked. Add the chicken pieces, including the liver, if available, chopped tomatoes, cinnamon and cardamoms and salt to taste. Continue cooking over a gentle heat for 10 minutes. Pour in half a cup of hot water and simmer gently until the chicken is almost cooked.

■ In a small basin crush the saffron and mix in a little hot milk. Stir the halved and stoned apricots and the saffron liquid into the chicken and continue cooking for 5 minutes until the apricots are tender but not too soft. Serve hot.

DHANIA MURGH

CHICKEN CORIANDER

1 medium chicken	1 teaspoon turmeric powder
600 ml/1 pint curd or yoghurt	20 green chillies
225 g/8 oz khoya (solidified milk)	225 g/8 oz coriander leaves
	600 ml/1 pint coconut milk extract
6 cloves garlic	4 tablespoons ghee
4.0 cms/1½ inch piece ginger	Salt to taste
50 g/2 oz almonds	
50 g/2 oz sultanas	

—— VERY VERY HOT ——

■ Joint the chicken. Grind the ginger and garlic together and smear the chicken pieces with the paste. Heat ghee and fry chicken pieces until browned, remove from the ghee.

■ Blend curd and khoya together to a smooth paste, add turmeric and salt and mix well. Blanch almonds and slice. Reheat ghee and fry almonds and sultanas, add curd mixture and chicken and cook until only a little liquid is left. Add slit green chillies and cook until dry. Stir in the coriander leaves and coconut milk, bring to the boil and reduce the heat. Simmer gently without stirring until the chicken is tender and ghee floats to the top. Serve with boiled rice, chappatis or any other bread.

CHICKEN
CHILLI FRY

1 medium chicken	*½ lemon*
2.5 cms/1 inch piece ginger	*Freshly ground black pepper*
6 cloves garlic	*Breadcrumbs*
8 green chillies	*Ghee or oil for frying*
4 eggs	*Salt to taste*

—— MEDIUM ——

■ Cut the chicken into five pieces (legs, wings and the rest of the body). Place in a heavy saucepan with ½ teaspoon salt and enough water to cover the meat. Cook until tender.

■ Mince the ginger, garlic and chillies together. Break the eggs into a mixing bowl and beat until frothy. Rub cooked chicken pieces with a squeeze of lemon. Coat them with the minced mixture and sprinkle with pepper. Season with salt if desired, and prick with a fork. Dip generously in egg, roll in the breadcrumbs and fry on both sides in hot ghee until crisp and brown. Serve immediately.

COORGI STEAMED CHICKEN

1 medium chicken. *1 large banana leaf*

GRIND TOGETHER:

225 g/8 oz coriander leaves *1 teaspoon cummin seeds*
1 large onion *$^{1}/_{2}$ teaspoon turmeric powder*
6 - 8 dry red chillies *Juice of $^{1}/_{2}$ lemon*
1 tomato *4 cloves garlic*
1 teaspoon peppercorns *4 tablespoons ghee*

—— *MEDIUM* ——

■ Make the ground paste and set aside in a bowl. Dress the chicken, making a few cuts with a sharp knife on either side. Spread the whole chicken generously with the paste, using a wooden spoon. Leave it in a cool place for 3 hours. Wrap the chicken in the banana leaf (or foil can be used) and steam for an hour. Cut into pieces and serve. Alternatively, heat ghee, cut chicken into large pieces and fry well on both sides.

TANDOORI CHICKEN

BARBECUED CHICKEN

2 spring chickens *300 ml/$^{1}/_{2}$ pint curd or yoghurt*
(675 g/1$^{1}/_{2}$ lb each) *150 ml/$^{1}/_{4}$ pint lemon juice*
4.0 cms/ 1$^{1}/_{2}$ inch piece ginger *2 teaspoons chilli powder*
1 small pod garlic *1 teaspoon black cummin seeds*
1 large onion *Salt to taste*

GRIND TOGETHER:

2 sticks cinnamon *3 cardamoms*
1 bay leaf *Salt to taste*
10 cloves *Ghee or butter*
8 black peppercorns

—— *MEDIUM* ——

■ Grind together the ginger, garlic and onion and blend in with the curd to a smooth paste. Apply the mixture to the inside and outside of the chickens, and leave to marinate for 5 hours.

■ Add the chilli powder, cummin seeds and ground spices to the lemon juice and mix well. Make three or four cuts with a sharp knife on each side of the chickens and smear them both with the mixture. Sprinkle with salt and allow to stand for 1 hour.

■ Skewer the chickens, brush them with a little melted butter and grill, for the best results, on an open charcoal stove. If this is not possible, grill under an electric or gas grill or cook in an oven for ½ hour taking care to cook on all sides. Serve sprinkled with a little garam masala and garnish with sliced lemon and onion rings, accompanied by tandoori roti.

CHICKEN BAFFATTE

1 medium chicken	450 g/1 lb potatoes
1 tablespoon vinegar	450 g/1 lb small onions (pickling
8 dry red chillies	variety)
2.5 cms/1 inch piece ginger	100 g/4 oz tamarind, soaked in
4 cloves garlic	hot water
1 teaspoon cummin seeds	Salt to taste
1 teaspoon coriander powder	300 ml/½ pint thick coconut
3 tablespoons ghee	milk
450 g/1 lb onions	

—— *MEDIUM* ——

■ Joint the chicken. Grind the chillies, ginger, garlic, coriander and cummin with the vinegar. Heat the ghee and brown the sliced onions, add ground spices and fry for 5 minutes. Add the chicken pieces and enough warm water to cover and simmer for 30 minutes.

■ Peel and quarter the potatoes and cook in boiling salted water for 15 minutes, add the potatoes with the small onions and cook for a further 10 minutes. Strain the tamarind and add the juice. Salt to taste. Cook for 10 minutes, add the coconut milk and when the chicken is tender, serve with rice or bread (chappatis etc.).

CHICKEN PIDEE

CHICKEN WITH RICE DUMPLINGS

1 chicken (1 kg/2lb)	*2 tablespoons coriander seeds*
2 coconuts	*1 teaspoon turmeric powder*
2 large onions	*1 teaspoon mustard seeds*
1 teaspoon black peppercorns	*225 g/8 oz rice*
6 dry red chillies	*2 tablespoons ghee*
2 sticks cinnamon	*Salt to taste*
6 cloves	

—— *MEDIUM* ——

■ Grate 1 coconut and extract the thick and thin milk separately. Chop half a coconut into very thin slices. Grate and extract the milk from the remaining half-coconut for the rice balls. Grind the pepper, chillies, cinnamon, cloves, coriander seeds and half an onion to a paste. Slice the remaining onions and fry in hot ghee until golden brown. Add the ground spices and fry for 5 minutes. Put in the chicken (cut into pieces) and fry until brown. Pour in the thin coconut milk, sprinkle with turmeric powder. Salt to taste and cook for at least an hour.

■ The rice should be washed and soaked in water overnight or 12 hours previously. Drain the rice and grind it to a thick paste, adding the thick milk from half a coconut or just half a grated coconut, if preferred. Season with salt. Prepare balls about the size of an egg from this paste. When the chicken is nearly tender add the rice balls and cook for about 30 minutes until the rice balls are ready. Heat 1 tablespoon ghee in a frying pan and fry the chopped coconut and mustard seeds. Mix them in gently with the chicken. Pour in the remaining thick coconut milk and cook for 5 - 10 minutes. Serve hot.

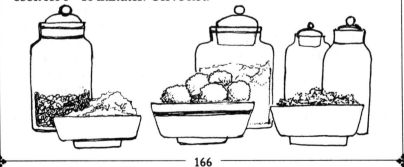

CHICKEN DO PIAZZA

CHICKEN WITH ONIONS

1 medium chicken	*6 cloves garlic*
450 g/1 lb onion	*6 dry red chillies*
675 g/1½ lb tomatoes	*2.5 cms/1 inch piece ginger*
8 small new potatoes	*½ teaspoon peppercorns*
1½ tablespoons coriander powder	*15 g/½ oz saffron*
1 tablespoon cummin seed powder	*Salt to taste*
	4 tablespoons ghee

—— MEDIUM ——

■ Joint the chicken. Slice the onions coarsely. Peel and chop the tomatoes. Peel the potatoes. Grind together the coriander, cummin, garlic, chillies and ginger.

■ Heat the ghee in a heavy saucepan and fry the onions until tender. Add the ground spices, peppercorns and tomatoes, mix and cook until thick and tender. Add the chicken and fry for 10 minutes. Pour in 600 ml/1 pint water and the saffron previously dissolved in 1 tablespoon water, cover and simmer until the chicken is almost tender. Add the potatoes and cook until they are soft and a thick gravy remains.

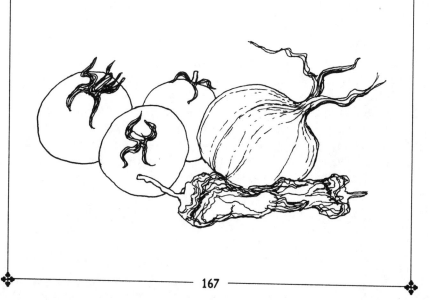

SHAHI PASAND CHICKEN

CHICKEN WITH VEGETABLE AND MUSHROOMS

1 medium chicken	*4 green chillies*
3 medium onions	*Salt and pepper to taste*
5 cms/2 inch piece ginger	*Ghee*

—— *MEDIUM* ——

■ Place the ghee in a pan over medium heat and, when hot, add the sliced onions, frying them until golden brown. Drain and keep on one side. Clean and joint the chicken and fry for 10 minutes setting aside the liver. At this stage of the cooking, add the sliced ginger, sliced chillies, salt and pepper and fry for another 5 minutes. Add 1 cup of almost boiling water and simmer over very gentle heat, stirring occasionally. When the chicken is tender, remove and allow to cool.

NOW TAKE:

1 small cauliflower (cut into pieces)	*2 tomatoes (halved)*
50 g/2 oz shelled peas (parboiled)	*50 g/2 oz dried black mushrooms (soaked in cold water until swollen)*
The chicken liver (finely sliced)	*100 g/4 oz cream cheese*
1 teaspoon whole cummin seed	*A bunch of coriander leaves*
4 dry red chillies	

■ In a heavy frying pan or skillet, pour in the gravy of the chicken curry already prepared. Add the cauliflower, peas, chicken liver, cummin seeds and chillies and cook for 10 minutes, stirring frequently. Add the tomatoes, mushrooms and cream cheese and continue cooking for another 5 - 7 minutes, stirring constantly. Arrange the pieces of chicken on a platter and pour the gravy over. Arrange the vegetables around the chicken. Garnish with coriander sprigs. Serve hot.

PIGEON VINDALOO

4 pigeons
2 large onions
12 dry red chillies
1 teaspoon cummin seeds
½ teaspoon mustard seeds
2.5 cms/1 inch piece ginger

1 teaspoon turmeric powder
6 cloves garlic
1 tablespoon vinegar
3 tablespoons cooking oil
Salt to taste

—— *VERY HOT* ——

■ Cut the pigeons into quarters. Grind together the chillies, cummin seeds, mustard, ginger, turmeric, garlic and vinegar to a paste. Slice the onions.

■ Heat the oil and fry the onions until translucent in colour. Stir in the ground paste and fry for 5 minutes. Add the pigeons and fry until lightly browned. Pour in enough water to cover the meat and cook gently until tender.

PALAK MURGHI

1 medium chicken
450 g/1 lb spinach
2 tomatoes
2 onions
4 cloves garlic
2 cloves

1 teaspoon coriander powder
½ teaspoon freshly ground
    black pepper
2 tablespoons ghee
Salt

■ Joint the chicken and slice the spinach. Melt the ghee in a saucepan and sauté the sliced onions and crushed garlic. Stir in the cloves, coriander, pepper, chopped tomatoes and spinach and cook for 5 minutes. Add the chicken and salt to taste. Cover and simmer until the chicken is tender.

PAHARI CHICKEN

1 medium chicken	2 cloves garlic, crushed
1.2 ltrs/2 pints curd or yoghurt	2 tablespoons ghee
6 green chillies	1 tablespoon chopped coriander
3 cardamoms	leaves
2.5 cms/1 inch piece ginger	Salt

—— MEDIUM ——

■ Joint the chicken. Chop the ginger and 2 green chillies finely. Slit the remaining chillies and fry in hot ghee with the cardamoms, ginger and garlic. Add the chicken pieces and fry until evenly browned.

■ Whip the curd and add to the chicken, lower heat and simmer gently without stirring. Salt to taste and cook until the chicken is tender and the gravy is thick and creamy. Garnish with coriander leaves and chopped green chillies. Serve with rice.

KERALA FRIED DUCK

1 medium duck	¼ teaspoon ground cinnamon
1 tablespoon chilli powder	1 egg
1 teaspoon freshly ground black	Breadcrumbs
pepper	Salt
1 teaspoon coriander powder	Ghee or oil
½ teaspoon turmeric powder	Grated coconut
¼ teaspoon ground cloves	Lemon slices

—— HOT ——

■ Joint the duck. Put the meat in a saucepan with the spices and about 900 ml/1½ pints water. Bring to the boil and simmer until the water has evaporated and the duck is tender. Heat ghee in a frying pan. Dip each piece of duck in beaten egg and breadcrumbs and fry in hot fat until golden brown on both sides. Serve garnished with grated coconut and slices of lemon.

DUCK VINDALOO

1 medium duck	2.5 cms/1 inch piece ginger
2 sticks cinnamon	1 teaspoon turmeric powder
2 cardamoms	3 tablespoons vinegar
6 cloves	1 tablespoon sugar
8 dry red chillies	½ teaspoon poppy seeds
6 green chillies	225 g/8 oz potatoes.
3 onions	3 tablespoons ghee or oil
1 tablespoon cummin seeds	Salt
1 pod garlic	

—— *HOT* ——

■ Joint the duck and put in a saucepan with enough water to cover the meat. Add the cinnamon, cardamoms, cloves and salt and cook until the meat is barely tender (approximately 1 hour). Peel and quarter potatoes.

■ Grind all the remaining ingredients with vinegar to a smooth paste. Heat the ghee in a large saucepan and fry the cooked duck until well browned on all sides. Remove and keep on one side. Add the ground paste to the same ghee and fry until dry. Pour in 300 ml/½ pint water and simmer until the liquid has evaporated. Add the fried duck, remaining paste and potatoes. Season with salt, sugar and vinegar, if desired, and cook gently until the potatoes are tender and the gravy has thickened.

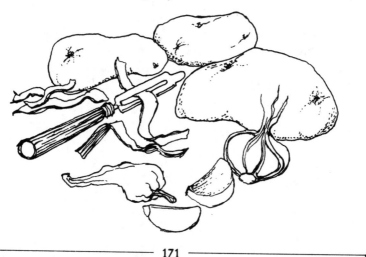

CHICKEN PIDIYAL

CHICKEN WITH SWEET CORN

1 medium chicken	*1 sprig curry leaf*
3 onions	*1 teaspoon mustard seeds*
1 teaspoon peppercorns	*225 g/8 oz maize flour or sweet*
6 dry red chillies	*corn kernels*
1 tablespoon coriander powder	*Salt to taste*
3 coconuts	*½ teaspoon garam masala*
½ teaspoon turmeric powder	*4 tablespoons ghee*

—— *MEDIUM* ——

■ Joint the chicken. With a very sharp knife separate the meat from the bone and chop into 5.0 cms/2 inch pieces. Heat a tablespoon of ghee and fry pepper, chillies, coriander and 1 sliced onion until brown. Grind this mixture.

■ Slice half a coconut very finely and extract the milk from the remaining 1½ coconuts. Mix the turmeric, ground paste and salt into the milk. Put the mixture together with the chicken pieces in a large saucepan and bring to the boil. Add the curry leaf, lower the heat and simmer until meat is tender. Remove from the heat.

■ Heat a tablespoon of ghee in a small saucepan, add mustard seeds and fry until they start crackling. Add 1 sliced onion and brown lightly. Pour into the chicken curry and keep covered.

■ Extract the milk from the last coconut and mix enough with the flour to make a thick dough, adding salt. Roll into marble-size balls. Boil ¾ pint water and put in the dough (or corn) balls to cook, for approximately 8 - 10 minutes, until tender. Re-heat the chicken curry, mix in the balls and simmer for 15 minutes. Serve garnished with sliced coconut, crisply fried onions and a sprinkling of garam masala.

GAJJAR MASALA MURGHI

1 large chicken (1.5 kg/3 lb)
2 large onions
450 g/1 lb carrots
4 cms/1½ inch piece ginger
8 cloves garlic
1 tablespoon coriander powder
2 teaspoons turmeric powder
2 teaspoons chilli powder
2 teaspoons garam masala

½ pint vinegar
2 black cardamoms
2 sticks cinnamon
1 bay leaf
6 hardboiled eggs
1 tablespoon chopped coriander
  leaves
4 tablespoons ghee
Salt to taste

—— MEDIUM ——

■ Quarter the chicken. Grate the carrots. Heat the ghee in a large saucepan and fry the chicken until well browned all over. Remove the chicken pieces and in the same fat, fry the sliced onions. Grind the garlic, coriander, turmeric, chilli, garam masala and vinegar together and add to the onions. Fry for 5 minutes. Put in the cardamoms, cinnamon, bay leaf and grated carrot and cook for a further 5 minutes. Add the chicken, salt and 300 ml/½ pint water and simmer until the chicken is tender.

■ Heat a little ghee in a separate frying pan and fry the halved hardboiled eggs until brown. Serve garnished with coriander leaves.

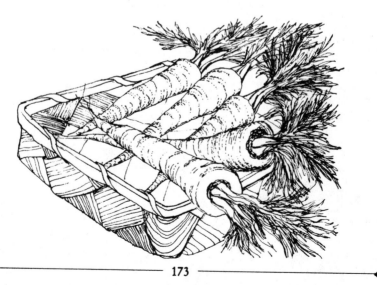

CHICKEN KORMA

1 medium chicken	*1 tablespoon chopped coriander*
300 ml/½ pint curd or yoghurt	*leaves*
4 large onions	*1 stick cinnamon*
6 green chillies	*2 cardamoms*
2.5 cms/1 inch piece ginger	*4 cloves*
¼ coconut	*1 lemon*
1 pod garlic	*3 tablespoons ghee*
1 tablespoon poppy seeds	*Salt to taste*
¾ teaspoon turmeric powder	

—— MEDIUM ——

■ Joint the chicken and slice 2 onions finely. Grind together the remaining onions, chillies, ginger, coconut, garlic, poppy seeds, turmeric and half the coriander leaves to a smooth paste.
■ Heat the ghee and fry the sliced onions until light brown. Stir in the ground paste and fry for a few minutes. Add the chicken and remaining spices, curd and salt and simmer gently, adding a little water if necessary. Cook until the chicken is tender. Season with lemon juice just before serving.

SHAHI MURG MUSAALAM

SPICE STUFFED CHICKEN

1 medium chicken	*50 g/2 oz pistachios*
225 g/8 oz green papaya	*50 g/2 oz poppy seeds*
4 onions	*2 teaspoons garam masala*
2.5 cms/1 inch piece ginger	*300 ml/½ pint curd or yoghurt*
2 cloves garlic	*8 tablespoons ghee*
2 green chillies	*4 hardboiled eggs*
2 tomatoes	*Salt to taste*
50 g/2 oz almonds	

—— MILD ——

■ Prepare and dress chicken for stuffing. Grind the papaya and smear the body of the chicken, including the cavity. Chop 2 onions, ginger, garlic and chillies finely and stuff the chicken with this mixture together with the hardboiled eggs.

■ Grind together almonds, pistachios, poppy seeds and garam masala and smear the chicken with this paste. Sew the chicken up well.

■ Heat the ghee in a heavy saucepan and slice and saute the remaining onions. Place the chicken in the pan and add the chopped tomatoes, curd and salt. Cover and seal well or cook in a pressure cooker and cook for 45 minutes on medium heat. Remove the string and serve immediately.

MURGH
MASAALAM

1 large chicken	4 cloves
1 onion	1/2 teaspoon whole black pepper
1 tablespoon coriander	5 cms/2 inch piece coconut
1 teaspoon aniseed	25 g/1 oz almonds
1 teaspoon cummin seeds	300 ml/1/2 pint curd
100 g/4 oz roasted gram dhal	Pinch of saffron
4 dry red chillies	6 tablespoons ghee
4 white cardamoms	Salt to taste
2 black cardamoms	

—— MILD ——

■ Slice the onion. Soak saffron in a spoonful of hot water. Roast all the remaining spices without any fat in a frying-pan and grind together. Heat half the ghee in a large saucepan and brown the chicken on all sides. Remove from the pan and pour in the remaining ghee. Fry the onions until brown, add the ground spices and ground coconut and fry for 5 minutes. Put the chicken back into the pan. Blend curd with 1.2 ltrs/2 pints water and pour into the pan together with salt. Cover tightly and cook until the liquid evaporates and the chicken is tender. Just before serving add saffron water and garnish with chopped almonds.

CHICKEN ROAST

1 medium chicken	4 tablespoons ghee
2 onions	Salt to taste
½ lemon	

FOR STUFFING MIX TOGETHER:

½ grated coconut	25 g/1 oz raisins
100 g/4 oz khoya (solidified milk)	25 g/1 oz finely chopped almonds
½ teaspoon salt	15 g/½ oz saffron

FOR GRAVY GRIND TOGETHER:

1 onion	1 teaspoon coriander powder
3 cloves garlic	2 cloves
2.5 cms/1 inch piece ginger	2 sticks cinnamon
1 teaspoon chilli powder	1 teaspoon vinegar
1 teaspoon turmeric powder	

—— MILD ——

■ Rub chicken with lemon juice and salt. Mix ingredients for stuffing and fill the cavity of the chicken. Sew the stomach up securely. Heat the ghee in a large saucepan and fry the sliced onions until golden brown. Put in the chicken and cook over a low heat, basting occasionally, until tender.

■ Grind together all the ingredients for the gravy. Remove cooked chicken from the saucepan and fry the paste in the same ghee until the ghee floats to the top. Put the chicken back, add 300 ml/½ pint water, salt to taste and cook for 10 minutes. Serve with roast potatoes and roti.

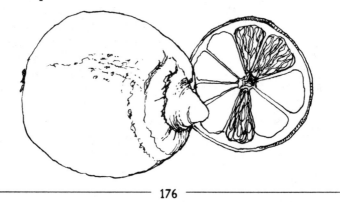

YAKHNI MURGH

1 large chicken	2 black cardamoms
225 g/8 oz minced lamb	2 sticks cinnamon
175 g/6 oz rice	100 g/4 oz raisins
225 g/8 oz onions	12 pistachios
2 dried figs	1 tablespoon curd or yoghurt
2.5 cms/1 inch piece ginger	150 ml/¼ pint cream
1 teaspoon aniseed	1 tablespoon fresh dill
1 tablespoon coriander powder	300ml/½ pint milk
1 teaspoon cummin seeds	Pinch of saffron
1 teaspoon whole black pepper	Salt to taste
1 teaspoon chilli powder	Sugar to taste
6 cloves	450 g/1 lb of ghee

—— MILD ——

■ Grind together ginger and figs and smear the paste over the outside and inside cavity of the chicken. Keep in a cool place for 3 hours. Chop 2 onions and slice the remainder into rings.

■ Heat 2 tablespoons ghee and sauté the chopped onion until tender. Add all the spices and fry for a few minutes. Stir in the lamb, saffron and salt and simmer until the meat is tender. Soak the rice in water for 10 minutes. Drain, wash in more cold water and add to the lamb. Fry for 2 minutes and pour in enough water to cook the rice. Put in raisins and pistachios, and cook until the rice is barely tender. Remove from the heat and allow to cool for at least 10 minutes. Mix into the curd, cream and dill. Fill the cavity of the chicken tightly with this mixture and sew up.

■ Heat the remaining ghee in a large saucepan, put in the chicken and fry on all sides until lightly browned. Pour in the milk, add sugar and cook gently until tender. Serve garnished with lightly sautéd onion rings.

SIRDARI CHICKEN

1 medium chicken	6 whole black peppercorns
350 g/12 oz tomatoes	2 small sticks cinnamon
225 g/8 oz onions	3 cardamoms
3 cloves garlic	1/2 teaspoon chilli powder
2.5 cms/1 inch piece ginger	1/2 teaspoon cummin seeds
150 ml/1/4 pint curd or yoghurt	1/2 teaspoon turmeric powder
75 g/3 oz aniseed	1/2 tablespoon ghee
8 almonds	Salt to taste

—— MILD ——

■ Joint the chicken. Grind the garlic and ginger together. Slice onions finely. Peel and chop the tomatoes. Heat the ghee in a heavy saucepan and fry the onions golden brown. Blend in the garlic/ginger paste and fry. Stir in the curd and simmer for 5 minutes.

■ Add tomatoes, aniseed, blanched almonds and remaining spices and cook for 10 minutes, stirring well. Put the jointed chicken pieces into this mixture and fry, turning, for 5 minutes. Pour in 600 ml/1 pint water, add salt and place in an ovenproof dish. Cook at 180°C/350°F/Gas mark 4 for 35 minutes until the chicken is tender and the gravy is reduced to about half.

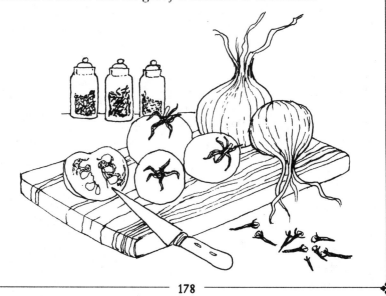

MOGHULAI CHICKEN

1 large chicken
600 ml/1 pint curd or yoghurt
5.0 cms/2 inch piece ginger
1 small pod garlic
15 g/½ oz saffron
2 tablespoons milk
1 tablespoon cream
100g/4 oz almonds

50g/2 oz charoli or pumpkin
 seeds
2 large onions
10 dry red chillies
2 cardamoms
8 tablespoons ghee
Salt

—— HOT——

■ Joint the chicken and prick the flesh with a fork. Grind the ginger and garlic and apply to the chicken pieces. Grind saffron with the milk and cream and mix with the curd in a large shallow bowl. Put the chicken pieces in the curd to marinate for at least 2 hours.

■ Grind the chillies to a smooth paste with 1 tablespoon of water. Slice the onions finely. Roast the nuts on a medium heat, remove the skins and grind to a smooth paste.

■ Heat the ghee in a large pan and sauté the onions until tender and translucent. Add the jointed chicken pieces and fry, turning, until they are lightly brown on all sides. Add the remaining curd mixture, chillies, cardamoms, nut paste, salt and a pint of water. Simmer for an hour stirring occasionally until the chicken is tender and the ghee floats to the surface. Serve with nan or roti.

PAPATU WITH CHICKEN CURRY

1 medium chicken	5 cloves garlic
2 onions	1 teaspoon cummin seeds
2 green chillies	10 dry red chillies
1 coconut	³/₄ teaspoon coriander seeds
2.5 cms/1 inch piece ginger	Tamarind or lemon juice to taste
1 teaspoon poppy seeds	Oil for frying

FOR THE PAPATU:

450 g/1 lb semolina (thicker variety)	¹/₂ coconut
450 ml/³/₄ pint milk	A pinch of cardamom powder
150 ml/¹/₂ pint water	Salt to taste

―― *VERY HOT* ――

■ Joint the chicken and wash well. Grate the coconut. Heat a little oil in a saucepan and fry 1 sliced onion until soft but not brown with the green chillies. Grind the rest of the ingredients together to form a fine paste. Add the jointed chicken pieces to the fried onions and brown the meat evenly on all sides. Season to taste with the salt. Stir in the ground spices and pour in 300 ml/¹/₂ pint water. Allow to simmer for approximately 35 minutes until the chicken is cooked and the gravy has thickened. Serve the curry hot with papatu.

■ Wash the semolina and drain off the water. Add salt, water, milk, cardamom powder and grated coconut. Divide the batter into 6 flat steaming dishes. Put them in an idli boiler and steam for 45 minutes. If an idli vessel is not available, steam each papatu separately using any recognised method steamer. When cooked, cool the cakes well, cut into quarters and serve with the chicken curry.

SHEESH KALEJI

CURRIED CHICKEN LIVERS

450 g/1 lb chicken livers	6 cloves
1 onion (minced)	2 sticks cinnamon
1 onion (sliced)	2 large cardamoms
1 pod garlic	2 green chillies
1 piece ginger	1 teaspoon turmeric powder
½ cup celery (minced)	2 tablespoons ghee
150 ml/¼ pint curd or yoghurt	Salt to taste

—— MILD ——

■ Grind the minced onion, garlic, ginger and celery to a fine paste. Chop the liver into neat 2.5 cms/1 inch pieces and arrange on cocktail sticks, skewers or toothpicks - the longer they are the better. Each one should take about 3 or 4 pieces. Leave the liver to soak in the curd.

■ In a saucepan, heat the ghee and fry the cloves, cinnamon and cardamoms. Stir in the ground spices, turmeric and chillies and cook well for at least 15 minutes. When the spices are brown and well cooked, add liver-sticks and the sliced onion. Simmer on a low heat for 15 minutes. If desired, tomatoes may be added at this stage of the cooking so that the liver cooks in the tomato juice. For extra spice add ½ teaspoon chilli powder to the paste of spices. Serve with tandoori roti.

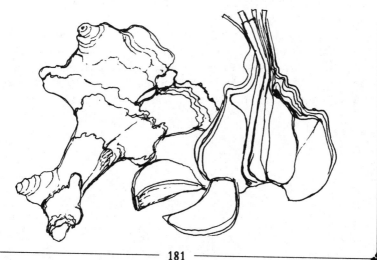

MAIMOOS

1 chicken (about 1.25 kg/2½ lb)
450 g/1 lb meat (lamb or beef)
4.0 cms/1½ inch piece ginger
1 pod garlic
4 green chillies
1 kg/2lb tomatoes
4 tablespoons red chilli powder
  (or to taste)
225 g/8 oz khoya (solidified
  milk)
2 tablespoons poppy seeds
2 tablespoons chironji (peeled
  melon seeds)

3 tablespoons almonds
3 tablespoons pistachios
3 onions
8 cardamoms
8 cloves
6 sticks cinnamon
150 ml/¼ pint milk
15 g/½ oz saffron
Small bunch mint leaves
Small bunch coriander leaves
Ghee
Salt to taste

—— *VERY HOT* ——

■ Heat the ghee and fry the sliced onions until crisp and brown, remove and crush. Grind the garlic, ginger and 2 green chillies to a paste. Heat the ghee, fry 4 cardamoms, 4 cloves and 2 cinnamon sticks. Slice the meat into 8 large pieces and coat with the spice paste. Leave it for 20 minutes in a cool place to allow the spices to permeate through the meat and add to the ghee.

■ Blend the red chilli powder and a ground paste of poppy seeds, chironji, almonds and pistachios and fry until brown adding the chicken and cooking for 5 minutes. Make a thick purée from the tomatoes and blend with the meat. Cook for 5 minutes.

■ When the gravy is thick, stir in the khoya blended with milk, saffron, powdered spices (4 cardamoms, 4 cloves, 4 cinnamon sticks), mint, coriander leaves and 2 green chillies. Cover the saucepan with a tight fitting lid and place over a low heat. Cook for 20 - 25 minutes. Remove and serve hot with nan.

PARSI TOOVAR DHAL BEDA

PARSI EGG WITH LENTILS

1 dozen eggs	*20 button onions*
225 g/8 oz dhal (oiled)	*4 garlic pods*
2 teaspoons salt	*1 large piece ginger*
1 teaspoon turmeric powder	*½ teaspoon cummin seeds*
Large bunch coriander leaves	*½ cup thick tamarind water*
15 green chillies	*1 kg/2 lb ghee*
18 large onions	

—— *VERY VERY HOT* ——

■ Wash the dhal well and cook with salt and turmeric until all the water has evaporated. Grind half the coriander leaves, chillies, large onions and button onions, garlic and ginger together with all the cummin seeds. Finely chop the remaining ingredients and fry the chopped onions in ghee. Stir in both the ground and the chopped ingredients and fry for 10 minutes. Blend in the cooked dhal. Beat the eggs and add to the mixture. Cook on a low heat until the eggs are well mixed, add the tamarind water, and allow to simmer until the ghee comes to the top.

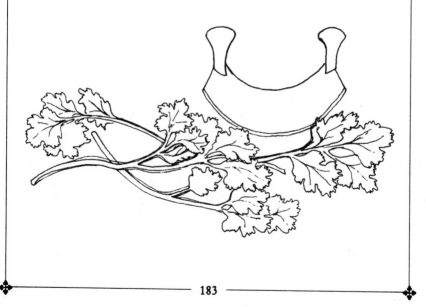

DUCKS EGG BALCHOW

18 duck eggs
675 g/1½ lb onions
1 teaspoon cummin seeds
1½ teaspoons peppercorns
12 dry red chillies
7.5 cms/3 inch piece turmeric
6 green chillies

1 pod garlic
2 pieces ginger
4 curry leaves
Coriander leaves
2 tablespoons ghee
Salt to taste

—— *VERY VERY HOT* ——

■ Scramble the eggs and keep aside. Mince the onions. Heat the ghee in a saucepan and fry the onions light brown. Grind together cummin seeds, peppercorns, red chillies, turmeric and add to the onions. Put in the scrambled eggs and brown the mixture over a low heat. Stir in the remaining finely sliced spices and allow the balchow to simmer until the ghee floats to the top.

EGG ROTI

Dough sufficient for 8 parathas
16 eggs
Salt and pepper to taste

Chilli powder (optional)
Ghee

■ Divide the dough into 8 sections. Roll a piece out into a round paratha. Heat the tava or frying pan and cook the paratha lightly on both sides. Break 2 eggs on to one side of the dough and let them spread out over the whole paratha. Sprinkle with salt, pepper and chilli powder. Add a little ghee to the edges of the paratha and turn when the eggs have slightly set. Fry to a golden brown on both sides. Serve with potato bhajias or meat kababs.

EGG HALWA

1 dozen eggs	2 teaspoons crushed cardamoms
450 g/1 lb sugar	50 g/2 oz raisins
100 g/4 oz almonds	Vanilla essence
100 g/4 oz pistachios	8 tablespoons ghee or butter
1 teaspoon saffron	

■ Blanch and slice the nuts. Roast the saffron and crush to a powder. Whip the eggs well for 5 minutes until frothy. Beat in the sugar and saffron and whip for a further 5 minutes. Heat the ghee in a saucepan and fry the cardamoms for 1 minute.

■ Remove from the heat and allow to cool. Stir in the egg and raisins and cook, stirring gently, until the ghee begins to separate. Add vanilla essence, stir and remove from the heat. Turn out into a flat thali or dish and spread evenly. Sprinkle with nuts and allow to cool and set. Cut into squares and serve.

EGG MALAI MASALA

6 eggs	Chopped coriander leaves
300 ml/½ pint milk	½ teaspoon garam masala
2 medium onions	Salt to taste
2.5 cms/1 inch piece ginger	2 tablespoons ghee
4 green chillies	

—— MILD ——

■ Hardboil the eggs, peel and halve. Grind the onions, ginger and chillies to a paste. Heat the ghee in a saucepan and fry this masala paste for one minute. Put in the hardboiled eggs, without breaking them, and fry gently for 2 minutes. Add the milk and salt and bring slowly to the boil. Stir in the finely chopped coriander. Simmer over a low heat until the gravy thickens. Sprinkle with the powdered garam masala and serve with parathas or tandoori roti.

EGG PATTIES

6 eggs	50 g/2 oz fresh breadcrumbs
4 potatoes	1 tomato
Small bunch of coriander	3 green chillies
leaves	Ghee
Small onion	Salt to taste

—— MILD ——

■ Boil the potatoes, peel, mash well and keep aside. Chop the onion, tomato and green chillies finely. Wash and chop the coriander leaves.

■ Heat a tablespoon of ghee and fry the onion until translucent. Add the tomato and cook for a few minutes. Stir in the salt and coriander and break in 5 eggs, stirring constantly until the mixture thickens and sets. Remove from the heat and allow to cool.

■ Beat the remaining egg into a bowl and keep on one side. Knead the potato dough again and make into flat cases. Place a heaped spoonful of the egg mixture in the centre and cover, folding in the sides of the dough to seal in the stuffing. Press between the palms to make a flat cake. Heat some ghee or oil in a pan. Dip each patty into the beaten egg, roll in breadcrumbs, if desired, and fry until nicely browned. Serve hot with tomato sauce or chutney.

EGG NARGIS KOFTA

4 eggs
1 - 2 slices bread
1 dessertspoon ghee

1 minced green chilli
1 teaspoon minced onion
Salt to taste

FOR THE TOMATO SAUCE:

1 small finely chopped onion
450 g/1lb ripe tomatoes (peeled)
1 dessertspoon chopped
    coriander leaves

$^1/_2$ teaspoon garam masala
1 teaspoon chilli powder
Ghee

—— *MILD* ——

■ Sauté the chopped onion in a little ghee. Add the tomato sauce ingredients and simmer until tender. Hardboil the eggs, shell and keep aside. Crumble the bread and soak in cold water for 10 minutes. When soft, drain, squeeze out all liquid and mash well with a fork. Cut the eggs in half lengthways and carefully remove the yolks. Mash the egg yolks into the bread and add the melted ghee. Stir in the onion, chilli and salt and mix well. Spoon this mixture into the halved egg whites. Place the stuffed eggs carefully in a flat ovenproof dish and pour the prepared tomato sauce over them. Cover the dish and place in a moderate oven. Cook just long enough for the sauce to simmer. Remove and serve immediately with hot chappatis.

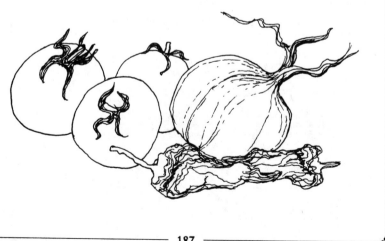

EGG
KORMA

6 eggs

6 medium onions

150 ml/ ¼ pint milk

2 tablespoons cashew nuts

Salt to taste

3 tablespoons ghee

GRIND TOGETHER:

8 green chillies

1 tablespoon grated coconut

3 tablespoons coriander
    powder

6 cloves

1 stick cinnamon

2 cardamom pods

2.5 cms/1 inch piece ginger

½ teaspoon turmeric powder

—— *MEDIUM* ——

■ Chop the onions coarsely. Separate the eggs and beat the white with an egg-whisk until stiff. Add yolks, milk and salt to taste. Beat the mixture again for 10 minutes. Pour into a shallow dish and steam until set. (A simple method is to place the dish with the egg mixture into a larger vessel containing a little water and boiling until the egg sets). Turn out the egg and cut into cubes.

■ Heat the ghee in a heavy saucepan and fry the chopped cashew nuts until golden brown. Add the sliced onions, ground masala paste and salt. Cook over a low heat, stirring occasionally, until the mixture is well cooked and the ghee floats to the top.

■ Add 300 ml/½ pint warm water and bring to boiling point. Stir in the egg cubes gently and cook, simmering, until the korma thickens. Serve with parathas or rice.

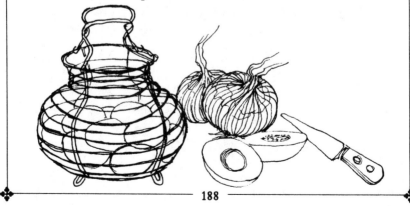

EGG AND BEAN CURRY

6 eggs
450 g/1 lb french beans
2.5 cms/1 inch piece ginger
6 cloves garlic
1 tablespoon chilli powder
1 dessertspoon coriander seeds

1 dessertspoon cummin seeds
1 teaspoon turmeric powder
1 onion
1½ tablespoons ghee or oil
Salt to taste

——— HOT———

■ Grind the garlic and ginger to a paste. Hardboil the eggs, shell and fry in hot ghee to a golden brown. Halve the eggs and keep aside. Remove the stringy edges from the beans and cut into 2.5 cms/1 inch pieces. Boil in salted water for 10 minutes, drain and keep aside. Chop the onion finely and fry in heated ghee. Blend in the spices, garlic-ginger paste and salt to taste. Stir constantly until the spices are well cooked and the ghee floats to the top. Pour in 300 ml/½ pint water and simmer gently to form a thickish gravy, adding extra water if more gravy is desired. Add halved eggs and beans and simmer for another 10 minutes.

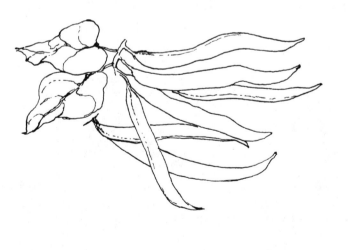

PARSI AKOORI

1 dozen eggs	½ teaspoon turmeric powder
3 medium onions	½ teaspoon garam masala
2 tomatoes	4 cooking bananas
3 green chillies	2 tablespoons ghee or oil
1 tablespoon chopped	Salt to taste
coriander leaves	

—— MILD ——

■ Boil 10 eggs, shell and chop coarsely. Chop onions finely, slice the green chillies and chop the tomatoes roughly. Boil the bananas, peel and divide lengthways. (If the fruit variety are used, do not boil but grill or fry lightly).

■ Heat the ghee and fry the onions lightly. Add tomatoes and spices and fry until cooked. Put in the chillies, coriander leaves, salt, boiled eggs and the remaining 2 eggs, lightly beaten. Fry, stirring constantly until the mixture thickens but does not evaporate. Serve piled in the centre of a flat dish with the cooked bananas arranged around it. It can also be eaten on toast.

AKOORI ON TOAST

6 eggs	3 chopped green chillies
2 small onions	1 teaspoon chopped green
1 tomato	mango
1 tablespoon chopped	¼ teaspoon turmeric powder
coriander leaves	Ghee or butter
½ teaspoon garam masala	Salt and pepper to taste

—— MILD ——

■ Chop the onions and fry until golden brown. Add all the remaining ingredients except the eggs and fry. Remove from the heat, break in the eggs, stir well and replace over a low heat. Serve on toast.

EGGS
AND KHEEMA

6 - 8 eggs
450 g/1 lb minced meat
   (kheema)
2 onions
1 piece fresh ginger
3 cloves garlic
1 tomato

1 teaspoon chilli powder
1 teaspoon coriander powder
1 teaspoon turmeric powder
1 teaspoon garam masala
2 tablespoons ghee
Salt to taste

—— MILD ——

■ Chop the onions, ginger, garlic and tomato. Heat the ghee in a saucepan and fry the onions, ginger and garlic until a golden brown. Add the meat (kheema) and spices and cook until dry. Stir in the chopped tomato and continue cooking, stirring occasionally, until the meat is tender, adding a little warm water if necessary. Place the meat in a frying pan or flat ovenproof dish. Break the eggs on top, side by side. Place in a hot oven and bake until the eggs are cooked. Serve immediately with nan.

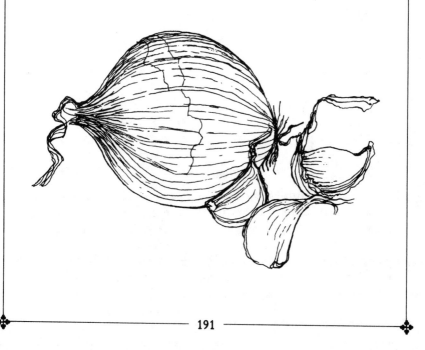

EGG CUTLETS

300 ml/½ pint milk
25 g/1 oz flour
1 tablespoon butter
50 g/2 oz boiled rice
4 hardboiled eggs
2 green chillies

1 pinch grated nutmeg
¼ teaspoon chopped parsley
or coriander
White breadcrumbs
1 egg

—— MILD ——

■ Melt the butter in a saucepan. Add the flour and cook, stirring constantly, for a few seconds. Pour in the milk and bring to the boil, stirring, for 5 minutes. Blend in the rice, chopped eggs, chopped green chillies, nutmeg, parsley and breadcrumbs. Mix well. Spread on a floured platter and allow to cool. Divide into equal portions and shape into cutlets. Coat in egg and breadcrumbs and deep-fry in hot fat. Drain well on kitchen paper and serve with tomato purée or chutney.

EGG VINDALOO

4 hardboiled eggs
225 g/8 oz onions
4 dry red chillies
5 cloves garlic
1 piece ginger
½ teaspoon cummin seeds

1 piece cinnamon
1 teaspoon garam masala
150 ml/¼ pint vinegar
1 tablespoon sugar
2½ tablespoons ghee
Salt to taste

—— HOT ——

■ Grind the chillies, garlic, ginger and cummin seeds with a little vinegar, and salt to taste. Heat the ghee in a saucepan, chop the onions and fry in the ghee. Stir in the cinnamon and ground paste. Cook for 5 minutes. Pour in 150 ml/¼ pint water and blend in the sugar, vinegar and garam masala. Shell the eggs, cut in half lengthways and add them to the curry. Cook until the gravy thickens and serve with rice or rotis.

MEAT

MEAT

Most Indian Hindus are still strict vegetarians, but North Indian families that have been influenced by the militant non-vegetarian Sikhs and Rajputs have a wealth of fine meat recipes. Some of the people of the southern coast have been influenced by the Christians and the meat curries from Kerala deserve a special word of praise. Some feel the choicest meat recipes of all are still to be found in the home of the Indian Muslim. The succulent meat dishes from Hyderabad, Delhi and Lucknow, the original centres of Muslim culture and cuisine, are relished throughout the country. The food prepared at a Muslim feast is a gourmet's orgy and even though most of the festivals are in some way or other associated with mourning, the feast is not. The two festivals are shared and celebrated with great enthusiasm by peoples of all religions.

A very elaborate and lavish feast is held on the Bakri Id or Id-ul-Zuha. It is in honour of Abraham, who, when subjected to the test of faith by God, offered to sacrifice his only son, Ismail - the person dearest to his heart. When his intention was established, it was revealed that it was only a test of faith and so a ram was sacrificed in the name of Allah. The offering thus made is commemorated each year on the tenth day of Zil Hijjah. Camels, cows, sheep and goats are sacrificed on Id, according to the means of the family, in memory of Abraham and his son. The Muslims also believe that the entrance to Paradise is guarded by a very narrow bridge, 'Pulsi Sirat', that offers a precarious footing. Devout Muslims believe that the animals sacrificed at Id will be present on that day to aid them across the bridge. Biryani, a dish cooked on Id, is an international favourite.

Id-ul-Fitr is the festival that marks the end of the Ramzan fast at the appearance of the new moon. It is also known as Ramzan-ki-Id. On this day, Muslims bathe, put on new clothes, apply kajal (antimony) to their eyes and perfume themselves with athar (a concentrated oil-based perfume). 'Fitr', which means five pounds of grain, is destributed among the poor and prayers are held all day at the mosques. Id dinner is served in all Muslim homes amid great gaiety and rejoicing and accompanied by entertainment. Singing parties - 'Qawalis' - are an all-night feature. Some of the dishes served during Ramzan (when all fast from sunrise to sunset) as the early morning breakfast, are particularly delicious. Paiya, or lamb's trotters, cooked in the form of a thick soup and served with hot buttered rolls is an especial favourite.

BADAMI GOSHT

MEAT WITH ALMONDS

1 kg/2 lb meat	*14 dry red chillies (or half the*
1 coconut	*quantity)*
100 g/4 oz almonds	*6 cloves*
225 g/8 oz onions	*4 cinnamon sticks*
4.0 cms/1½ inch piece ginger	*4 cardamoms*
6 cloves garlic	*½ teaspoon caraway seeds*
1 teaspoon turmeric powder	*6 tablespoons ghee*
300 ml/½ pint curd or yoghurt	*Salt to taste*

—— *VERY HOT* ——

■ Wash the meat and chop into 4.0 cms/1½ inch cubes and soak in a mixture of curd and turmeric for one hour. Grate the coconut and extract the milk twice. Soak the almonds in hot water, wash, peel and grind them to a fine paste. Grind the garlic and ginger. Grind the red chillies along with the salt to a fine paste. Slice the onions.

■ Heat the ghee in a saucepan, add the cloves, cinnamon, cardamoms, caraway seeds and onions. Fry until the onions are translucent, stir in the ground ginger and garlic and add the ground chillies. Continue to cook until the onions are brown, add the meat and cover the saucepan with a tight lid. Stir in a little warm water halfway through cooking. Add the coconut milk and continue cooking until the meat is tender. Put in the ground almond paste. This should be kept on a very low heat until the ghee floats to the top. Serve hot with parathas.

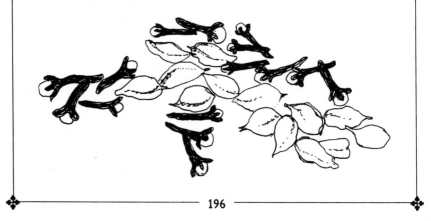

NARGISI KABABS

750g/1½ lb minced meat
1 onion
½ teaspoon turmeric powder

1 dozen hardboiled eggs
3 eggs
Salt to taste

GRIND TO A PASTE:

1 small piece ginger
1 teaspoon turmeric powder
1 teaspoon cummin seed
    powder

3 green chillies
1 teaspoon garam masala
Salt to taste

—— *MILD* ——

■ Chop the onion, boil with the minced meat and turmeric powder in 300ml/½ pint water until dry. Shell the hardboiled eggs, trying not to break the whites. Grind the spices, add the cooked meat and grind again until very soft. Mix in the raw egg and salt to taste. Coat the eggs with the mixture using up all the meat. Heat the ghee for shallow frying and fry on all sides until well browned. Remove and serve with slices of lime and raw onion. Nargisi kababs may also be served in a thick sauce prepared from ripe tomatoes.

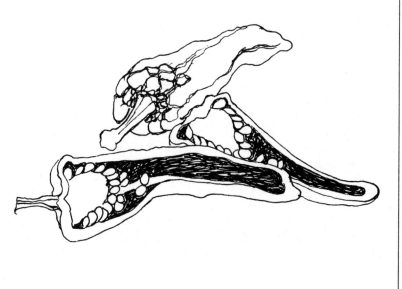

SHAMI KABABS

750 g/1¹/₂ lb minced meat	Ghee
100 g/4 oz gram dhal	Salt to taste
1 egg	

CHOP COARSELY:

1 hardboiled egg	1 dozen blanched almonds
1 medium onion	1 teaspoon chopped coriander
2 green chillies	

GRIND TO A PASTE:

1 piece ginger	1 teaspoon coriander powder
3 cloves garlic	1 teaspoon garam masala
1 teaspoon turmeric powder	1 dry red chilli

—— *MILD* ——

■ Clean and wash the dhal, boil it with the meat in enough water till cooked and dry. Grind together with the masala paste finely, break in the raw egg and mix well. Shape into balls or flat cakes and put a little of the chopped masala in the centre of each kabab. Heat ghee for shallow frying fry till richly browned. Serve with onion rings and slices of lime.

HYDERABAD MASALA GHOST

HYDERABAD SPICED MEAT

450 g/1 lb meat	300 ml/¹/₂ pint curd or yoghurt
1 large onion	6 peppercorns
4 cms/1¹/₂ inch piece ginger	3 pieces cinnamon
10 cloves garlic	2 cardamoms
3 dry red chillies	4 cloves
1 teaspoon turmeric powder	2 tablespoons ghee

—— *MILD* ——

■ Wash the meat, slice the onion and chop the garlic and ginger finely. Beat the curd well and mix in the turmeric. Break the chillies into 3 pieces each. Heat the ghee until it smokes, put in the meat and all the other ingredients. Seal the saucepan with a tight lid or with flour paste and leave to cook on a low heat. No water is needed. Allow to cook for 45 minutes. Unseal the saucepan, add more ghee and fry uncovered until the meat is reddish brown. Serve hot.

KUCHHA KORMA

1 kg/2 lb breast of lamb	*8 - 10 cloves*
5 tablespoons ghee	*10 - 15 peppercorns*
225 g/8 oz onions	*2 teaspoons dry coriander*
600 ml/1 pint curd or yoghurt	*powder (ground to a paste*
2 curry leaves	*with a little water)*
2 pieces cinnamon	*Salt to taste*
6 large black cardamoms	*6 dry red chillies*

—— *MILD* ——

■ Put all the above ingredients into a saucepan after washing and cutting up the meat and slicing the onions. Mix well. Pour in enough cold water to cover the mixture. Cook on a low heat until the meat is soft, stirring well from time to time. When the onions are very soft and the ghee comes to the top, thus forming a gravy, serve hot with chappatis. The gravy should not be too thick and water may be added during cooking if necessary.

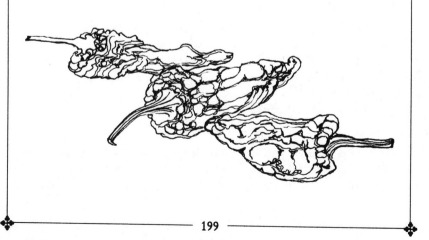

KALEJI-DO-PIAZA

1 kg/ 2 lb liver	1 teaspoon chilli powder
450 g/1 lb onions	2 teaspoons fresh garam masala
450 g/1 lb tomatoes	150 ml/¼ pint curd or yoghurt
2 teaspoons turmeric powder	3 tablespoons ghee
8 cloves garlic	1 bunch coriander leaves
2.5 cm/1 inch piece ginger	Salt to taste
4 green chillies	

—— MEDIUM ——

■ Wash the liver and cut into medium-sized pieces. Cut onions into thick slices and cut tomatoes into 8 pieces each. Place a large saucepan on the heat and warm the ghee. Add the onions, tomatoes and turmeric and fry until reddish brown. Put in the chopped ginger, garlic and green chillies and fry for 5 minutes.

■ Add the liver pieces and cook until nicely browned. Stir in the curd and the remaining spices and cook on a low heat until the liver is tender and the ghee floats to the top. Sprinkle with a little water if necessary. Garnish with chopped coriander leaves. Serve with hot tandoori rotis.

'BHARUCHI' BRAISED LAMB (KID)

1.8 kg/4 lb lamb	2.5 cm/1 inch piece cinnamon
1 kg/2 lb potatoes	1 pod garlic
8 tablespoons ghee	1.3 cm/½ inch piece ginger
275 g/10 oz onions	2 dry red chillies
300 ml/½ pint milk	15 g/½ oz saffron
150 ml/¼ pint thick coconut	Juice from ½ lemon
milk	Salt to taste
Seeds of two cardamom pods	

—— MILD ——

■ Fry the finely-sliced onions in deep fat until brown and crispy. Crush to a powder. Soak the saffron in the lemon juice and allow to stand. Clean the meat and cut into 12 pieces. Smear with a paste made of ground ginger and garlic, salt and the onion. Marinate for an hour. Boil the potatoes, peel, cut into halves and fry.

■ Grind the rest of the spices except chillies and saffron. Heat the ghee and fry the lamb pieces. Blend in the chillies and ground spices. Reduce the heat and cook until the meat is tender. Stir in the saffron, potatoes, coconut milk, and salt if needed. Serve hot.

SHIKAMPOOREE KABAB

450 g/1 lb finely minced meat	½ teaspoon garam masala..
1 onion	1 large pinch ground cinnamon
2 cloves garlic	1 large pinch ground
1.3 cm/½ inch piece fresh	cardamoms
ginger	1 small pinch ground cloves
6 dry red chillies	1 tablespoon gram flour (besan)
1 teaspoon coriander powder	Salt to taste
1 teaspoon turmeric powder	1 tablespoon thick coconut milk
½ teaspoon cummin powder	150 ml/½ pint thick curd
½ teaspoon ground almonds	1 teaspoon chopped fresh mint

—— MEDIUM ——

■ Mince the onion, garlic and ginger and fry with chillies in a little ghee for 3 - 4 minutes. Stir in the ground turmeric, coriander, cummin powder, almonds and the other spices. Mix this thoroughly and continue cooking over a low heat for about 5 minutes. Add the gram flour (besan), minced meat, coconut milk and salt to taste. Cook for 10 minutes, turn out the contents of the pan and grind the mixture into a fine paste.

■ Blend together the thick curd and some of the mint with a pinch of salt. Take sufficient meat paste to form a small ball and flatten it out in the palm of the hand. Put ½ teaspoon of the curd mixture in the centre. Gradually work the meat upwards until the curd is covered and a round flat cutlet is formed. Fry in hot ghee until the kabab is golden brown.

LAMB
CHILLI FRY

675 g/1 ½ lb lamb	1 teaspoon turmeric powder
20 dry red chillies	3 tablespoons coriander seeds
20 cloves garlic	300 ml/½ pint sour curd
4 onions	Juice of 1 ripe lemon
6 cardamoms	6 tablespoon ghee
6 cloves	Salt to taste
2 sticks cinnamon	1 small bunch of coriander
10 cms/4 inch piece ginger	leaves

—— *VERY VERY HOT* ——

■ Wash and cut up the meat into 5 cm/ 2 inch cubes. Slice the onions into thin long pieces. Finely slice the ginger and then the garlic. Heat a teaspoon of ghee on a tava and roast the chillies until dark in colour. Fry the coriander seeds, garlic and ginger separately in the same way, using 1 teaspoon ghee for each ingredient. Keep these fried spices aside.

■ In a large saucepan, heat the remaining ghee and fry the onions until golden brown and crispy, drain and keep aside. Add the cloves, cardamoms and cinnamon to the ghee and fry. Stir in the lamb, turmeric powder and salt. Cover and cook until the meat is half cooked stirring occasionally. Add curds and remaining spices. Mix and cook on a low heat until the meat is tender. If necessary, add a cup of warm water. Just before serving mix in the lemon juice and fried onion slices. Serve garnished with chopped coriander leaves.

LAMB
IN CURD

450 g/1 lb lamb
600 ml/1 pint curd or yoghurt
1 lemon

2 tablespoons ghee
Salt to taste

GRIND TO A PASTE:

8 green chillies
1 onion
1 heaped tablespoon poppy
   seeds
1 tablespoon coriander seeds
1 teaspoon chopped coriander
   leaves

2.5 cm/1 inch piece green ginger
¼ coconut
6 cloves garlic
1 tablespoon Bengal gram
5 cloves
1 piece cinnamon

—— HOT——

■ Cut the meat into small pieces. Put the curd, meat and salt in a saucepan and cook on a low heat until the meat is tender and almost dry. Blend in masala paste and stir, cover and cook for 10 minutes. Add ghee and fry until the meat turns a reddish brown. Stir in the lemon juice and serve with uppams or dosais.

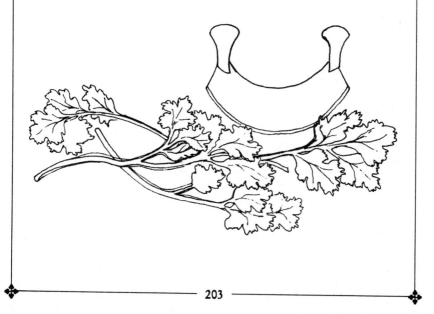

KERALA LAMB
IN COCONUT MILK

*675 g/1 ½ lb tender lamb
    chops
1 coconut
5 cms/ 2 inch piece ginger
6 cloves
6 cardamoms
1 stick cinnamon
4 large onions*

*225 g/8 oz very small potatoes
12 green chillies
1 sprig curry leaves
1 lemon
1 tablespoon ghee
1 tablespoon butter
1 tablespoon flour
Salt to taste*

—— VERY HOT ——

■ Grate the coconut finely into a bowl. Stir 300 ml/½ pint hotwater into the gratings. Mix well and squeeze out the coconut milk. when the gratings have been squeezed dry, add 1.2 ltrs/ 2 pints hot water, mix and allow to cool. When cool, strain and squeeze out the liquid into a separate bowl.

■ Slice the onion finely. Heat the ghee in a large saucepan and fry the sliced onion, cloves, cardamoms and cinnamon until brown. Stir in the second extraction of coconut milk and bring to the boil over a medium heat. Cut the meat into 4.0 cms/1 ½ inch pieces. Add the meat to the boiling coconut milk. Stir in salt to taste, cover the saucepan and let the contents simmer on a low heat.

■ Boil the potatoes and peel them. Split chillies lengthways. Divide the remaining onions into four pieces each. Grate the ginger finely. When the meat is almost tender add the quartered onions, chillies and ginger and continue cooking until tender. Add the boiled potatoes.

■ Mix the flour into the thick coconut milk (first extraction) and add this mixture to the curry. As soon as the gravy thickens, remove from the heat. Stir in the butter, juice of the lemon and curry leaves. Mix gently and serve hot with dosais or idlis.

PALAK MEAT

MEAT WITH SPINACH

450 g/1 lb meat
225 /8 oz spinach
4 green chillies
150 ml/¼ pint milk
1 teaspoon sugar
Chilli powder

Salt to taste
2 teaspoons ground coriander
  seeds
1 teaspoon turmeric powder
2 teaspoons garam masala
3 tablespoons ghee

—— MILD ——

■ Wash the spinach leaves and chop into small pieces. Boil the spinach and green chillies until absolutely tender. Drain, allow to cool and grind to a thin paste. Heat the ghee in a saucepan and stir in a teaspoon of sugar. When the sugar rises, stir in the pieces of meat and continue to stir. When the meat begins to stick to the bottom of the saucepan, pour in the milk and continue to cook. Stir in the salt, chilli powder and ground coriander and cook until the mutton is well browned.

■ Blend in the spinach paste and cook for a further 5 minutes. Add turmeric and a cup of water. Allow to simmer until the meat is quite tender. Once the water has evaporated and the ghee rises to the top of the saucepan, add the garam masala and cook, covered, on a very low heat to allow the flavour of the spices to permeate thoroughly. Serve hot with chappatis.

MASUR
MA GOSHT

PARSI MEAT COOKED WITH MASUR

450 g/1 lb black masur dhal
450 g/1 lb lamb or chicken
6 onions
½ pod garlic
1 teaspoon turmeric powder
½ dessertspoon cummin seeds
½ dessertspoon coriander
   seeds
1 dessertspoon chilli powder

1 dessertspoon sambhar masal
   or garam masala
1 large lemon
1 small bunch coriander leaves
3 large tomatoes
3 green chillies
1 tablespoon ghee
Salt to taste

—— MEDIUM ——

■ Clean the masur dhal and soak in water for an hour. Cut the chicken or lamb into small pieces.

■ Heat 1 tablespoon ghee in a large saucepan, add the finely-sliced onions and garlic and fry until they are golden brown. Stir in the turmeric powder, coriander and cummin seeds, red chilli powder, sambhar masala and lemon juice. Cook over a low heat until the spices are cooked.

■ Put the chicken or lamb into the spice mixture and fry for 5 minutes. Drain any liquid into a bowl and blend the masur dhal into this. Add the finely chopped coriander leaves, green chillies and tomatoes. Pour in 600 ml/1 pint water. Cover the saucepan and cook over a low heat until tender. Serve hot with chappatis.

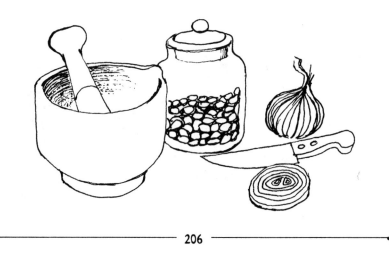

PORK VINDALOO

1 kg/2 lb fatty pork
300 ml/¹/₂ pint vinegar
10 dry red chillies
¹/₂ teaspoon turmeric powder

1 onion
1 tablespoon ghee
Salt to taste

GRIND TO A FINE PASTE IN VINEGAR AND HOT WATER:

1 pod garlic
7.5 cms/3 inch piece ginger
2 tablespoons cummin seeds

3 teaspoons prepared mustard
2 teaspoons coriander

—— *HOT* ——

■ Rub each piece of pork thoroughly with the ground masala and cut into 2.5 cms/1 inch cubes. Leave in a glass jar for 24 hours in a cool place. The following day, roast the chillies and grind with vinegar to a fine paste. Chop the onion finely and brown in a saucepan with the ghee. Stir in the turmeric powder and fry for 5 minutes. Put in the pork and chilli paste and cook over a low heat until the meat is tender. Add the salt to taste. Pork prepared in this way can be kept for a week.

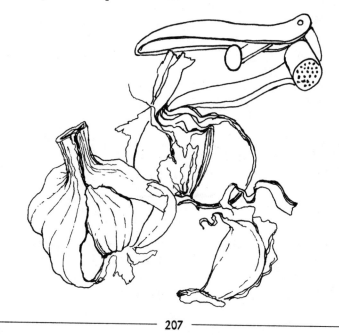

HALEEM

450 g/1 lb wheat	1 teaspoon fresh chilli powder
450 g/1 lb meat	1 tablespoon garam masala
3 onions	3 eggs
2 tablespoons garlic and ginger paste	Ghee
1 teaspoon turmeric powder	Salt to taste
1 tablespoon chopped coriander leaves	

GRIND TO A FINE PASTE:

1 tablespoon coriander seeds   1 teaspoon cummin seeds

—— MILD ——

■ Soak the wheat in water for 24 hours and spread on a clean cloth to dry (approximately 20 minutes). Pound the wheat in a mortar or blend in a blender until the outer skin is removed. Keep aside.

■ Slice 1 onion. Heat some ghee in a saucepan and fry the onion until brown. Add the garlic and ginger paste and fry for 1 minute. Add the ground masala, turmeric, salt and meat and cook for 5 minutes. Stir in the wheat, coriander leaves, chilli powder and 1.75 ltrs/3 pints warm water.

■ Cook slowly over a low heat until the wheat grains are soft and very pulpy. This will take approximately 1 hour. When ready, add the garam masala and 3 - 4 tablespoons ghee. Continue to cook until the ghee floats to the top and the dish is golden brown. Garnish with the remaining onions (sliced and fried) and slices of hardboiled egg.

TAMARIND CHOPS

450 g/1 lb lamb chops	1 small ball of tamarind
8 onions	1/2 teaspoon mustard powder
1 large potato	1 tablespoon ghee
6 green chillies	1/2 dessertspoon salt, or to taste

—— MEDIUM ——

■ Soak the tamarind in a little water for 5 minutes. Extract the juice and keep aside. Peel and halve the onions and potatoes. Slit the chillies. Wash the chops and put into a pan with the ghee, potato, onions, chillies, mustard and salt. Cover with boiling water and cook gently over a medium heat until tender. Add the tamarind juice and simmer for 5 minutes. Serve with nan roti.

COORGI PORK

1.5 kg/3 lb pork	3 tablespoons coriander powder
30 dry red chillies (or to taste)	1 tablespoon peppercorns
12 onions	3 tablespoons vinegar
1 tablespoon cummin seeds	4 medium potatoes
2 pieces turmeric or 1½ teaspoons turmeric powder	Salt to taste

—— VERY VERY HOT ——

■ Cut the pork into pieces, mix with the ground chillies and salt. Marinate for about 15 minutes. Slice 10 onions and cook in a saucepan with the pork and a little water. Cover the pan as this preserves the flavour. Allow to simmer for approximately 30 minutes until the meat is tender. Grind the 2 remaining onions, cummin seeds, turmeric, coriander and pepper, and stir into the meat. Blend in the vinegar and continue cooking for a further 15 minutes. Add the boiled potatoes, peeled and cut into cubes. Cook for a few minutes and serve hot.

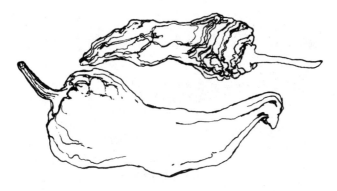

SHAHI
KOFTA

450 g/1lb minced lamb   1 large onion
1 egg

GRIND TO A SMOOTH PASTE:

1 medium onion   1 bunch coriander leaves
2.5 cm/1 inch piece ginger 4 green chillies
6 peppercorns   Salt to taste
1.4 cms/½ inch stick cinnamon

GRIND TO A SMOOTH PASTE:

1 tablespoon coriander seeds 1 dessertspoon of mace
1 teaspoon turmeric powder 3 small cardamoms
1 tablespoon cummin seeds Salt to taste
Red chilli powder to taste   Ghee

—— MILD ——

■ Beat the egg slightly and mix well with the minced lamb to bind. Shape this mixture into small balls of about 1.9 cms/ ¾ inch diameter. In a heavy frying pan, place 8 tablespoons ghee and place over a high heat. Fry the meat balls until they are light brown. Drain and keep aside. In the same ghee, fry the sliced onion to a golden brown. Add both sets of ground ingredients and fry for approximately 7 minutes. Put in the meat balls along with ½ cup warm water and cook over medium heat until the gravy is reduced to a thick consistency, making sure the balls do not break up. Serve hot.

LAMB CUTLETS MOGHLAI

8 lamb cutlets	8 cloves garlic
2 medium potatoes	150 ml/¼ pint lemon juice
5 cms/2 inch piece ginger	2 medium onions
6 dry red chillies	Salt to taste
1 teaspoon turmeric powder	Ghee

—— *MEDIUM* ——

■ Grind to a smooth paste the ginger, chillies, turmeric and garlic. Mix well with the lemon juice and salt. Pound the cutlets gently to shape and soften them. Marinate the cutlets in the paste for at least 2 hours.

■ Heat 8 tablespoons ghee in a deep frying pan and sauté the cutlets until thoroughly brown. Drain and set aside. Parboil the potatoes and slice them into rounds. Fry the potatoes to a golden brown in the same fat in which the cutlets were fried. Add the chops and continue to cook for 5 minutes.

■ Keep warm in a low oven. Before serving, fry the sliced onions to a crispy golden colour in the same fat and sprinkle over the cutlets. Serve hot.

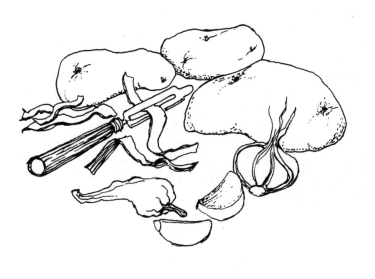

KEBAB CURRY

450 g/1 lb meat
1 large piece ginger
225 g/8 oz pearl onions
6 green chillies or red peppers
1 pod garlic
1 large onion

2 large tomatoes
2 large potatoes
Tamarind juice
Ghee
Salt to taste

GRIND TO A FINE PASTE:

3 red chillies
5 cloves of garlic
1 piece ginger
1 teaspoon coriander
¼ teaspoon cummin seeds
2 tablespoons raw rice or
    poppy seeds

1 stick cinnamon
3 cloves
3 cardamoms
1 small piece turmeric

—— MEDIUM ——

■ Cut the meat into cubes. Slice the ginger. Peel the onions. Halve the garlic and cut the chillies into 1.3 cms/½ inch pieces. On a cocktail stick or skewer place a piece of meat, a slice of ginger, pieces of garlic and chilli and a pearl onion. Repeat the process until all the meat has been used.

■ Heat 1 tablespoon ghee in a saucepan and brown 1 sliced onion. Stir in the chopped tomatoes and cook until soft. Blend in the ground masala and cook until the ghee floats on the top. Carefully put in the kababs, and stir with a fork until they are well coated with masala. Add salt to taste and sufficient water to cook the meat. When the meat is nearly cooked, quarter the potatoes and add to the kababs. Allow the curry to simmer over a low heat until the meat and potatoes are tender.

■ Add the tamarind juice. Boil for 2 minutes and remove from the heat. Serve hot, garnished with chopped coriander and halved hardboiled eggs.

KACCHA KABAB

450 g/1 lb minced lamb
1 teaspoon corander powder
1 teaspoon aniseed
¼ teaspoon black cummin
    seeds
6 cloves
12 peppercorns

1 small stick cinnamon
1 teaspoon garam masala
6 cardamoms
½ a slice of green papaya
1 tablespoon gram
Salt and chillies to taste

■ Roast the coriander and aniseed on a tava. Grind or blend all the spices together. Mix the spices with the papaya and minced meat and grind or blend to a paste. Place the mixture in a saucepan and cook over a high heat until the mixture is thoroughly browned. Remove from the heat and allow to cool. Add the coarsely ground gram to the meat and mix well. Form into kababs and fry on both sides in smoking hot ghee.

■ To try the traditional way of cooking Kaccha Kabab use a barbecue and make a small hole in the mixture and place a piece of live (red hot) charcoal in the centre. Pile onion skins over the charcoal and add a little ghee to the coal. Seal with a tight fitting lid so that the smoke generated by the coal and onion skins cannot escape. When the smoking stops, remove the coal and onion skins. This gives the kabab its unusual, smoked meat flavour.

PORK SORPOTEL

1 whole pig's liver	*18 cloves garlic*
1 kg/2 lb fatty pork	*2.5 cms/1 inch piece ginger*
12 dry red chillies	*4 small onions*
2 teaspoons turmeric powder	*1 small ball tamarind*
1½ teaspoons cummin seeds	*Vinegar*
16 - 20 peppercorns	*Pinch of salt*
5 cms/2 inch cinnamon stick	*Pinch of sugar*
16 cloves	

—— *VERY VERY HOT* ——

■ Cook the liver and salt in 900 ml/1½ pints water and a little salt until tender. Allow to cool, drain, reserving the liquid and cut into small cubes.

■ Grind the rest of the spices to a smooth paste and mix with the pork and liver. Add the chopped onions, tamarind water, a little vinegar to taste, the reserved liquid from the pork and liver, a pinch of salt and sugar and boil until the gravy is thick. Serve with bread and salad.

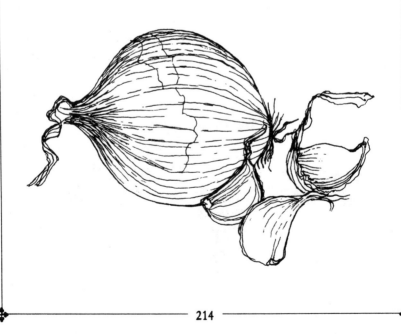

KOFTA CURRY

675 g/1½ lb minced meat
3 medium onions
1 egg
2.5 cms/1 inch piece ginger
1 stick cinnamon
3 - 4 green chillies
8 peppercorns
1 tablespoon chopped
   coriander leaves
2 teaspoons coriander powder
1 teaspoon turmeric powder

1 teaspoon ground cummin
   seeds
1 teaspoon chilli powder
2 black cardamoms
3 cloves
3 cloves garlic
1 sprig curry leaves
Small bunch coriander leaves
1 ripe tomato
Ghee
Salt to taste

—— MILD ——

■ Slice 2 onions and garlic very finely, and chop the tomato. Grind together the chillies, ginger,1 onion, peppercorns and half the coriander leaves, chopped. Mix together the meat, egg, ground spices and salt. Roll the mixture into balls about the size of a small egg. Heat the ghee in a frying pan and deep-fry the koftas until nicely brown. Drain and keep aside.

■ Heat 1 tablespoon ghee in a saucepan. Add sliced onions and remaining spices and add salt to taste. Fry for 5 minutes until the onions are translucent. Add the tomato and cook the mixture until the ghee floats to the top, adding a little water if necessary. Put in the koftas and 600 ml/1 pint water and cook until the gravy thickens. Serve garnished with chopped coriander.

MOGHLAI LAMB MALAI

1 kg/2 lb lamb (preferably the leg in one piece after the bone has been removed)	½ teaspoon ginger powder
	6 cloves
	6 cardamoms
1.2 ltrs/2 pints milk - full cream	10 cms/4 inch stick cinnamon
25 g/1 oz almonds	1 teaspoon aniseed
25 g/1 oz pistachios	15 g/½ oz saffron
50 g/2 oz raisins	1 tablespoon ghee
1 wine-glass sherry	Asafoetida (size of tamarind
2 teaspoons chilli powder	seed)
1 teaspoon black pepper	Salt to taste

—— *MILD* ——

■ Blanch the almonds and grind to a fine paste and dissolve in the milk. Put in a shallow pan over a low heat. Remove when a thick layer of cream forms on the top. Make a slit in the side of the cream and gently drain out the milk. Pour milk back on top of the cream and replace on a very low heat. Repeat this until all the milk has been used. Turn the cream out onto a plate and allow to cool.

■ Smear a pastry board with ghee and pound the meat. While pounding, sprinkle the meat with the spices and sherry alternately and sprinkle with a little salt. When the meat is flattened to almost 5 cm/¼ inch thickness, cut the cream in strips and lay on the meat, leaving a 1.3 cm/½ inch border all round. Sprinkle cream with raisins, pistachios and saffron. Roll tightly, fasten with rows of cocktail sticks , skewers or toothpicks then tie with twine or string. Allow to stand for 30 minutes.

■ Steam the meat roll until tender. Fry or roast gently, basing well in a little ghee until lightly browned. Alternatively, cook in a rotisserie grill until done. Remove toothpicks and string before serving.

MOGHLAI KORMA

1 liver	225 g/8 oz shelled peas
4 kidneys	2 teaspoons salt (or to taste)
5 onions	1 teaspoon sugar
8 green chillies	A little saffron
1 handful coriander leaves	6 tablespoons ghee
1 large piece ginger	½ teaspoon garam masala
7 cloves garlic	1 dessertspoon turmeric powder
2 frying bananas (medium ripe)	1 teaspoon ground black pepper
225 g/8 oz potatoes	1 tablespoon Worcester sauce
225 g/8 oz yam	(optional)
100 g/4 oz pumpkin	3 tablespoons vinegar

—— MEDIUM ——

■ Clean and chop the liver into small pieces. Slit the kidneys and quarter. Grind together the ginger, garlic, coriander leaves and green chillies. Slice the onions finely and fry them in 2 tablespoons ghee until translucent. Put in the ground ingredients and brown well. Add the liver and kidneys and half the salt and cook, stirring, until the meat has browned, add 1.75 ltrs/3 pints water and cover the saucepan. Cook over a medium heat for 25 minutes.

■ Scrub and cut the potatoes into pieces. Cut the yam, pumpkin and bananas into chunks. Boil the peas adding ¼ teaspoon salt. In the remaining ghee fry the vegetables separately. Add the remaining salt to ¼ cup of water and sprinkle on the fried vegetables. Remove the vegetables from the frying pan. Stir in the turmeric, garam masala and pepper and fry. Heat the saffron until it becomes brittle and then crush it. Mix the saffron with 1 tablespoon water and add to the fried spices. Put the peas and fried vegetables back into the mixture. When the meat is cooked add the vegetables to it and mix well. Mix in the vinegar, sauce and sugar. Bring the entire dish to the boil, remove from the heat and serve hot.

SOUTH INDIAN LAMB FRY

450 g/1 lb leg lamb
3 tablespoons ghee
3 large onions
A few sprigs coriander leaves

4 pods garlic
1 piece ginger
1 sprig curry leaves

POWDER TOGETHER:

1 dessertspoon cummin seeds
6 dry red chillies
6 cloves
3/4 of a cinnamon stick

1 teaspoon aniseed
1 small piece turmeric
1 pinch mustard seeds

—— MEDIUM ——

■ Powder all the spices together finely and sieve to enable the stalks, etc. to be separated from the powder. Cut the mutton into medium sized cubes. Slice the onions and chop the coriander leaves, garlic and ginger separately. Place the ghee in a saucepan and add most of the onions and the curry leaves. Fry until the onions are golden brown. Add the powdered spices. Fry well and sprinkle with a little water so that they do not burn.

■ Add the chopped coriander, ginger, garlic and remaining onions, with enough salt to taste. Finally, stir in the mutton and fry for several minutes. Pour in sufficient water to cover the meat and simmer until quite tender. Remove the lid and let the meat cook gently until practically all the water has evaporated and a small quantity of gravy is left, sufficient to coat the meat. Serve at once.

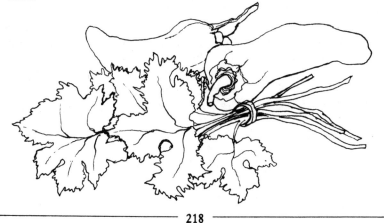

MUTYEA

MEAT WITH MILLET DUMPLINGS

1 kg/2 lb millet flour
1 kg/2 lb lamb
225 g/8 oz salted dry fish
1 coconut
1 tablespoon coriander seeds
1 tablespoon garam masala
12 cloves garlic

5 cms/2 inch piece ginger
225 g/8 oz onions
1 tablespoon turmeric powder
A few sprigs of coriander leaves
Dry red chillies to taste
Ghee
Salt to taste

■ Mix a little ghee and salt into the millet flour. Grate the coconut, mix half of it into the flour and knead well. Allow the dough to stand for 30 minutes and then take a handful of the dough and form the mutyeas, i.e. shape the dough into sausage shapes. Keep the mutyeas aside. Grind all the spices finely with remaining grated coconut.

■ Fry the sliced onions in ghee and add first the ground spices, then the finely minced lamb. Fry until the liquid evaporates. Add 1.75 ltrs/3 pints water and bring to the boil. Carefully add mutyeas one by one, and cook on a low heat for 15 minutes. Chop the coriander leave finely and sprinkle over the dish. The salted fish should be washed and fried, and served separately with the mutyeas.

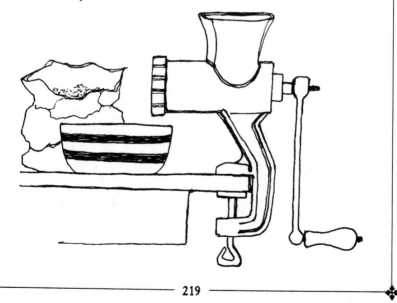

MUTTON SINDHI

450 g/1 lb lamb or mutton
2 onions
1 large tomato
2 pods garlic
¹/₂ pint curd or yoghurt
3 cardamoms

6 cloves
2 tablespoons ghee
¹/₂ teaspoon garam masala
¹/₂ teaspoon turmeric powder
Salt to taste

■ Cut the lamb into medium sized pieces. Slice the onions, tomato and garlic and put them with the meat into a large saucepan and mix the curd into it. Add all the spices, mix and leave for 30 minutes. Just before putting on the heat, add ghee to the mixture. Cover the saucepan and seal tightly to ensure that the steam cannot escape. Place on a medium heat and cook for 2 hours. (If it is more convenient, this dish can be cooked in the oven, covered, at 180°C/350°F/Gas mark 4 for 2 hours, until the meat is very tender).

MUSSALAM RAAN

CURRIED LEG OF LAMB

1 leg lamb (or mutton) about	*1 pinch saffron*
1.8 kg/4 lb	*1 tablespoon garam masala.*
50 g/2 oz almonds	*5cms/2 inch piece ginger*
50 g/2 oz piece dry coconut.	*1 small pod garlic*
50 g/2 oz raisins	*150 ml/½ pint curd or yoghurt*
36 dry red chillies	*1 lemon*
1½ tablespoons coriander	*5 cms/2 inch piece green papaya*
seeds	*1 tablespoon salt or to taste*
1 sprig curry leaves	*8 tablespoons ghee*

—— *VERY VERY HOT* ——

■ Grind the coriander seeds, chillies, saffron and curry leaves into a fine paste and mix it with the garam masala. Similarly, grind the coconut, almonds and raisins to a fine paste and keep aside.

■ Grind the ginger, garlic, lemon juice and papaya together. Mix the curd and salt with this mix. Squeeze in the lemon juice and keep this aside. Wash the leg of lamb and with a sharp knife make numerous slits on both sides. Fill them with the garlic, ginger, papaya, curd and lemon juice mixture and allow to marinate for 10 minutes.

■ Spread the first ground mixture over the whole leg of lamb and finally spread a layer of almonds, coconut and raisins mixture over the layer of ground spices. Heat the ghee in a large roasting pan and place the leg of mutton in it. Allow to cook over a low heat. Keep turning the lamb until it is a light brown. Cover the pan, place in the oven at 200°C/400°F/Gas mark 6 for 20 minutes per pound of weight. Remove from the oven when it becomes reddish brown in colour and the meat is tender. Serve with roast potatoes and rotis.

HUSSEINI SEEKH KABABS

MOGHLAI STYLE

1 kg/2 lb meat	40 g/1 ½ oz almonds
1 2.5 cms/1 inch piece ginger	4 cardamoms
8 cloves garlic	600 ml/1 pint cream
1 teaspoon roasted cummin seeds	600 ml/1 pint milk
	450 g/1 lb baby pickling onions
6 dry red chillies	Few coriander leaves
2 - 3 tablespoons ghee	Salt to taste
25 g/1 oz pistachios	

—— *MEDIUM* ——

■ Grind the ginger, garlic, cummin seeds, chillies and coriander to a fine paste. Add the salt to taste. Cut the meat into cubes and rub the paste over it. Marinate for 2 - 3 hours.

■ Fix the meat cubes on skewers, placing an onion between each cube of meat. Grill over a low heat until tender and brown.

■ In a saucepan, heat the ghee, add the milk, cream, finely grated almonds and pistachios. Mix well and cook until slightly thickened. Garnish with ground cardamoms and serve with the kababs. If preferred the kababs may be removed from the skewers and the sauce poured over them before serving.

PASAND KABABS

1 kg/2 lb minced meat	2 teaspoons black pepper
5 cms/2 inch piece ginger	1 dozen cloves
12 green chillies (or to taste)	1 teaspoon turmeric powder
1 bunch coriander leaves	Butter or ghee
2 onions	Salt to taste
600 ml/1 pint curd or yoghurt	

—— HOT——

■ Grind the meat on a curry stone or use a mincing machine or blender until the meat is extremely fine. Mince the ginger and squeeze out the juice. Chop the chillies and coriander leaves finely. Slice the onions and fry in 2 tablespoons ghee until a golden brown. Tie the curd in a piece of muslin and drain out the liquid. Mix the ginger juice into the meat. Add the curd, pepper, salt, powdered cloves, turmeric, coriander, chillies and browned onions. Mix well and marinate for 2 - 3 hours.

■ Make small balls of the meat mixture and pass the skewers through them. Dip in melted butter or ghee and grill over a barbecue or under a grill until brown on all sides. Serve with onion rings and lemon slices.

KASHMIRI ROGAN JOSH

1 kg/2 lb meat (chops or leg of lamb)
1 heaped teaspoon aniseed
½ teaspoon ginger powder
1 teaspoon caraway seeds
2 teaspoons chilli powder
1 lump of asafoetida (size of a cherry stone)
6 cloves

10 cms/4 inch stick cinnamon
6 large cardamoms.
1 sprig curry leaf
1 teaspoon saffron
150 ml/½ pint thick beaten curd
8 tablespoons ghee or oil
Salt to taste

—— MILD ——

■ Put the ghee in a heavy bottomed saucepan and heat until smoking. Add the asafoetida and the meat previously cut into large pieces. With a flat wooden spoon stir the meat until well coated with the hot ghee.

■ Continue to stir and when the meat separates from the bone and turns brown, add the beaten curd and fry again until all the curd is absorbed. Add 600 ml/1 pint boiling water and all the spices. Simmer for 2 hours over a low heat. Increase the heat so that the water in the gravy evaporates and the ghee floats to the surface. Serve with tandoori rice.

KHEEMA MATTER

MINCE WITH PEAS

450 g/1 lb minced lamb	3 green chillies
225 g/8 oz peas	4 cloves garlic
4 ripe tomatoes	1 teaspoon turmeric powder
1 large onion	1 small piece ginger
3 - 4 curry leaves	Salt to taste
2 sticks cinnamon	$\frac{1}{2}$ teaspoon garam masala
6 cloves	Coriander leaves
1 large black cardamom	2 tablespoons ghee

—— *MEDIUM* ——

■ In 2 tablespoons ghee, fry cinnamon, cloves, cardamom and green chillies. Add the finely chopped onion and the remaining spices and fry for about 5 minutes until the onions are brown. Add the chopped tomatoes and then the minced meat, mix well and cover with a tight lid. Cook gently, stirring occasionally, until the meat is tender. The peas must be boiled beforehand and then added just before the meat is quite cooked. Sprinkle with garam masala when ready. Just before serving, garnish with chopped coriander leaves.

HUSSEINI SEEKH

BAKED KABABS

450 g/1 lb steak cut into small pieces	1 large tomato
5 cms/2 inch piece ginger	3 tablespoons ghee or butter
1 unripe fig or slice of green papaya	A sprig each of coriander and mint leaves
1 tablespoon salt, or to taste	2 teaspoons red chilli powder
2 medium onions	3 eggs

—— *MEDIUM* ——

■ Clean and grind the ginger, fig (or papaya) and salt, to a smooth paste. Mix well into the meat and leave to marinate for

2 hours. Chop the onions and fry to a crisp golden brown and grind. Peel the potatoes, cut into quarters and fry. Chop the coriander and mint. Cut the tomato into tiny pieces. Mix all these ingredients plus 1 tablespoon ghee or butter and chilli powder with the meat.

■ Spread the meat in a deep heat resistant dish. Beat the eggs and pour on the top of the meat. Cover with a tight lid and bake in a hot oven for 35 minutes.

LAMB (MUTTON) AND CABBAGE CURRY

SERVES 4

450 g/1 lb lamb or mutton	*6 pepper corns*
1 coconut	*3 cloves garlic*
1 small cabbage about	*½ teaspoon mustard seeds*
450 g/1 lb	*2 onions*
5 dry red chillies	*2 teaspoons vinegar*
1 teaspoon cummin seeds	*2 tablespoons ghee*
1 teaspoon coriander powder	*Salt to taste*
1 piece turmeric	

—— *MEDIUM* ——

■ Grate the coconut and extract both the thick and thin milk from half of it. Chop up and wash the meat and cook in 3 cups of thin coconut milk. Wash the cabbage, discarding the stem and thick leaves, chop and add to the meat with salt to taste. Roast each spice separately and grind them all together with 1 onion and the other half of the grated coconut.

■ Blend in the spices paste and vinegar to the meat and boil. Add the ghee and 1 chopped onion. Stir in the thick coconut milk and simmer for 15 - 20 minutes. Serve hot.

SUKA BRAIN

CURRIED BRAINS

4 sheeps brains	1 green chilli
2 tablespoons ghee	1 small piece ginger
1 small onion	Salt and pepper to taste

—— MILD ——

■ Clean the brains thoroughly and divide each into six. Heat the ghee and fry the ginger in it. Grind the onion with 1 green chillie, fry with the ginger. Add the pieces of brain and seasoning. Allow to cook on a low heat until the brains turn light brown.

BHINDI MEAT CURRY

225 g/8 oz lady's fingers (bhindi, okra)	½ teaspoon turmeric powder
450 g/1 lb meat	3 - 4 dry red chillies
225 g/8 oz tomatoes	½ teaspoon coriander powder
2 large onions	½ teaspoon black cummin seeds
4 cloves garlic	½ teaspoon black pepper
2 small piece ginger	1½ teaspoons salt (or to taste)

—— MEDIUM ——

■ Wash the meat and cut into cubes. Put the tomatoes in boiling water for a minute. Remove, peel and mash. Chop onions and fry in ghee until light brown. Stir in the garlic and ginger. Put in the pieces of meat, turmeric, coriander, red chillies, black pepper, ground cummin seeds and salt. Cook the meat, adding water if necessary. In the meantime wash and dry the bhindi and fry lightly. When the meat is brown, add bhindi and mashed tomatoes.

■ Allow to simmer, adding a little water, until the meat is tender and the tomato completely absorbed, thus giving the curry an attractive, reddish colour. Garnish with finely chopped coriander leaves and the garam masala.

PORK
KORMA

450 g/1 lb pork
3 onions
4 cloves garlic
$^1/4$ teaspoon ground cummin
   seeds
3 - 2.5 cms/1 inch cinnamon
   sticks
3 - 4 bay leaves

300 ml/$^1/2$ pint curd or yoghurt
5 large ripe tomatoes
$^1/2$ teaspoon ground black
   pepper
12 cloves
6 cardamoms
4 tablespoons ghee
Salt to taste

■ Wash the meat and cut up into 2.5 cms/1 inch cubes. Slice the onions finely. Heat the ghee and fry the onions, garlic and spices until deep brown. Add the meat and allow to simmer until it is brown on all sides. Add the tomato, curd and salt, simmer until the meat is tender.

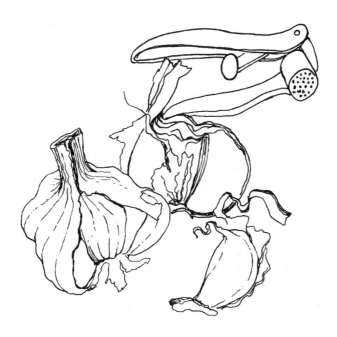

CAULIFLOWER GHOSH CURRY

MEAT AND CAULIFLOWER CURRY

1 small cauliflower about	2 large onions
450 g/1 lb	1 ripe tomato
1 kg/ 2 lb meat	1/2 teaspoon turmeric powder
8 cloves garlic	Coriander leaves
1 2.5 cms/1 inch piece ginger	Salt to taste

GRIND THE FOLLOWING SPICES:

6 dry red chillies	2.5 cms/1 inch piece cinnamon
6 peppercorns	4 cloves
2 tablespoons coriander	1 tablespoon dessicated coconut

—— *MEDIUM* ——

■ Clean and cut the meat into small pieces. Grind the garlic and ginger to a fine paste. Rub the paste on to the meat and keep aside. Clean the cauliflower and cut up. Chop the onions finely and fry in hot ghee until light brown. Add ground spices and fry. Add the meat, chopped tomato and cauliflower. Fry for a minute then add the turmeric and 600 ml/1 pint water for the meat to cook in. Cover with a well-fitting lid and cook until the meat is tender. Sprinkle with salt. Cook for a further 10 minutes. Before serving, garnish with chopped coriander leaves. Serve hot with chappatis.

MOGHLAI SHAMI KABABS

MEAT CUTLETS

450 g/1 lb minced mutton or	2 small pods garlic
beef	2 onions
1 dessertspoon garam masala	1 tablespoon gram flour
1/2 teaspoon ground turmeric	3 eggs
3 - 4 chopped green chillies	Ghee
1/2 teaspoon chopped green	Lemon juice to taste
ginger	Salt to taste

—— *MEDIUM* ——

■ Fry all the spices and 1 chopped onion lightly in the ghee for 3 - 4 minutes. Add the finely minced meat and cook for 10 minutes with the pan uncovered. Stir in gram flour, salt and lemon juice.

■ Turn the mixture out to cool, then grind or pound it to a fine paste. Hardboil eggs and dice into small pieces. Chop the second onion into fine pieces. Shape the meat in round cutlets with a mixture of onion and egg in the centre of each cutlet. Fry in hot ghee until brown and serve with onion rings and slices of lemon.

COORGI MULLIGATAWNY

COORGI MUTTON SOUP

450 g/1 lb breast of lamb (mutton)	*1 large grated coconut*
	1 dessertspoon ghee

GRIND TO A FINE PASTE:

4 dry red chillies	*1 teaspoon mustard seeds*
1 dessertspoon coriander	*4 cloves garlic*
1.4 cms/¹/₂ inch piece of turmeric	*1 large onion*
	A few dry curry leaves
1.4 cms/¹/₂ inch piece of ginger	*1 teaspoon salt or to taste*
1 dessertspoon cummin seeds	

——— MILD ———

■ Cut the meat into small cubes. Extract the milk from the coconut with only 2 tablespoons hot water. Set this aside and extract the second milk using 600 ml/1pint hot water. Boil the meat in the milk together with the ground ingredients and salt. When the meat is tender, remove it from the gravy. Fry it in the ghee. Put the meat back into the gravy. Simmer for a further 5 minutes. Serve with boiled rice and slices of lemon.

DUM GOSHT

STEAMED MEAT

1 kg/2 lb lamb (cut into steak
   sized pieces)
1 tablespoon poppy seeds
1 tablespoon melon seeds
6 almonds
2 teaspoons ginger-and-garlic
   paste
1 teaspoon peppercorns
4 cardamoms

1 tablespoon chopped coriander
   leaves
A small piece of green papaya
3 sticks cinnamon
1/2 teaspoon cummin seeds
   (optional)
Salt to taste
1 teaspoon turmeric powder
8 tablespoons ghee

■ Roast the poppy seeds, melon seeds and almonds and grind them to a paste. Grind the ginger-garlic paste, cardamoms, pepper, papaya and coriander leaves.

■ When all the masala is ready, wash meat and beat it lightly on a board or grinding stone. Mix all ground masala along with the cinnamon sticks and cummin seeds (whole). Spread over the meat and rub in. Allow to marinate for 1 hour. Take a large saucepan with an air-tight lid and heat the ghee in it. When hot add the masala mixed lamb and cook for 5 minutes, stirring constantly. Reduce the heat and allow to simmer over a low heat for 15 minutes. Place in the oven at 180°C/350°F/Gas mark 4 and cook for an hour. When the meat is tender, sprinkle with a little turmeric and serve hot.

SUNDIA

FRIED MEAT BALLS

1 kg/2 lb lamb
1 teaspoon turmeric powder
3 teaspoons coriander powder
2 teaspoons chilli powder
6 large onions
2.5 cm/1 inch piece ginger
2 large pods garlic

1 coconut
2 teaspoons poppy seeds
100 g/4 oz gram dhal
2 cardamoms
3 lemons
Oil or Ghee
Salt to taste

—— *MILD* ——

■ Chop the meat into chunks. Boil it with the turmeric, chilli and coriander powder, adding just enough water to cover the meat. Remove when the lamb is tender, pound and shred it fibre by fibre or chop finely in a blender. Chop the onions, ginger and garlic and grate the coconut. Separately fry the poppy seeds, gram dhal and cardamoms, in oil or ghee.

■ Add the ingredients to the shredded lamb and squeeze in the juice of 3 lemons. Stir in salt to taste. Mix well, make into small balls and deep-fry in hot ghee over a low heat. This dish can also be prepared with pork and the meat balls may be used in a Kofta Curry as a variation (see page 215).

COORGI PORK

1.5 kg/3 lb pork	*3 teaspoons coriander seeds*
15 dry red chillies (freshly ground)	*1 dessertspoon peppercorns*
	1½ tablespoons vinegar
12 onions	*4 boiled potatoes*
1 tablespoon cummin seeds	*Salt to taste*
1 small piece turmeric	

—— *VERY VERY HOT* ——

■ Cut the pork into small pieces. Mix the pork with the chilli powder and salt and let stand for about 15 minutes. Slice 10 onions, add to the pork and put it on the heat in a heavy based saucepan with a cup of water. Remember to cover the vessel as this preserves the flavour. Let it simmer for an hour, or until the meat is cooked. Grind the 2 remaining onions, cummin seeds, turmeric, coriander seeds and pepper and add this paste to the meat. Add the vinegar and salt and cook for a further 15 minutes. Add the boiled potatoes, peeled and cut into quarters.

MASALA KALEJI

CURRIED LIVER

450 g/1 lb liver	*¹/₂ teaspoon turmeric powder*
1 onion	*¹/₂ teaspoon cummin seeds*
1 small piece ginger	*1 stick cinnamon*
1 clove garlic	*1 large ripe tomato*
1 teaspoon coriander seeds	*Salt to taste*
¹/₂ teaspoon chilli powder	*2 tablespoons ghee*

—— MILD ——

■ Grind the onion, garlic and ginger to a smooth paste. Blend in the spices, with the exception of the cummin seeds and cinnamon. Remove the skin from the liver and chop into small pieces. Heat the ghee and fry the cummin seeds and cinnamon and add the masala paste. Cook the masala thoroughly, keeping the vessel covered to retain the aroma. Pour in a little water and cook until the masala turns a rich brown colour. Stir in the liver pieces and let them cook in their own juice. Add the chopped tomato to the liver when well cooked. Simmer very gently until the tomato pieces have turned into a thick gravy.

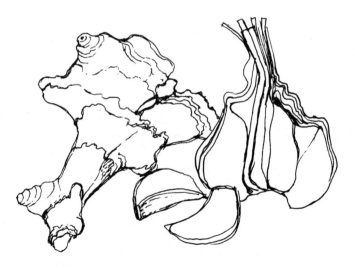

SWEETS

SWEETS

There are innumerable festivals celebrated by the people of India, but the most festive is Divali or Dipavali - the festival of the lights. (Dipa - a lamp, Avali - a row). Divali, which falls in October or November, is the first day of Kartik, the first month of the Hindu Calendar. It is indeed a festival of joy and all the communitities join in the Divali celebrations.

One of the most popular legends concerning the origin of the festival is that Rama was crowned on this day, after his return from exile and his subjugation of Lanka (the ancient name for Ceylon) - now named Sri - Lanka. Another legend, originating in South India, says that when Vishnu killed Navaksur, the giant demon, his people decorated and illuminated the city to welcome him on his return. Divali is a most auspicious day for the Banias, the trading community of India. On the eve of the auspicious day, they collect all their treasures together in their homes and shops and worship them in the name of Laxmi, goddess of wealth (also known as Saraswati, goddess of learning, the arts and sciences). All the merchants close their books and buy new ledgers in which a credit account is opened. All the servants are given an extra Divali bonus, in the hope that the day's generosity will bring returns in the coming year.

Preparations for Divali are begun weeks in advance. Large quantities of flour, rice, sugar, coconuts, nuts and other ingredients used in making sweetmeats are bought, and the kitchen hums with activity. The choicest family recipes are prepared for the occasion. The traditional sweetmeats served on Divali are Laddoos, Barfi, Mesoor, Gulab Jamuns and Jalebis. Nimkis (salted snacks made of gram flour) are also prepared. The mithaiwala (sweetmeat-seller) probably earns the better part of his income for the year on this day, and his shop is piled with the most fabulous, mouth-watering delicacies, impossible to resist.

The Divali festival lasts four days and nights. Houses are cleaned, whitewashed and illuminated. Rangoli, traditional Divali patterns, are made with coloured rice flour on the ground in front of doorways. New clothes are bought for every member of the family and children are supplied with firecrackers.

On the morning of the New Year, Hindus wake up before sunrise and have a traditional Divali bath of scented oils and hot water. New clothes are worn by everyone and the family sit down to a light breakfast of sweetmeats and fruit. The older members of the family have a second bath and proceed to the temple to pay homage to the goddess. They spend all morning visiting friends and relatives, distributing sweets and exchanging greetings. Elders and children have an elaborate Divali lunch and when completed the children start on the firecrackers.

RASOGOOLAS

1.2 ltrs/2 pints milk
1 kg/ 2 lb sugar

1 tablespoon flour
600 ml/1 pint sour whey

■ Make chhana of the milk and whey (see Glossary 4). Add flour to the chhana and knead it with the palms of the hands until it is smooth and pliable. Divide the dough into eight or sixteen small portions. In each portion put a grain or two of sugar candy and roll to form a ball. Make a thin syrup by combining the sugar and 1.75 ltrs/3 pints water and cooking over a low heat until a thin syrup forms. Add 2 tablespoons milk to the boiling syrup so that the froth comes to the top of the syrup, remove with a spoon. Drop the rasogoolas in the clean boiling syrup, and boil for 10 minutes. Sprinkle water onto the boiling syrup every 2 minutes, remove from the heat and cool. Flavour with rosewater, if desired.

SANDESH

1.2 ltrs/2 pints milk
600 ml/1 pint sour whey
225 g/8 oz castor sugar

Flavouring (e.g. lemon,
rosewater etc.)

■ Make chhana of the milk and whey. Combine it with the sugar, knead well between the palms of the hands until very smooth. Place a kerai over a medium heat and stir the mixture in this with a spatula until all the water evaporates. Remove from the heat and keep stirring with the spatula. Cool and put in the colouring. Divide into equal portions and press each portion in a pastry mould to give it shape. Remove from the mould. This sandesh can also be made of date-palm gur instead of sugar.

SUSEUM

225 g/8 oz sweet potatoes
2 pods cardamom (powdered)
25 g/1 oz grated coconut
100 g/4 oz sugar or jaggery
½ teaspoon salt or to taste

75 g/3 oz rice flour
3 tablespoons water
⅛ teaspoon turmeric powder
Oil

■ Boil the potatoes, peel and mash them. Mix cardamom, sugar, coconut and salt with the potatoes. Make small balls from this paste. Mix flour, turmeric and salt to taste, with a little water and beat in a bowl to make a thick batter. Dip the small potato balls into the batter and fry in oil. Serve hot.

KALKASS

150 g/5 oz flour (maida)
1 coconut
8 tablespoons ghee

450 g/1 lb sugar
1 teaspoon cardamom powder

■ Grate the coconut and grind it. Squeeze out all the milk, adding a little hot water if necessary. Mix the flour and coconut milk and knead to a soft dough. Take a marble-sized piece of the dough, flatten it out on a fork and roll it off so that the forkmark is imprinted on the dough. Make as many little rolls as possible from the mixture.
■ Heat the ghee in a pan. When hot, fry all the rolls to a golden brown. Make a thick syrup of the sugar, by putting into a heavy bottomed saucepan with 1 cup of water over a high heat and boiling until thick. Put all the rolls in a bowl and pour the syrup over them making sure that the syrup covers all the rolls completely. Sprinkle with cardamom powder and allow to cool before serving.

CHANA DHAL KHEER

225 g/8 oz chana dhal	*1 tablespoon ghee*
1 coconut	*A few cardamoms*
450 /1 lb jaggery	

■ Wash, clean and soak the dhal in water for 10 minutes. Drain and put in a pan with 900 ml/1½ pints water and bring to the boil. Cover partially, and simmer gently for 1 hour or until soft. Take a piece of coconut, cut it into small pieces and keep it aside. Grind the rest of the coconut and extract the milk. Grind the gratings again and extract the milk a second and third time.
■ When the dhal is almost cooked, add the thinner milks and jaggery, stir and cook over a low heat for 20 minutes. Remove from the heat and allow to cool for 5 minutes. Stir in the thick coconut milk. Fry the coconut bits in ghee until brown and add to the kheer along with crushed cardamoms. Serve cold.

SWEET POTATO BONDAS

450 g/1 lb sweet potatoes	*225 g/8 oz gram flour (besan)*
100 g/4 oz sugar	*Oil or ghee*
6 small cardamoms	*Salt to taste*

■ Boil sweet potatoes, peel and mash. Peel the cardamoms and crush to a fine powder. Boil the sugar and 2 tablespoons water to make a thin syrup. Add the mashed potato, mix well and add the cardamom powder. Keep on one side. Make a thin batter of the gram flour (besan) by adding a little water. Add salt and mix well. Divide the mashed potato into small balls, dip in batter and fry each until light brown. These quantities will make about 40 small bondas.

BADAM KHEER

350 g/12 oz almonds
1.75 ltrs/3 pints milk
225 g/8 oz sugar (or to taste)

Powdered cardamom
A pinch of saffron

■ Soak the almonds in hot water for some hours. Peel and slice. Heat the milk in a large saucepan, add the sugar and boil until thickened. Add the almonds, saffron and cardamom powder. Serve hot with fresh hot puris.

MALABAR BANANA DESSERT

6 ripe Malabar bananas
2 eggs
150 ml/½ pint milk
50 g/2 oz sugar
1 dessertspoon crushed
   almonds

225 g/8 oz grated coconut
2 teaspoons raisins
Vanilla essence
2 tablespoons butter
12 cloves

■ Wash the bananas and steam them, without removing the skins, until soft. Cool, peel and lay them in a flat dish. Cut each lengthways and carefully remove the string of seeds. Mash with a fork to a smooth dough adding a little butter. Shape into 12 balls. Beat the eggs and stir in the milk, sugar and almonds. Blend well together with the coconut and raisins. Melt a little butter and scramble the egg mixture until frothy. Add a dash of vanilla essence.

■ Take each banana ball, flatten it in the palm of your hand and pile a teaspoon of the egg mixture in the centre, cover the stuffing carefully and roll into a ball again. Stick a clove into the top. Place in a dish and chill overnight. Serve with cream. If desired the balls may be dipped in batter, fried in hot ghee and served hot.

PURAN POLI

450 g/1 lb flour	*12 cardamoms ground*
450 g/1 lb gram dhal	*4 cloves*
450 g/1 lb sugar	*Ghee*

■ Clean and wash the gram dhal well. Put in a pan with 900 ml/1 ½ pints water and bring to the boil. Simmer and cook until tender, approximately 1 hour. If there is excess water, drain thoroughly. Add the sugar to the cooked gram dhal and cook again. Stir in the ground cardamoms and whole cloves and cook until a thread-like syrup is formed. Remove from the heat and allow to cool.

■ Meanwhile, sieve the flour and mix in about 2 teaspoons ghee. Add a little water at a time and knead to a thick dough. Knead well and divide into equal portions. Roll into walnut sized balls approximately 5 cms/2 inches in diameter. Keep aside.

■ Grind the gram mixture to a very thick paste and roll into the same number of balls as the flour balls. This should be done in the palm of your hands. The gram balls should be almost double the size of the flour balls.

■ Flatten out the flour balls and carefully fill with the gram balls. Seal carefully and roll out like the ordinary paratha. Place on a tava and fry on both sides using as little ghee as possible.

PARSI CUSTARD

3 ltrs/5 pints milk	*6 eggs*
1.75 ltrs/3 pints milk cooked	*1 dozen egg yolks*
into khoya	*1 coffeespoon ground*
225 g/8 oz sugar (or to taste)	*cardamoms*
100 g/4 oz mixed almonds and	*1 coffeespoon ground nutmeg*
pistachios	*2 teaspoons vanilla essence*
100 g/4 oz pumpkin or chironji	
(melon) seeds	

■ Boil the milk, adding the sugar, until half its original quantity remains. Grind the almonds and pistachios very finely and blanch the chironji seeds. Mix the khoya and almonds paste into the milk. Beat all the eggs and egg yolks and stir into the milk mixture.

■ Add the cardamom and nutmeg powder and vanilla essence. Pour into a greased baking dish, garnish with the chironji seeds and bake for 30 minutes at 180°C/350°F/gas mark 4 until set and the seeds turn dark brown. When cold, serve. Alternatively, this pudding may be steamed.

PARSI RAVA

2.4 ltrs/4 pints milk	8 tablespoons pure ghee
100 g/4 oz raisins	½ teaspoon nutmeg powder
175 g/6 oz almonds	½ teaspoon cardamom powder
100 g/4oz pistachios	¼ cup rosewater (or any other
225 g/8 oz semolina (sooji)	flavouring)
225 g/8 oz sugar (or to taste)	Silver paper (varak)

■ Soak the almonds, pistachios and raisins in hot water. When soft, slice the nuts. In a frying pan heat 1 tablespoon ghee and fry the nuts and raisins. Boil and thicken 1.2 ltrs/2 pints milk till reduced to 600 ml/1 pint. Boil the remaining milk with the sugar in a separate saucepan.

■ Take a large saucepan and heat the remaining ghee and fry the semolina over a low heat stirring constantly. Gradually add the thickened milk and continue stirring. Add the sweetened milk, about half at a time, stirring all the time. Blend in the rosewater, nutmeg and cardamom powder. Mix in half the fried nuts and raisins. Turn out on a flat dish or thali and garnish with remaining nuts and raisins and strips of silver paper. Cut into squares and serve. Alternatively, do not thicken the mixture as much and then serve in individual glasses.

PUMPKIN HALWA

1 large ripe red pumpkin	100 g/4 oz almonds
300 ml/½ pint milk	100 g/4 oz pistachios
225 g/8 oz khoya (solidified milk)	100 g/4 oz pumpkin seeds
	Pinch of saffron soaked in a little water
600 ml/1 pint cream	Rose essence
8 tablespoons ghee	
450 g/1 lb sugar	

■ Cut up the pumpkin. Remove the seeds and pith and grate the flesh. Put to boil with the milk and cook gently until all the milk evaporates. Heat the ghee in a large saucepan and fry the mixture until it turns reddish in colour. Add the sugar and khoya and fry gently over a low heat. Blanch the nuts and chop finely. Pour the mixture out on to a large thali and spread evenly with a wooden spoon.

■ Sprinkle the saffron water, rose essence and nuts on the surface. Whip the cream and make an even pattern of swirls on the top. When cool, cut in squares so that you have a peak of cream on each piece.

BADAM KI BARFI

350 g/12 oz almonds	4 tablespoons ghee
600 ml/1 pint milk	1 teaspoon powdered cardamom
675 g/1½ lb sugar	

■ Soak the almonds in a jugful of warm water for 2 hours. When soft, remove the skins and grind the almonds to a paste. (If you are using a grinding-stone, take care to wash it properly first so that no previous flavours linger!). Mix the almond paste with the milk and sugar and cook in a heavy saucepan over a medium

heat. Stir constantly until the sugar melts and the mixture boils.
■ Add the ghee and cook until the mixture comes away from
the sides of the saucepan. Stir in the cardamom powder. Pour
mixture into a greased thali and flatten it out. Cool and cut into
strips.

COCONUT
BARFI
COCONUT FUDGE

2 large coconuts
600 ml/1 pint milk
1.2 kg/2lb sugar

A few drops of any desired
colouring
1 tablespoon ghee

■ Grate the coconut and grind very finely. Add the sugar to the
milk in a large saucepan and place over a low heat. Blend in the
ground coconut and stir gently until the mixture solidifies. Stir in
a little essence and colouring, if desired, and spread the mixture
on a greased thali. When cool, cut into desired shapes.

MALPURAS

350 g/12 oz flour (maida)
350 g/12 oz semolina
350 g/12 oz sugar
½ teaspoon cardamom powder

1.2 ltrs/2 pints diluted curd or
yoghurt
A pinch of saffron (kesar)
Ghee

■ Blend all the ingredients together in a large saucepan and mix
into a thickish batter. Cover and leave overnight. The next day,
add ½ cup of semolina and mix well. Heat the ghee in a flat pan
and drop a tablespoon of the batter into it. When the edges turn
brown, turn over and cook on the other side. Drain well and cool.
The edges should be crisp and the centres soft.

MYSORE PAK

450 g/1 lb gram flour (besan)	450 g/1 lb sugar
675 g/1½ lb ghee	Cardamom powder

■ Add a little water to the sugar and melt it to a syrup. Add 6 tablespoons ghee. Leave for 10 minutes and stir in the gram flour and the remaining ghee.

■ Continuously stir over a medium heat to avoid the mixture sticking to the pan. As the mixture melts and the ghee begins to appear on the surface, remove and pour the contents onto a greased thali and sprinkle with cardamom. Allow to cool and cut into 2.5 cms/1 inch squares.

DHAL HALWA

LENTIL SWEET

1 kg/2 lb green gram dhal	100 g/4 oz melon seeds
675 g/1½ lb sugar	48 powdered green cardamoms
450 g/1 lb khoya (solidified milk)	12 silver leaves (varak)
48 finely sliced almonds	675 g/1½ lb ghee

■ Wash and clean the dhal and soak in water overnight. Wash the dhal twice again in fresh water and grind to a paste. Heat sugar together with a cup of water until it forms a thin syrup.

■ Break up the khoya and roast on a tava for 5 minutes, remove and keep aside. Heat the ghee in a kerai and fry the dhal paste. Cook until the ghee separates from the dhal, stirring constantly to prevent the mixture from sticking to the pan. Add the khoya, almonds, melon seeds and cardamoms. Fry for 5 minutes and stir in the syrup. Continue to cook, stirring constantly, until the syrup dries up. Turn out in a thali and decorate with silver leaves. This dish is at its best served hot.

NUT
HALWA

1.5 kg/3 lb nuts
450 g/1 lb sugar
½ teaspoon powdered
  cardamom

Pinch of saffron
50 g/2 oz raisins
175 g/6 oz chopped cashew nuts
1 kg/2 lb ghee

■ Soak the nuts in water for an hour. Wash with fresh water, peel and grind in a mortar or an electric blender. Pour the thick liquid into a heavy vessel and bring to the boil over a medium heat. Cook until the paste is reduced to half the original quantity. Add the ghee, sugar, cardamom powder, saffron and raisins. Cook, stirring constantly until the mixture thickens. Turn out onto a greased dish and garnish with chopped, fried cashew nuts. Cut into cubes, serve hot or cold.

JALEBIS

450 g/1 lb flour (maida)
1 teaspoon baking powder
1.5 kg/3 lb sugar

A little saffron (kesar)
450 g/1 lb ghee

■ Sift the flour with the baking powder. Add enough warm water to make a thin batter. Make the sugar into a syrup, by putting one cup of water into a saucepan, adding the sugar and boiling until thick. Keep on one side. Add the saffron mixed with a little hot water, to the syrup. Heat the ghee to boiling-point. Pour the batter into a jalebi mould and press it out in coiled circles into the hot ghee. Fry to a nice golden brown on both sides. Remove and put immediately into the syrup. Allow to soak in this syrup for 5 - 10 minutes.
■ If a jalebi mould is not available, use a forcing bag or icing nozzle and squeeze out the batter in small spirals.

KELA JALEBIS

BANANA JALEBIS

1.8 kg/4 lb bananas (cooking
variety)
1 kg/2 lb sugar
2 lemons

Pinch of saffron (soaked in a
little water)
Ghee

■ Divide each banana in half lengthways, without removing the skin. Bring to the boil in enough water to cover the banans, cook until tender. Cool and peel. Chop and grind the banana pulp to a thick paste adding a little water, if necessary. Knead well with a little ghee.

■ Heat the sugar with a cup of water until it forms a syrup, add the lemon juice and strain. Add the saffron and keep aside.

■ Heat the ghee. Put some dough through a jalebi mould and form round jalebis in the ghee. If a jalebi mould is not available, pipe through an icing nozzle or forcing bag. Deep-fry on both sides until brown and immerse in the syrup to soak for 5 - 10 minutes. Serve hot or cold.

MANGO HALWA

1.75 ltrs/3 pints ripe mango
juice
1 kg/2 lb sugar
450 g/1 lb khoya or 4 pints milk
450 g/1 lb pure ghee

100 g/4 oz sliced almonds
50 g/2 oz chopped pistachios
50 g/2 oz raisins
Silver leaves for garnishing
(varak)

■ In a large saucepan, heat the mango juice, sugar, crushed khoya or milk. Cook over medium heat, stirring constantly, until the mixture begins to thicken and attains a paste-like consistency. Add the ghee, a spoonful at a time, stirring well so that the mixture does not stick to the sides of the pan. Grease a thali or dish lightly and pour the mixture into it. flatten out evenly and garnish with nuts, raisins and silver leaves. When cool, cut into diamond-shaped pieces.

PISTACHIO
KULFI

1.2 ltrs/2 pints milk
225 g/8 oz sugar
½ oz cornflour
75 g/3 oz khoya or 1.2ltrs/
  2 pints thick cream

50 g/2 oz blanched pistachios
Pinch of saffron

■ Boil the milk until it is reduced to 750 ml/1¼ pints. Add the cornflour previously dissolved in a little cold milk and cook till the consistency is of a thin sauce. Add sugar and stir until completely dissolved. Remove from the heat and add the crushed khoya or cream, chopped pistachios and saffron. Fill the kulfi moulds with the mixture and screw the tops securely. If kulfi moulds are not available, use ice-cube trays. Place the moulds in the freezer or the deep freeze compartment of a refrigerator and leave for 3 - 4 hours.

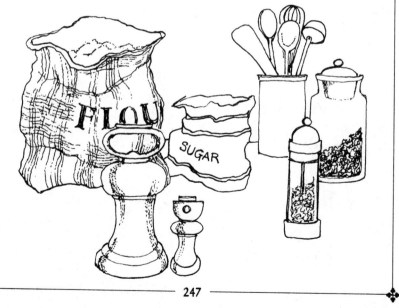

ALU MATTAR HALWA

450 g/1 lb potatoes	*225 g/8 oz mixed chopped nuts*
450 g/1 lb shelled peas	*50 g/2 oz raisins*
175 g/6 oz sugar	*1 teaspoon cardamom powder*
8 tablespoons ghee	

■ Peel the potatoes, wash and grate them. Bring 600 ml/1 pint water to the boil in a saucepan, add the grated potato and cook for 5 minutes. Strain. Boil the peas in 600 ml/1 pint water until tender. Drain, allow to cool a little and coarsely mash. Keep aside. Put the sugar in a saucepan, add one cup of water and allow to boil to a thick syrup. Remove from the heat. Fry the nuts in a little ghee and put aside.

■ Heat the remaining ghee, add the potatoes and coarsely mashed peas. Fry for 5 minutes, stir in the syrup and cook, stirring, for 15 minutes. Add the nuts and raisins and mix well. Stir in the cardamom and remove from the heat. Serve warm, garished with a few leaves of silver (varak).

MARROW FIRDAUS

1 large marrow or squash	*600 ml/1 pint cream*
600 ml/1 pint milk	*Chopped almonds and*
225 g/8 oz khoya (solidified	* pistachios*
* milk)*	*Saffron essence or cardamom*
8 tablespoons ghee	* for flavouring*
450 g/1 lb sugar	

■ Scrape the marrow, cut in half and remove the seeds. Grate on a medium grater and then boil with the milk until it is absorbed and the marrow is tender. If necessary add a little water. Heat the ghee in a kerai or frying pan and fry the cooked marrow together with sugar, khoya and saffron essence over a low heat. When the mixture forms a thick mass, pour out into a thali and spread evenly. Spread the cream over the halwa and sprinkle with nuts. Cut into squares and serve.

CARROT MURABHA

450 g/1 lb carrots
450 g/1 lb sugar
4 cloves
2 sticks cinnamon

2 green cardamoms
300 ml/½ pint water
Pinch of citric acid

■ Scrape and wash the carrots. Cut into slices 2.5 cms/1 inch thick and boil in the water until tender. Drain and keep aside. In the same water, dissolve the sugar, add citric acid, cloves, cinnamon and cardamom and ¼ cup of water. Cook until the syrup is of one-thread consistency. Add the carrots to the syrup and boil once more until the syrup reaches the one-thread consistency again. Remove and allow to stand overnight.
■ If the syrup becomes a little watery, boil once again. Bottle in an air-tight jar if the carrot murabha is to be preserved. If serving immediately, the citric acid may be omitted.

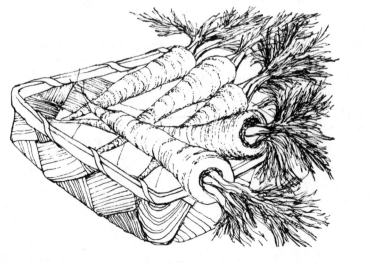

BEETROOT HALWA

4 beetroots
225 g/8 oz sugar
4 tablespoons ghee
50 g/2 oz raisins

50 g/2 oz blanched, chopped
cashew nuts
1 teaspoon cardamom powder

■ Peel the beetroots and wash well. Chop into small cubes. Place in a saucepan with 600 ml/1 pint water and cook until tender. Drain and then mash or grind until smooth. Put the beetroot and the sugar into a pan and cook over a low heat until the mixture thickens. Gradually, add the ghee, stirring until the halwa is almost solid. Add the nuts, raisins and cardamom. Spoon into a serving dish and allow to cool before serving.

MOOLEE KI KHEER

2 large white radishes
1 tablespoon ghee
1.25 ltrs/ 2¼ pints milk

450 g/1 lb sugar
50 g/2 oz raisins
1 teaspoon powdered cardamom

■ Wash and grate the radishes and boil in a little water until tender. Drain off excess water and keep aside. Heat the ghee and fry the radishes until lightly browned. Heat the milk in a separate pan, add the radishes and cook over a low heat until the milk begins to thicken. Add the sugar and raisins and cook, stirring constantly until you have the desired consistency. Remove from the heat, add cardamom and leave to cool, covered. Serve hot or chilled.

RA VA LADDOO

225 g/8 oz semolina (sooji)   300 ml/½ pint milk
3 teaspoons ghee   1 tablespoon currants
225 g/8 oz sugar   1 tablespoon cashew nuts

■ Fry the semolina in a saucepan over a low heat until it turns slightly brown in colour. Add the sugar, ghee and milk and fry until the mixture becomes sticky. Chop the nuts and stir them along with the currants, into the mixture. Remove the pan from the heat and form the dough into small balls. Serve when dry.

BALUSHAHI
SUGAR COATED PASTRY ROLLS

675 g/1 ½ lb flour   6 tablespoons ghee
1 kg/2 lb sugar

■ Work the ghee into the flour. Gradually add water to obtain a soft dough. Divide dough into small balls, flatten and form dents in the centre. Prepare a thick syrup by placing the sugar with 1 cupful of water into a saucepan, bring to the boil, turn the heat down and simmer until syrupy. Heat the ghee in a deep frying pan and put in the balushahis. Remove the pan from the heat until the ghee stops simmering.
■ Repeat the process of removing the pan from the heat each time the ghee boils and replacing when cool, until the balushahis are well risen and layers appear. When all the dough is used, place the balushahis on a rack and pour thick, hot syrup over them. Shake the vessel and when the syrup is cold it should leave an even coating.

GULAB JAMUN

SCENTED ROLLS SOAKED IN SYRUP

1.2 ltrs/2 pints milk
100 g/4 oz flour
450 g/1 lb sugar
A few drops essence (vanilla or
   rose)

A pinch of salt
½ teaspoon baking powder
Ghee

■ Boil the milk and simmer until it thickens to the consistency of a thick batter. Stir constantly to avoid burning. Knead the milk in the flour, baking powder and salt to make a smooth dough. If the dough is sticky, add a little more flour.
■ Prepare a thin syrup with the sugar and a cupful of water. Add a little essence to the syrup, and keep on one side.
■ Heat the ghee, form small rolls or balls with the dough and fry until brown on all sides. Drain the jamuns on a sheet of absorbent paper and put to soak in the syrup.

KATAHAL KI KHEER

3 ltrs/5 pints milk
450 g/1 lb semi-ripe katahal
   (jackfruit)
225 g/8 oz sugar
100 g/4 oz almonds

100 g/4 oz chironji seeds (melon
   seeds)
100 g/4 oz sugar candy
15 g/½ oz cardamoms
Rosewater

■ Select a semi-ripe and sweet-smelling jackfruit. Boil the milk over a low heat and stir it continuously until it becomes thick. Add the sugar and stir for another 10 minutes.
■ Clean the jackfruit, stone and cut into small pieces. Stir these pieces into the boiled milk. Allow to remain simmering over a low heat for 30 minutes. Stir occasionally to ensure the milk does not burn at the bottom.

■ When the jackfruit is soft, remove the kheer from the heat. Garnish with powdered cardamom, chironji seeds, chopped almonds and crushed sugar candy. Sprinkle with rosewater, and spread over five or six gold or silver leaves, if desired.

LABANGA LATIKA

225 g/8 oz sugar
600 ml/1 pint water
225 g/8 oz flour

24 cloves
Ghee

FOR THE FILLING:

600 ml/1 pint milk
50 g/2 oz sugar

25 g/1 oz raisins
4 cardamoms

■ Dissolve the sugar in the water and allow to boil until it forms a fairly thick syrup. Keep aside.
■ Make the filling by boiling the sugar and milk until it forms soft lumps. Add the raisins, remove from the heat and sprinkle with cardamom powder.
■ Add water to the flour and make a dough of fairly stiff consistency. Divide the dough into about 10 or 12 small balls and roll them out into circular shapes. Place the filling in the centre and fold round the edges to form a rectangle. Seal by sticking 2 cloves on either side of the rectangle to prevent it from opening. Fry the rectangles of dough in ghee over a low heat until they are crisp and light golden brown in colour. Arrange on a platter and when cold, pour the syrup over them.

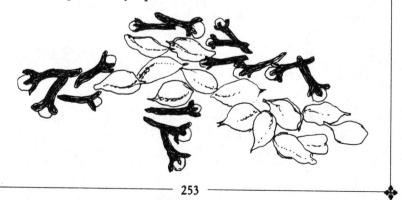

LOTUS SEED KHEER

1.2 ltrs/2 pints milk
100 g/4 oz lotus seeds
100 g/4 oz sugar

8 cardamoms
Silver paper for garnishing
(varak)

■ Remove hard covering from the seeds. Break the seeds into small coarse pieces. Set the milk to boil and add the seeds. Continue boiling until the seeds are soft and mixed thoroughly with the milk. Add the sugar and bring to the boil once more.
■ Sprinkle with cardamom powder. Serve garnished with silver paper.

BESAN LADDOO

GRAM FLOUR SWEETMEATS

1 kg/2 lb gram flour (besan)
1/2 teaspoon cardamoms
675 g/1 1/2 lb castor sugar

Enough ghee to bind flour
Cashew nuts and pistachios

■ Heat the ghee, gradually add the flour. Fry until brown and set aside. Add the powdered cardamom, and stir in the sugar and chopped nuts. Mix and form into small balls while still warm.

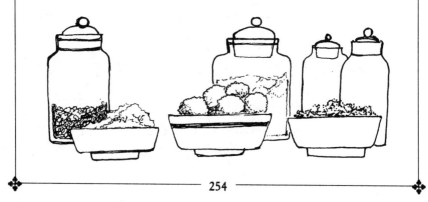

PUDALAMBOO

1 coconut
225 g/8 oz black gram dhal
50 g/2 oz cashew nuts
6 cardamoms

450 g/1 lb sugar
300 ml/½ pint almond oil (or
    8 tablespoons ghee)

■ Soak the dhal in water for 1 hour, drain well and grind to a paste with a little water. Add the ground cashew nuts and cardamoms and keep aside. Extract thick milk from grated coconut and dilute it with water to measure 600 ml/1 pint. Add the sugar and stir well. Make small balls of the dhal paste and fry in oil to a golden brown. Leave these to soak in the coconut juice for 1 hour, then serve.

CASHEW NUT
HALWA

350 g/12 oz cashew nuts
1 coconut
675 g/1½ lb sugar

1 tablespoon ghee
4 drops vanilla essence

■ Soak the cashew nuts in cold water. Finely grate the coconut and then grind with the cashew nuts to a thin paste.
■ Melt the sugar in 300 ml/½ pint water and heat until the mixture has a syrupy consistency. Add the paste, ghee, vanilla essence and mix until the halwa is semi-solid. Remove from the heat, spread on a large plate and cut to the required sizes. Serve.

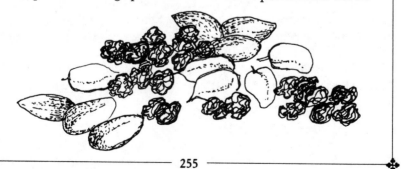

CAULIFLOWER KHEER

450 g/1 lb white cauliflower
tops or flowerets
2.4 ltrs/4 pints milk
225 g/8 oz sugar

50 g/2 oz each almonds, raisins,
pistachios and dried coconut
6 cardamoms
Silver paper (varak)

■ Grate the flowerets of fresh cauliflower. (Approximately 1.8 kg/4 lb cauliflower will give you 450 g/1 lb flowerets. For every 450 g/1 lb of grated cauliflower tops, take 2.4 ltrs/4 pints milk). Put the grated cauliflower and 4 whole cardamoms into the milk and allow to cook until the milk turns very thick. Stir in the sugar, sliced almonds, raisins and the dried coconut and cook for another 10 minutes. Remove from the heat and pour into a bowl. Decorate with silver paper (varak), cardamom powder and chopped pistachios. Stir in a few drops of rosewater or any other essence if desired.

VERMICELLI KHEER

75 g/3 oz vermicelli
450 ml/³/4 pint milk (boiled)
75 g/3 oz sugar, or to taste

25 g/1 oz sultanas
3 small white cardamoms
2 tablespoons pure ghee

■ Heat the ghee in a saucepan and add the vermicelli. Fry stirring constantly, until golden brown. Pour in the milk and bring to the boil over a very low heat and simmer for 5 - 10 minutes. Add the sugar and sultanas and stir occasionally. When the desired thickness is obtained, remove from the heat and sprinkle with cardamom powder. Place in a serving dish and keep covered. If desired, decorate with silver paper (varak).

RABARHI

1.2 ltrs/2 pints milk
50 g/2 oz sugar
1 teaspoon rosewater

1 teaspoon cardamoms
Almonds and pistachios

■ Bring the milk to the boil and cook slowly over a low heat for at least 2 hours. Stir frequently and let the cream thicken at the edge of the pan. Add the sugar and stir until the milk is less than quarter the original amount. Scrape the cream formed on the sides back into the milk.

■ When ready, stir in the rosewater and pour into a glass dish. Garnish with chopped almonds, pistachios and ground cardamoms. Rabarhi may be served either hot or chilled.

BHAPI DAHI

1.2 ltrs/2 pints curd or yoghurt   1 tin sweetened condensed milk

■ Beat the curd well and gradually mix in the condensed milk. Pour the mixture into a bowl or an oven-proof dish with a tight lid and place it in a saucepan with water coming to a little less than half the depth of the bowl. Boil gently for 1 hour. Chill and serve. If curd is too sour then use less. The best method to prepare this dish is by using a perforated steamer.

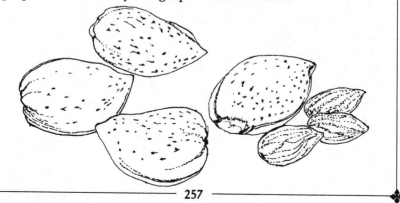

ICED
CUSTARD-APPLE

75 g/3 oz sugar

1.75 ltrs/3 pints milk

15 g/½ oz cornflour

6 custard apples

■ Add sugar to milk and heat until a quarter has evaporated. Blend the cornflour first with a little milk and then with the rest of the milk. Reheat until the milk is thick, stirring constantly. Remove from the heat, add fruit pulp, and cool. Keep in the refrigerator until set. Whip and serve.

SHAHI
TUKRI

12 slices white bread

600 ml/1 pint milk

10 green cardamoms

225 g/8 oz sugar

½ teaspoon saffron

225 g/8 oz khoya

2 teaspoons essence

4 silver leaves (varak)

25 g/1 oz almonds

15 g/½ oz pistachios

4 preserved cherries

Ghee

■ Cut the bread into rectangular squares, discarding the hard crust, and fry in ghee until golden brown. Remove from the ghee and drain on kitchen paper. Boil milk with crushed cardamoms and dissolve sugar and saffron in it. Soak the fried bread in this prepared milk for a few minutes. Remove the slices with a flat spoon and keep aside.

■ Mix the khoya into the milk and heat for 5 minutes. Add the bread slices and continue to cook over a low heat until the mixture thickens. Turn the slices over several times with a flat spoon. Add the essence, remove from the heat and leave to cool for 15 minutes. Spread it carefully in a serving dish, garnish with silver leaves. Chop and sprinkle almonds, pistachios and cherries on top. Serve cold.

SOHAM HALWA

1 kg/2 lb sugar
1.2 ltrs/2 pints water
225 g/8 oz cornflour
Red or yellow colouring
225 g/8 oz almonds

100 g/4 oz pistachios
50 g/2 oz green cardamoms
8 tablespoons ghee
150 ml/¼ pint milk
1 tablespoon lemon juice

■ Dissolve the sugar in half the water and allow to boil for 5 minutes. Add the milk and leave to boil for a further 5 minutes. Remove from the heat and strain through a muslin cloth.

■ Dissolve the cornflour in the remaining water and add to the syrup. Cook over a medium heat and when the mixture starts turning into lumps, add the colouring previously soaked in lemon juice. Stir continuously, adding a little ghee every time the mixture starts sticking to the bottom of the pan. When the mixture leaves the sides of the pan and forms one whole piece, add the crushed cardamoms and finely-sliced almonds and pistachios, keeping aside a few nuts for garnishing.

■ Put the halwa on a greased thali and flatten it out. Decorate with the remaining almonds and pistachios. When cooled, cut into desired shapes and sizes. This halwa will keep for months if packed in air-tight tins.

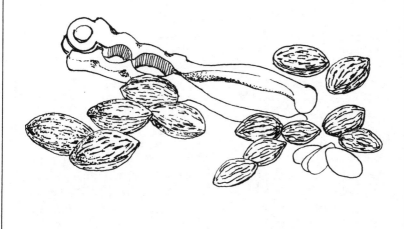

GAJJAR BARFI

CARROT FUDGE

1 kg/2 lb carrots
1.25 ltrs/2¼ pints milk
Few shreds saffron (kesar)
675 g/1½ lb sugar
1 cup dried fruit (chironji,
raisins or chopped
pistachios)

½ teaspoon cardamom powder
50 g/2 oz blanched chopped
almonds
Few silver leaves (varak)

■ Wash and cut up the carrots lengthways and put them through a mincer. Boil the minced carrot in 300 ml/½ pint milk. When tender remove from the heat and allow to cool. Make a paste of saffron with a little milk. Place a pan on the heat, pour in the milk, add the carrot and saffron and cook well, stirring frequently. When all the milk has evaporated, add sugar, and continue stirring until the mixture thickens. Remove from the heat. Stir in the dried fruit, almonds and cardamom and mix well. Spread out the mixture on a large dish. Garnish with silver leaves. When cool, cut into squares and serve. It will keep for a week or more.

CARROT HALWA

450 g/1 lb carrots
600 ml/1 pint milk
450 g/1 lb sugar

Chopped nuts
Cardamom powder
1 tablespoon ghee

■ Wash and grate the carrots. Cook the grated carrot with the milk over a medium heat until the carrot is soft. Add the sugar and cook uncovered, stirring at intervals until the mixture begins to solidify. Keep stirring until the mixture turns a reddish brown. Add the ghee, nuts and cardamom and fry until dry. Serve hot.

KERWAI

12 ripe frying bananas
75 g/3 oz almonds
40 g/1½ oz charoli or peanuts
40 g/1½ oz raisins
1 teaspoon cardamom

½ teaspoon nutmeg powder
½ teaspoon vanilla
450 g/1 lb ghee
75 g/3 oz sugar

■ Blanch the almonds, chop finely and fry them in a little ghee with the charoli and raisins. Heat more ghee in another pan and fry the peeled bananas until they are light brown. Add the sugar and continue stirring until the mixture forms a ball. Remove from the heat and mix well.

■ Take enough of the fried banana mixture to form a small ball. Flatten it out and fill in the fried nuts and raisins flavoured with cardamom, nutmeg and vanilla. Close in and press the edges firmly. Heat the ghee in a pan and fry the balls to a brown colour on both sides. Serve hot.

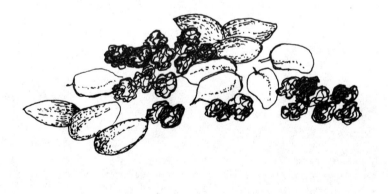

SNACKS AND
SAVOURIES

SNACKS AND SAVOURIES

All kinds of snack and savouries are prepared in the Indian kitchen. There are more titbits prepared in Indian cookery than in any other cuisine all over the world. The social cup of tea or coffee is always accompanied with a variety of nibbles and the Indian housewife can always produce 'chevda', 'sev' and various 'nimkis' without hesitation from her larder. The 'samosa' - spiced minced meat or vegetables wrapped in thin pastry and crisply fried in hot fat - and the 'bajia' or 'pakora' are perennial favourites.

Navratri, which means 'nine nights', and Dassara, the ninth day, is held in honour of Durga, warrior-goddess of the Hindu pantheon. The first seven days of Navratri are usually spent in fasting and domestic and public worship. People wake before dawn to have a light meal of snacks, savouries and sweets to fortify themselves for the rigid fast of the day. On the last day, however, feasting and merrymaking is allowed.

Navratri, known as the Puja holiday, is the national festival of Bengal. It is true to say that Bengal observes and celebrates the most festivals in India. The most impressive attraction of Calcutta is a colony of sculptors in the very heart of the old city. These artisans claim to be descendants of the artists who sculpted the beautiful Hindu temples of Orissa and Bihar. They are busy all the year round chiselling clay images of gods and goddesses for the next festival. Their studios are always alive with sculptures of Durga, Kali, Ganesh, Shiva, Parvati, Saraswati and many other gods from Hindu mythology.

The Navratri is the busiest time for these artisans, as Durga Puja is celebrated with great pomp and ceremony. During Navratri, the goddess, wife of Lord Shiva, is worshipped in her nine warlike manifestations. In the eighth manifestation she killed a demon called Durga and hence got her name. Durga is the symbol of triumph of Good over Evil, and on the tenth day of the festival, Vijoya (victory), the goddess is borne away in a spectacular procession and immersed in the river.

This festival is particularly sacred to the fighting castes and ruling clans. The princely Hindu States, now integrated with the rest of the country, still celebrate Dassara in a right royal fashion. In olden days, most of the military campaigns of the Hindu kings against their neighbours started on Dassara. It is still an important day for the Indian army and an offering of animal sacrifices is made to the goddess on this day.

It is only natural that with so much festivity in the country, the opportunity for between-meals eating is vast. The recipes in this chapter could be a great success at both cocktail and tea-parties.

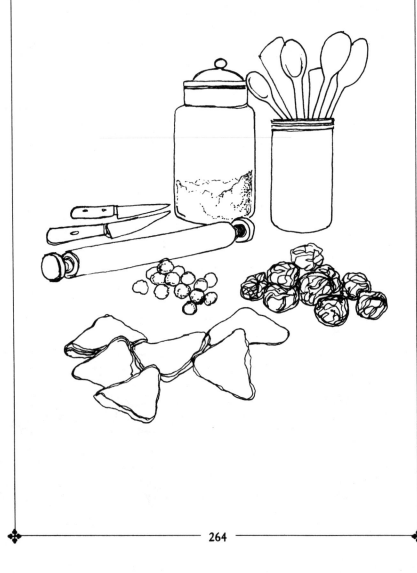

SEV

225 g/8 oz gram flour
150 ml/¼ pint water
Salt to taste

Pinch of bicarbonate of soda
1 teaspoon ghee
Oil

■ Make a batter from the gram flour and water, adding salt to taste. To prepare the sev, the dough must be reasonably stiff. Knead the batter with warm water, bicarbonate of soda and 1 teaspoon ghee. When smooth, fill into the sevanazhi. or piping nozzle. Heat the oil in a kerai. Hold the gadget above the oil and let the batter fall in long strips. Deep fry until brown. Cool and when crisp place in an air-tight container. A number of variations are possible when making this dish: for example, the batter can be spiced with chilli powder.

NIMKIS

225 g/8 oz wheat flour
2 tablespoons ghee

Oil
Salt to taste

■ Sift the flour with salt. Rub ghee into the flour. Add sufficient water to make a soft dough. Roll out into thin puris, sprinkle a little flour on each puri, fold in half and then in quarters. Dampen the corners and press together. Fry in oil until golden brown.

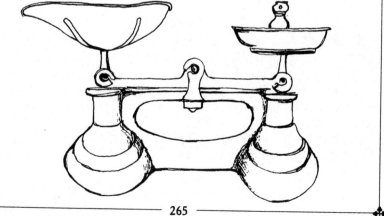

CHEESE BONDAS

100 g/4 oz flour	3 eggs
100 g/4 oz cooking cheese	1 teaspoon chilli powder
300 ml/½ pint milk	Ghee
75 g/3 oz butter	Salt to taste

—— MILD ——

■ Beat eggs until stiff, then grate the cheese. In a large saucepan, warm the milk and gradually add the flour stirring constantly so that no lumps form. Add butter and when the mixture thickens, remove from heat and add grated cheese. Blend well. Add salt, chilli powder and beaten eggs. When cool, the mixture should be thick enough to shape. Heat the ghee. Make balls the size of a lemon from the mixture and put into the hot ghee. Fry until golden brown all over. Drain and remove from the ghee. Serve piping hot with tomato sauce.

SHRIMP PAKORAS

450 g/1 lb shrimps, cleaned and shelled	1 teaspoon dried pomegranate seeds
50 g/2 oz gram flour	Pinch of bicarbonate of soda
2 large onions	Ghee or oil
6 green chillies	Salt to taste

—— MEDIUM ——

■ Try to buy the smallest shrimps available so that they may be mixed into the batter whole. In a mixing bowl put the flour and add 2 tablespoons water to make a batter. Slice the onions finely and chop the chillies. Add the onions, chillies, pomegranate seeds, bicarbonate of soda, salt and shrimps to the gram flour batter. Blend well.

■ Heat the ghee in a kerai until really hot. Drop a teaspoon of batter at a time into the ghee and fry in batches of 6 - 8 pakoras. Deep fry until evenly brown. Serve hot with tomato sauce or any kind of chutney.

FRIED CORN

2 *tender corn cobs*	3 *teaspoons ghee*
300 *ml/¹/₂ pint milk*	*Salt and pepper to taste*

Remove the corn from the cobs. Heat the milk and bring to the boil. Add the corn. Cook until the corn is dry and the milk has evaporated. Remove from the heat. Heat the ghee in a deep frying pan and add the cooked corn. Fry gently until the aroma rises, approximately 5 minutes. Sprinkle with seasoning and serve hot.

PURIS

Makes 48

1 *kg/2 lb fine flour (maida)*	*Oil*
Ghee	*Salt to taste*

■ Sieve the flour into a thali or flat tray and add salt to taste. Add a little water and knead to make a stiff dough. Blend in a dash of ghee.

■ Roll out thinly on a large board, with the help of a little dry flour to avoid sticking. Cut out small round shapes about the size of a lemon with a biscuit-cutter or a small katori. Deep fry in hot oil until the puris rise like little balloons. Cook until brown, drain and remove. These puris should remain crisp when cooled.

■ For the crisp but flat puris used in bhel and sev puri roll the dough out much thinner so that they do not puff up.

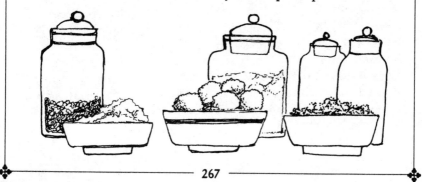

SEV PURI

2 dozen flat, crisp puris	1 chopped green mango
1 cup sev (1)	Hot chutney
1 large onion	Sweet chutney
4 boiled potatoes	Coriander leaves

■ Chop the onion finely. Peel and chop the potatoes. Chop the coriander leaves. Arrange the puris on a plate and add a layer of chopped potatoes on top of them. Sprinkle the onions on the potatoes. Top generously with crisp sev. Add the chutneys to taste and garnish with finely-chopped green mango and coriander leaves. Serve immediately.
■ (1) See recipe for sev on page 265. For chutney recipes see pickles section.

BATATA PURI

Makes 24

2 dozen puris	Pinch of roasted, ground
6 potatoes	cummin seed
150 ml/¼ pint curd or yoghurt	Chilli powder
Sweet chutney	Green gram sprouts (mung)
Hot chutney	Salt to taste
Chopped coriander leaves	

■ Peel, boil for 20 minutes and chop the potatoes into small cubes. Beat the curd. Arrange the puris on a flat plate. Make a hole in the centre of each puri and stuff with potato cubes. Sprinkle salt and chilli powder to taste and add the hot chutney. Pour a little curd on each puri and add the sweet chutney if desired. Garnish with mung sprouts and chopped coriander and a dash of the cummin seed powder. Serve immediately before the puris become soft.

PANI PURI
or 'GOL GAPPAS'

Puffed puris as required
100 g/4 oz tamarind
1.2 ltrs/2 pints water
1 small bunch coriander leaves
1 teaspoon chilli powder
$1/2$ teaspoon roasted ground
   cummin seeds

$1/2$ teaspoon black pepper
75 g/3 oz sprouted green gram
   (mung)
Jaggery or sugar to taste
Salt to taste

—— MEDIUM ——

■ Boil the tamarind in the water until soft. Strain and add the ground spices, salt and chopped coriander leaves. If the mixture is too thick, dilute with a little water. Make a small hole in each puri and stuff with some mung sprouts. Serve the pani and puris separately so that each guest can serve himself by dipping the puri into the pani. Chutneys may also be served with this dish if preferred.

BHEL

2 cups puffed rice (murmura)
$1^{1}/2$ cups sev
12 crushed crisp puris
1 onion
3 potatoes, boiled in their skins

Hot chutney
Sweet chutney
Green mango
Coriander leaves
1 tomato

■ In a large bowl mix the puffed rice, sev (see page 265) and crushed puris. Add the finely choppped onion, and peeled, chopped potatoes, chopped mango and chutneys to taste. Mix well and garnish with chopped coriander leaves and chopped tomato. Serve immediately.

MINCED CURRY PUFFS

PASTRY:

225 g/8 oz self-raising flour
Salt to taste
75 g/3 oz cooking fat or ghee

Cold water to mix to a stiff
dough

FILLING:

225 g/8 oz minced meat
2 teaspoons garam masala
2 onions
1 tablespoon ghee

$^1\!/_2$ teaspoon chilli powder
15 g/$^1\!/_2$ oz cornflour
Salt to taste
Oil for deep frying

—— MILD——

■ Mince the onions and fry half of them in a saucepan with one tablespoon ghee until they are brown. Add the meat and fry for 2 minutes. Add the remaining onion, garam masala, salt to taste and mix well to prevent sticking. Cover and simmer until the meat is tender and the water evaporates. Add a little water if required and the chilli powder (optional). Mix the cornflour to a smooth paste with a little water and mix into the meat. Bring to the boil and lower the heat. Allow the mixture to simmer for 3 minutes.

■ Make the pastry by blending the flour, salt, ghee and water to a stiff dough. Roll out thinly. Cut into round 10 cms/4 inches across. Put mince on one half and fold the pastry over, sealing the edges with a little water. Heat the oil until smoking hot and fry the puffs until brown on both sides. Drain well on absorbent kitchen paper. Alternatively, these curry puffs can be baked at 180°C/350°F/Gas mark 4 for 30 minutes.

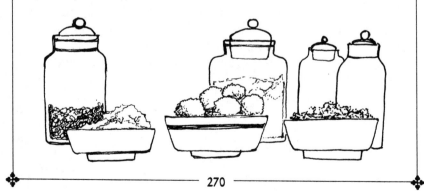

KHANDWI

300 ml/½ pint sour curd or
    yoghurt
275 g/10 oz gram flour
6 green chillies
1 piece ginger
½ teaspoon turmeric powder

1 teaspoon mustard seeds
1 tablespoon til oil (sesame)
2 teaspoons chopped coriander
    leaves
2 teaspoons grated coconut
Salt to taste

—— *MEDIUM* ——

■ Beat the curd with an egg beater, add 600 ml/1 pint water and beat until milky. Mix in the gram flour and stir until all the lumps disappear. Grind the chillies and ginger and add to the curd paste. Add the salt and turmeric. Pour into a saucepan and place over a low heat to cook. Bring to the boil and cook for approximately 15 minutes until the gram flour loses its strong flavour. Remove from the heat and pour a thin layer into a large thali. When cool, cut into strips and roll. Carefully place the rolls in a serving dish. Before serving heat the oil and fry the mustard seeds until they start spluttering. Pour over the khandwi rolls. Garnish with chopped coriander leaves and grated coconut and serve immediately.

VEGETABLE SAMOSAS

100 g/4 oz whole wheat flour	*2.5 cms/1 inch piece ginger*
(ata)	*½ teaspoon turmeric powder*
225 g/8 oz plain flour	*¼ teaspoon coriander powder*
100 g/4 oz shelled peas	*¼ teaspoon cummin seed*
100 g/4 oz carrots	*powder*
100 g/4 oz potatoes	*1 lime*
1 large onion	*Few sprigs coriander leaves*
2 green chillies	*Salt to taste*
2 pods garlic	*Oil*

—— MILD ——

■ Cut the carrots and potatoes into small pieces. Heat the oil and fry the sliced onion until brown. Grind the remaining spices into a paste. Add the peas, carrots and potatoes to the browned onion and fry for 3 minutes. Stir in the ground spices and salt and add 2 tablespoons water. Cover and cook until the vegetables are tender and the water is absorbed. Add the coriander leaves and fresh lime juice. Keep aside. Mix both flours with a little salt and knead well. Make a soft dough and divide it into small balls. Roll each ball out into a thin round shape, about 7.5 cms/3 inches in diameter. Cut in half and form cones. Dampen side edges and press together. Fill with the vegetable mixture and seal carefully. Deep fry in hot oil over a medium heat until brown.

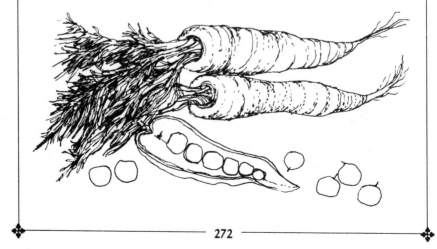

CHAKLIS

100 g/4 oz gram flour	1 tablespoon til seeds (sesame)
350 g/12 oz rice flour	2 tablespoons butter
3 teaspoons chilli powder	Oil
½ teaspoon asafoetida	Salt to taste

—— HOT ——

■ Mix both flours with chilli powder, asafoetida, butter and salt. Wash the til seeds and add to the flour mixture. Slowly add water, mixing together thoroughly, to make a soft dough. Place a kerai on the heat and heat the oil in it. When it is smoking hot, take pieces of dough (the size of small balls) and put them one by one through a chakli mould or soriya (if not available, use a forcing bag and force the batter to form small spirals), hold it over the kerai and press the lever. When the chaklis are crisp and brown, drain off the oil and remove. These chaklis will keep for a fortnight.

ALU
CHAT

1 kg/2 lb small potatoes	1 teaspoon roasted ground
4 green chillies	cummin seeds
1 teaspoon amchoor (dry	150 ml/¼ pint tamarind juice
powdered mango)	Chopped coriander leaves
1 teaspoon fresh garam masala	Salt to taste

—— MILD ——

■ Wash the potatoes and boil them in their skins. Peel and slice into small rounds. Place in a serving bowl and mix in all the ingredients. Lemon juice may be used instead of tamarind if preferred.

SAGOLET

100 g/4 oz sago
1 large potato
1 small onion
2 green chillies
2 tablespoons grated coconut

A few dried mint leaves
1 tablespoon lemon juice
$^1/_4$ teaspoon powdered black
    pepper
Salt to taste

—— MILD ——

■ Soak the sago with the salt in 600 ml/1 pint warm water for 30 minutes. Boil, peel and mash the potato. Chop the onion and green chillies. Roast the grated coconut in a frying pan to a light brown. Drain the excess water from the sago and mix all the ingredients well together. Take a tablespoon of the mixture and shape into balls. Deep fry the sagolets to a golden brown. Serve with tomato sauce.

CASHEW NUT PAKORAS

450 g/1 lb cashew nuts
450 g/1 lb gram flour (besan)
1 teaspoon turmeric powder
1 teaspoon chilli powder

150 ml/$^1/_4$ pint oil
1 sprig curry leaf
Ghee
Salt to taste

—— MEDIUM HOT ——

■ Mix the chilli powder, salt and turmeric into flour. Heat the oil and when it smokes, pour into the flour and blend well. Add the chopped nuts and curry leaves and mix. Heat the ghee in a kerai or frying pan for deep frying. Prepare small balls from the flour mixture and fry in hot ghee to a golden brown. Serve hot or cold. The Samosas will keep for a week if stored in a refrigerator.

GROUND-NUT UPUMA

350 g/12 oz ground-nuts	A little asafoetida
¼ teaspoon mustard seeds	2 tablespoons grated coconut
5 green chillies	1 tablespoon oil or ghee
1 large onion	1 tablespoon chopped coriander
1 teaspoon turmeric powder	Salt to taste

—— MEDIUM HOT ——

■ Use fresh ground-nuts that are still tender. Otherwise, boil peanuts in enough water, drain and chop coarsely. Heat the ghee and fry the mustard seeds. Add the chillies, sliced onion, turmeric and asafoetida. Cook until brown and add the nuts and coconut. Mix well. Cover the mixture and cook for 3 minutes. Uncover and fry, stirring continuously, for 3 - 5 minutes. Add chopped coriander and serve at tea-time.

PAKORAS

225 g/8 oz gram flour	1 teaspoon garam masala
150 ml/¼ pint water	Diced vegetables
½ teaspoon turmeric powder	Salt to taste
1 teaspoon chilli powder	
1 tablespoon pomegranate	
seeds	

—— HOT ——

■ Make a batter from gram flour, salt and water. Blend the turmeric, chilli powder, pomegranate seeds and garam masala into the batter. Dip the diced vegetables into the batter and fry until evenly brown on all sides. Any vegetable may be used (e.g. potatoes, onion and parboiled carrots or, as a special delicacy, try quartered hardboiled eggs.)

POTATO
BONDAS

450 g/1 lb potatoes	2.5 cms/1 inch piece ginger
225 g/8 oz gram flour (besan)	1 sprig curry leaves
1/2 teaspoon mustard seeds	1 teaspoon chilli powder
1 tablespoon black dhal	1/4 teaspoon turmeric powder
2 tablespoons chopped cashew	1/2 lemon
nuts	3 tablespoons oil or ghee
2 medium onions	Salt to taste
6 green chillies	

—— HOT ——

■ Boil the potatoes, peel and cut into tiny cubes. In a saucepan heat 3 tablespoons oil and add the mustard seeds. When the mustard seeds begin to splutter, stir in the black dhal and cashew nuts. Cook until the dhal and nuts turn to a golden brown, add the turmeric powder, finely chopped onions, green chillies, ginger and curry leaves and cook, stirring, for 5 minutes until the onion is well cooked. Add the potatoes and salt. Cook for a further 2 minutes and remove from the heat.

■ Stir in the lemon juice and mix well. Make small balls out of the mixture (approximately 25 - 30 balls) and keep aside.

■ Make a thick batter from the gram flour, chilli powder, salt and 150 ml/1/4 pint water. Heat the oil in a frying pan. Gently dip the potato balls one by one in the batter, making certain that all the sides are coated evenly. Drop the balls carefully into the smoking oil. About 4 - 5 bondas can be fried at a time. Keep turning them constantly and when they are a golden brown, remove from the oil and drain on absorbent kitchen paper.

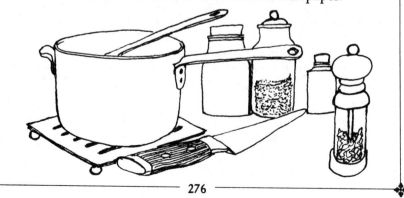

SAGO VADAI

225 g/8 oz sago	A sprig of curry leaves
250 g/8 oz ground nuts	150 ml/¼ pint curd or yoghurt
2 potatoes	1 teaspoon cummin seeds
6 - 7 green chillies	Ghee or oil
1 bunch coriander leaves	Salt to taste
1 tablespoon grated coconut	

FOR THE CHUTNEY:

½ coconut	½ bunch coriander leaves
6 - 7 green chillies	Salt to taste
A little tamarind	

—— *VERY HOT* ——

■ Wash the sago and soak it in a little water for at least 2 hours. Fry the ground nuts, peel and grind them to a powder. Boil and peel the potatoes, mash them and mix well with the sago and powdered ground nut, to form a dough. Crush the coriander leaves, curry leaves, green chillies and grated coconut and mix well into the sago dough. Blend in the salt, curd and the cummin seeds.

■ Heat the ghee in a saucepan until smoking hot, take a small ball of dough, flatten it on the palm of your hand and fry it in the ghee until it turns crisp. Serve with chutney.

■ To make the chutney, grind all the ingredients together to a very fine paste.

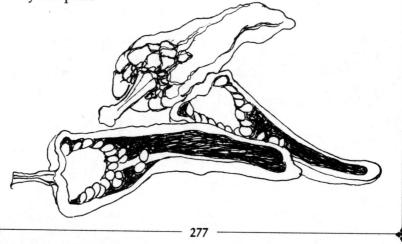

MASALA UPUMA

225 g/8 oz semolina
1 dessertspoon mustard seeds
40 g/1½ oz each Bengal and
   black gram
50 g/2 oz cashew nuts or
   ground nuts
2 large onions

1 bunch coriander leaves
100 g/4 oz grated coconut
Salt to taste
4 tablespoons refined oil, or
   pure ghee and refined oil
   in equal proportions

MASALA INGREDIENTS:

2 sticks cinnamon
1 teaspoon coriander seeds
1 pinch cummin seeds

4 dry red chillies
40 g/1½ oz turmeric
4 large lemons

—— MILD ——

■ Fry the masala ingredients in a pan on an even heat and then grind them. Mix the turmeric in 600 ml/1 pint of warm water and soak for about 15 minutes. Extract the juice from the lemons and keep aside. Strain, add the ground masala either to the turmeric or lemon juice. Add the remaining juices to the mixture. Roast the semolina over a low heat for about 4 - 5 minutes and keep aside.

■ Put the oil or ghee in a saucepan and heat until it smokes. Stir in the mustard seeds. Add the black and Bengal gram and the cashew nuts or ground nuts. Stir in the chopped onions and leave to cook for about 5 minutes, and add the coriander leaves. Continue cooking and pour in 450 ml/¾ pint boiling water, blending well. Stir in the salt, grated coconut and the masala solution to this mixture and boil for about 10 minutes. Gradually, add the semolina to the boiling mixture, stirring constantly until it is well mixed and becomes a thick paste. Stir the paste several times, cover with a lid and leave to cook on a very low heat for 3 - 4 minutes. Serve hot.

MOGHLAI SAMOSA

450 g/1 lb minced meat	1 teaspoon turmeric powder
2 large onions	1 lemon
6 cloves garlic	1 tablespoon ghee
4 green chillies	Salt to taste
1 bunch coriander leaves	

PASTRY:

275 g/10 oz flour	Salt to taste

PASTE TO SEAL:

1 dessertspoon flour	1 dessertspoon water

—— MILD ——

■ Put the minced meat, finely chopped onions, garlic, chillies and coriander leaves into a pan with the ghee, salt and turmeric. Stir and cook without water until the meat is dry and tender. Add the juice of ½ lemon and allow to cool.

■ Make the pastry by mixing the flour and salt with water into a stiff but pliable dough. Knead well. Divide the dough into small balls the size of walnuts. Take two of these balls and flatten between the palms into circular pieces. Lay one on a floured board, spread thinly with melted ghee and lay the other piece on top, pressing lightly together with the fingers. Flour a rolling pin, and roll out the circles of dough until very thin. Bake on a medium hot tava, and cook until the chappatis are dry but taking care not to brown them as they have to be fried again. While still hot pull the two pieces of dough apart (they will come apart quite easily) and you will have two thin pieces of pastry. Lay flat and cut into strips 4 cms/1½ inches wide. Continue in the same manner with all the dough until you have a pile of pastry strips.

■ Fold the straight edge of the pastry strip into the shape of a triangle twice. Put a spoonful of mince into the pocket thus formed and fold over and over again until all of the strip is used up. Mix the dessertspoons of flour and water together and seal the edges of the pastry with the paste. Fill the rest of the strips in the same way.

MYSORE KODUMBALAI

1 kg/2 lb rice flour	*2 onions*
225 g/8 oz flour (maida)	*¼ teaspoon asafoetida*
100 g/4 oz fine semolina (sooji)	*25 g/1 oz jaggery*
1½ large coconuts	*2 teaspoons cummin seeds*
12 medium sized green chillies	*450 g/1 lb ghee*
1 bunch fresh coriander	*Salt to taste*

—— *VERY VERY HOT* ——

■ Mix the rice flour, flour and semolina well and leave on one side in a large bowl. Grate the coconuts and grind with the chillies, coriander leaves, sliced onions, asafoetida and jaggery to a chutney consistency, in a mortar or blender. Add salt to taste and the cummin seeds. Melt 3 tablespoons of ghee in a frying pan and pour into the flour. Add the ground ingredients to the flour and knead well, stirring in as much water as is necessary to form a stiff dough. Take a small piece of dough and roll it into a long noodle. Form into a spiral on a greased plate. Heat the remaining ghee in a pan and fry to a rich brown colour. Continue with the rest of the dough.

PAYASAM

SUMMER DRINK

6 ripe mangoes	*A few cashew nuts*
1 coconut	*A little saffron*
½ teaspoon cardamom powder	*Ghee*
100 g/4 oz sugar	

■ Peel the mangoes, squeeze well and keep the pulp. Add a little hot water to the mango stones and wash them clean of all the pulp, adding the water to the fleshy pulp. Grate the coconut and extract the milk. Grind a second time and extract the thinner milk. Stir the sugar, coconut milk, cardamom powder and saffron to the mango pulp and blend. Fry the cashew nuts in a little ghee and add them to the kheer and mix well. Serve cold with ice cubes.

BADAM SHERBET

175 g/6 oz almonds
12 green cardamoms
1 kg/2 lb sugar
300 ml/¹/₂ pint water

5 - 6 drops kewra or rose
essence
Almond essence to taste

■ Soak the almonds overnight in enough water to cover them. The following day blanch and grind in a mortar or blender with a little water to a fine paste. Remove to a large saucepan and stir the water into the paste. Blend in the sugar and cook over a low heat stirring all the time. Grind the cardamoms together with their skins in a tablespoon of water. Strain through a muslin cloth and add to the almond syrup. Stir the mixture removing the skin from the top. Cook until the syrup thickens and remove from the heat. Strain and allow to cool. Add the kewra and almond essence. Dilute a quantity of badam sherbet with iced water and crushed ice.

ICED ANISEED TEA

2 tablespoons aniseed
2 cups strong black tea

Milk or cream
Sugar to taste

■ Boil the aniseed in a cupful of water until tender. Drain the liquid and pour into the black tea. Add milk and sugar to taste and pour into glasses filled with crushed ice.

ROSE FLAVOURED NIMBU PANI

3 lemons
1½ tablespoons sugar

3 teaspoons rosewater

■ Squeeze the juice from the lemons and add the sugar to the juice. Stir until the sugar is completely dissolved. Add the four glasses of iced water and the rosewater. Pour into serving glasses and serve with crushed ice.

FALOODA

1.2 ltrs/2 pints boiled milk
Prepared falooda (cornflour vermicelli)
50 g/2 oz falooda seeds
100 g/4 oz blanched chopped almonds and pistachios

300 ml/½ pint malai (cream from the top of the milk) or ice-cream
Rose syrup

■ To prepare the falooda, dissolve 100 g/4 oz cornflour in 150 ml/¼ pint water. Add 600 ml/1 pint water and cook over a medium heat, stirring constantly for 15 minutes. The mixture will turn thick and bluish in colour and then turn thinner and translucent. Remove from the heat. Have a basin of cold water ready. Put the cornflour paste into a vermicelli machine or sevanazhi and turn out the long threads over the basin of cold water. Repeat until all the paste has been used. The falooda will set into soft vermicelli strings. Leave in water until required. Soak the falooda seeds in a little water and keep aside for an hour.

■ To prepare six glasses of falooda, pour a large quantity of rose-syrup into the bottom of a glass, add a helping of falooda and 2 - 3 teaspoons of falooda seeds. Stir in a cupful of slightly sweetened chilled milk and a tablespoon of cream. Top with chopped nuts and crushed ice. Use ice-cream instead of malai when preparing falooda for children. Falooda is also delicious with kulfi and can be coloured by adding a drop of cochineal.

HONEY
MILK

300 ml/½ pint milk   *A dash of nutmeg*
1 tablespoon clear honey

■ Bring the milk to the boil. Remove from the heat and stir in the honey. Chill and serve with grated nutmeg or cardomom sprinkled on top

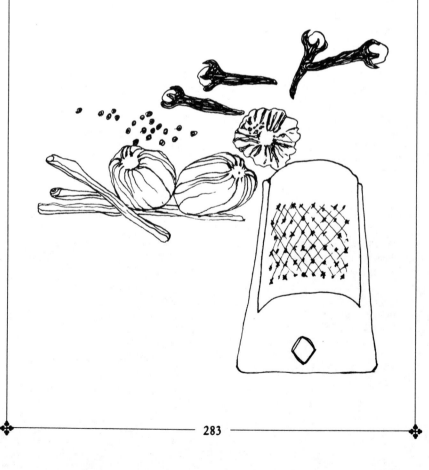

INDEX